CHINA'S WORKERS
UNDER ASSAULT
UNDER ASSAULT

─── ASIA AND THE PACIFIC ───

Series Editor: Mark Selden, Binghamton University

Exploring one of the most dynamic and contested regions of the world, this series includes contributions on political, economic, cultural, and social changes in modern and contemporary Asia and the Pacific.

CHINA'S WORKERS
UNDER ASSAULT

The Exploitation of Labor in a Globalizing Economy

ANITA CHAN

AN EAST GATE BOOK

M.E. Sharpe
Armonk, New York
London, England

An East Gate Book

Copyright © 2001 by M. E. Sharpe, Inc.

Library of Congress Cataloging-in-Publication Data

Chan, Anita.
    China's workers under assault : the exploitation of labor in a globalizing economy / by
Anita Chan.
        p. cm.—(Asia and the Pacific)
    "An East gate book."
    Includes bibliographical references and index.
    ISBN 0-7656-0357-8 (alk. paper)—ISBN 0-7656-0358-6 (pbk. : alk. paper)
        1. Labor—China. 2. Working class—China. 3. Labor mobility—China. 4. Labor
market—China. 5. Industrial relations—China. I. Title. II. Series.

HD8736.5 .C35 2001
331′.0951—dc21   2001020050

Printed in the United States of America

BM (c)   10   9   8   7   6   5   4   3   2   1
BM (p)   10   9   8   7   6   5   4   3   2   1

For my husband, mate, and colleague,

Jonathan Unger

Contents

Acknowledgments

Many people have provided valuable help to enable this book to come to print. Gratitude is due first to staff members of the Hong Kong Christian Industrial Committee, in particular to Shek Ping-kwan, for helping with the voluminous collection of newspaper and journal clippings; and to Apo Leung, May Wong, and Vivien Liu of the Asia Monitor Resource Center for their attempts to seek funding for the project, for their patience in providing me with further information on a couple of the cases collected in this volume, and for giving me some of the photos included here. The National Labor Committee has also graciously allowed me to use photos from its collection; and the Cartography Unit of the Research School of Pacific Studies of the Australian University has drawn the maps. Jeffrey Ballinger, Tim Connor, Gail Dreyfuss, Phil Kaplan, Keir Jorgensen, George White, and many others have helped me in a variety of ways.

I am greatly indebted to colleagues and friends who helped with the translations: Christopher Buckley, Kevin McCready, Eva Hung, Jonathan Hutt, Paul Levine, and Liu Dongxiao; and to the *China Labor Bulletin* and the International Transport Workers Federation for providing several translated materials.

I am particularly grateful to Mark Selden for offering to include this book in his series, and for his unfailing encouragement, his always speedy e-mail responses, his reading of the manuscript, and his perceptive comments; and to Douglas Merwin, who has kindly accepted the manuscript for publication. A big thanks goes to Robert Senser, who has imparted to me his wisdom on labor issues. His e-mail postings and messages are invariably sources of inspiration.

I am grateful to Sarah Leeming for copyediting the manuscript and to Heli Brecht for formatting it. Above all, their interest in the subject matter and their suggestions to improve the manuscript are greatly appreciated.

I owe much to my husband, Jonathan Unger, for his encouragement, critical comments, slash-and-burn style of professional editing, and love. Comfort comes from my daughter, Carla Unger, who understands that her mother's research has to do with the plight of the workers who make so many of the products that fill our stores.

This book is part of a larger project on Chinese labor and management, funded by an Australian Research Council Fellowship and an Australian Research Council Large Grant, for which I am truly grateful. Thanks also go to the Fairbank Center at Harvard University, where portions of the manuscript were written.

Anita Chan

Abbreviations

ACFTU	All-China Federation of Trade Unions
ACWF	All-China Women's Federation
AFL-CIO	American Federation of Labor and Congress of Industrial Organizations
CCP	Chinese Communist Party
CNMI	Commonwealth of the Northern Marianas Islands
FLA	Fair Labor Association
HRWA	Human Rights Watch/Asia
ICFTU	International Conference of Free Trade Unions
ILO	International Labor Organization
ITF	International Transport Workers Federation
NGO	Non-Governmental Organization
OSH	Occupational Safety and Health
PNTR	Permanent normal trade relations
PRC	People's Republic of China
PSB	Public Security Bureau
SEZ	Special Economic Zone
UN	United Nations
UDHR	Universal Declaration of Human Rights
WTO	World Trade Organization

U.S.$/Yuan Exchange Rate, 1990–1999

Year	1U.S.$/Yuan
1990	4.7838
1991	5.3227
1992	5.5149
1993	5.7619
1994	8.6187
1995	8.3507
1996	8.3142
1997	8.2898
1998	8.2791
1999	8.2798

Map 1: Location of Cases in China

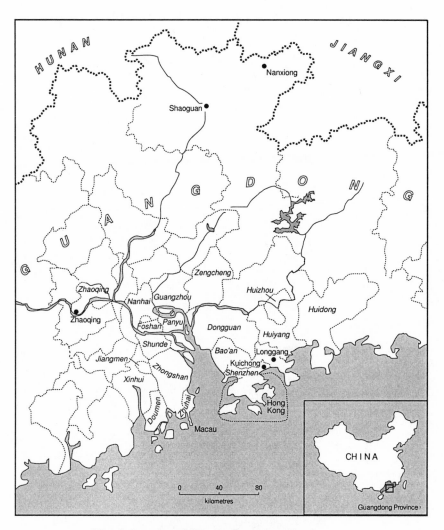

Map 2: Location of Cases in Guangdong Province

CHINA'S WORKERS
UNDER ASSAULT

Chapter 1

Introduction

The social science profession requires that we be rigorously "objective," and therefore, dispassionate. Social scientists are to extract hidden meanings from empirical facts and articulate them in generalizations and abstractions. Better still, we are to theorize and, somewhere along the way, throw in some jargon to show off our learnedness. These constructed texts are usually dry, but can be informative, and even may excite the intellect. But often, they do not have much of a feel for the people being studied. I have been guilty of this same pursuit after social-science professionalism in most of my previous work on labor, management, and industrial relations in China.

Over the past seven years, I have waded through Chinese journals and newspapers, interviewed managers, workers, and union officials in China, and conducted surveys. These investigations have formed the basis for more than a dozen papers that have all been aimed at academic readers. Then one day, while going through my expanding files of Chinese-language newspaper clippings, I felt deeply moved by these articles. Story after story of workers being mistreated leapt to life. I came to believe that these stories needed to be brought to a more general readership so that the harsh realities that millions of workers in China face can be made known in a way that will be vivid and informative.

This volume can be used to complement academic articles on Chinese labor. When inundated with facts and figures about rising unemployment, escalating industrial disputes, protests, labor go-slows, and strikes, these stories put flesh and blood on reified, bare-bones quantitative data. The investigative articles published in Chinese newspapers and magazines that have been collected for this book were selected from nearly a decade of clippings from some fifty different Chinese newspapers and periodicals, as well as a few from Hong Kong and Taiwan. In choosing the articles, I wanted to illustrate the range of labor-rights abuses that have been occurring in China in enterprises of different kinds of ownership.

A New Role of the Chinese Media

Not so many years ago, Chinese journalists had to write in communist slogans, and specialists had to read between the lines while dismissing the media as official propaganda. But in the 1980s, journalism gained greater freedom and a new genre of investigative reporting began to appear. The stories in these reports are usually very detailed, containing dates, names, and place names, and sometimes they include even the reporters' probing questions and the telling answers of cornered interviewees, usually managers and bureaucrats. This type of journalist was unknown in the Maoist era. The obsession for precision seems a reaction to the previous sloganizing that used to pass for journalism in China.

Only Chinese reporters and Chinese government investigators are able to unearth such detail. It is nearly impossible for Western reporters or academics, or even Chinese academics, to carry out this kind of investigative research. Nor is it easy for Chinese newspaper reporters, who often encounter intense resistance from local authorities and enterprise managers, to gather information, and still more difficult for them to write up their findings truthfully. Some risk their personal safety by disguising themselves as migrant workers to observe conditions firsthand (see, for instance, cases 2 and 6).[1] In case 2, where a woman journalist went undercover into a factory to confirm rumors of serious mistreatment of workers, her newspaper was so concerned about her safety that it sent a colleague to visit her every day pretending to be her relative.

Readers may wonder why a country notorious for its tight control over the media would allow such detailed reports on the mistreatment of workers to appear in print. After all, these represent serious failings of the political system—a system that still uses the rhetoric that China is a socialist workers' state, praising its workers as "masters of the enterprises" or "masters of the state."

There are a number of reasons why these extraordinary reports came to see the light of day. First, the Chinese government is not monolithic. Some government bureaus are quite aware of and concerned about the maltreatment of workers. The official trade unions and the local government labor bureaus are the most likely to be sympathetic to labor (see, for example, cases 1, 3, and 18). Most of the cases in this book come from newspapers and journals published by the All-China Federation of Trade Unions (ACFTU) and the Ministry of Labor (for example, the *Shenzhen Special Economic*

Zone News, the *Zhuhai Labor News, Chinese Workers,* and *China's Labor News*), or by quasi-government institutions like the Communist Youth League and the All-China Women's Federation. These last two organizations take a reasonably liberal stance in their publications and are willing to test the limits of censorship (for instance, the *Shenzhen Youth News* and *Chinese Women News*). These are not the kinds of reports that are ever likely to appear in China's economics and business newspapers.

Finally, precisely because the government continues to call itself "socialist," it needs to bolster its legitimacy by showing that it cares for workers' interests. Taking advantage of this, reporters and editors who want to expose social injustice have some space to maneuver. In fact, as can be seen in cases 1, 2, 3, and 16, mistreated workers often seek help from the media. The reports instigate a public outcry, which in turn applies moral pressure on the authorities (often the local authorities) to help the abused workers.

Unfortunately, follow-up reports are not common in the Chinese press. Going through the newspapers after the original reports were published usually yields nothing. Readers are left wondering how some of these cases ended, especially those that ended up in court. When circumstances permitted, I did some follow-up research by going through other kinds of documentation to put a particular case into perspective, or by visiting the area to gain a better understanding of the case and interviewing some of the people concerned. For example, in case 13, which involved the deaths of eighty toy factory workers, I have kept in touch with non-governmental labor organizations in Hong Kong to follow the struggle for compensation that has been going on for seven years. For case 18, concerning the imprisonment of Chinese seafarers on charges of "leaking state secrets," I visited the International Transport Federation in London, which had lodged a complaint to the International Labor Organization (ILO) on the seafarers' behalf. For case 19 on the export of Chinese labor to the Commonwealth of the Northern Marianas Islands (a U.S. territory), I have kept in close contact with the law firm that is handling applications from some of the workers seeking asylum in the United States. The report on serious health hazards in the footwear industry in Putian city (case 11) prompted me to go to Putian to interview workers, villagers, and the trade union. Such supplementary research appears in some of the introductions and commentaries that accompany the cases.

How representative are the cases selected for this book? As I shall note in separate introductions to each of the cases, some are common occurrences, whereas others represent unusual and serious cases of violence or abuse. Case 4, where migrants were lured to an isolated area with the promise of a job, then were made to work in slave-like conditions and risked being shot when they tried to escape, surely does not happen every day. This case was chosen because the text reveals how the owners of the kiln, the local authorities, and the local police colluded to trap the workers. Less extreme are stories such as cases 1 and 6, where workers are kept under tight surveillance during and after work hours by private security guards hired by the factories. In some parts of southern China, these controls are not uncommon. All of these examples were brought to the attention of the media and the authorities only when the exploitation became intolerable and the workers began to openly protest. There is every reason to believe that these cases are only the tip of the iceberg.

The earliest of these articles go back to 1991. It would be hoped that conditions have improved since then, but not much has changed.[2] Studies of toy and shoe factories in Shenzhen city by two Hong Kong–based labor NGOs reveal that conditions for workers in these factories did not improve over time—the same long working hours, the same low wages, the same myriad of fines for breaking arbitrary factory rules, and the same toxic fumes on the shop floor.[3] In fact, in many factories conditions have worsened. The dramatic increase in the number of officially recorded labor disputes is a reflection of this trend (see chapter 6). Given the Asian economic crisis, declining foreign investment in China in the late 1990s, wage pressures from Asian competitors, and massive unemployment in the state sector, China's workers in 2000 seem even more vulnerable. The number of foreign-funded factories and state enterprises that owe wages or pensions to workers rose rapidly in the late 1990s. Industrial conflicts have risen. The biggest conflict is over unpaid wages: in 1996 the Guangdong Labor Bureau secured 21 million yuan of owed wages for the workers,[4] in 1997 it was 150 million yuan, and in 1998 it was 450 million yuan.[5] The money was owed to migrant workers mainly by Asian investors. A survey conducted by the ACFTU in 1997 of 10,000 state enterprise production-line workers all over China found that 25 percent of workers reported being owed wages. Of these, 20 percent said their wages were over two months in arrears, and 30 percent up to three months in arrears.[6]

To fully comprehend the situation facing China's factory workers today, it is imperative to first understand that there are two main groups of workers. Before economic reforms began and China opened itself to the outside world, all of China's industry was publicly owned, by either state or collective enterprises, and factory employees were called *zhigong* (*zhi* meaning staff, *gong* meaning worker). This term implies a white- or blue-collar urban worker who enjoys lifetime employment and lifelong benefits provided by the work unit. It also implies that workers have residency rights where the work unit is located. Since the economic reforms, more and more of these workers have been laid off. Their urban residency status provides them with a minimal safety net, but it is fraying badly.

As the market economy emerges, a different type of factory worker has arisen. Unlike the *zhigong*, these workers work "for a boss" in the non-state and non-collective sector. In Chinese, this is known as *dagong*. To *dagong* has a pejorative connotation in Chinese socialist ideology. Such workers are called a *dagongmei* if a woman (the suffix *mei* means little sister, as a way of signaling their low status), and if a man, a *dagongzai* (*zai* means boy). They tend to come from the poorer parts of the country-side and many have traveled long distances to work on a temporary basis in the multitude of factories that have mushroomed in the coastal regions. Because they have a temporary work status, they are usually referred to in English as "migrant workers."[7]

The Plight of China's Migrant Workers

As will be seen from the reports collected in this volume, migrant workers are the main victims of the most serious labor-rights violations. Migrant workers numbered about 80 million in 1999,[8] a group almost as large as the urban state-enterprise and urban collective workforce combined. Most migrant workers are attracted to the more developed regions in China, especially the special economic zones and coastal cities, and are hired by foreign-funded enterprises, private enterprises, and rural collectives. They constitute a cheap and flexible source of labor in the new free labor market that has so often been hailed as the cornerstone of China's economic success. In keeping with the format and thrust of this book, and in order to effectively convey how the rights of many of the migrant workers are being violated, I will cite a letter cosigned by more than twenty workers of a foreign-funded footwear factory that was sent in 1995 to the editor of the *Workers' Daily*, the official trade union's newspaper:

Dear Comrade Editor,

We are staff and workers of Guangdong's Zhaojie Footwear Company. The company docks our pay, deducts and keeps our deposits, beats, abuses, and humiliates us at will.

Zhaojie Company is a joint venture. It sends people to Sichuan, Henan, and Hunan provinces to recruit workers. Even children under sixteen are their targets.

We people from out of province only knew we had been cheated after getting here. The reality is completely different from what we were told by the recruiter. Now even though we want to leave, we cannot because they would not give us back our deposit and our temporary residential permit, and have not been giving us our wages. This footwear company has hired over one hundred live-in security guards, and has even set up teams to patrol the factory. The staff and workers could not escape even if they had wings. The only way to get out of the factory grounds is to persuade the officer in charge of issuing leave permits to let you go. A Henan worker wanted to resign but was not allowed to by the office. So he climbed over the wall to escape, but was crushed to death by a passing train. Although it means forfeiting the deposit and wages and losing their temporary residential permits, each year about one thousand workers somehow leave this place.

Being beaten and abused are everyday occurrences, and other punishments include being made to stand on a stool for everyone to see, to stand facing the wall to reflect on your mistakes, or being made to crouch in a bent-knee position.

The staff and workers often have to work from 7:00 a.m. to midnight. Many have fallen ill. It is not easy to even get permission for a drink of water during working hours.

> Signed: Guangdong Zhaoqing City Zhaojie Company,
> *Yang Shuangqi, Li Xiaohua, and some twenty others*

When the *Workers' Daily* received this letter, it decided to publish it in a classified periodical limited to government officials. This resulted in the provincial labor bureau and the provincial trade union conducting investigations of the allegations. But it was several months before the *Workers' Daily* released the findings to the public (see case 1).

This short letter is reprinted here because it embodies the different kinds of labor-rights violations that migrant workers experience in China's foreign-funded factories, particularly those that are Asian. What is unusual in this case is that a single factory contained so many violations, and that the violations were so extreme. But to varying degrees, this type of treatment of migrant workers is also found in other types of factories. Abuses are also common in privately owned factories, to a lesser extent in factories owned by the local governments in rural villages and townships, and even in the enterprises owned by the central state.[9]

As the letter illustrates, Chinese peasants working in urban areas hold a very different status from the local urban residents.[10] They are required to possess a "temporary residential permit" and are trapped if the employer takes it away from them. Their residential status is similar to foreign nationals living as guest workers. They are not entitled to any of the benefits enjoyed by the local residents such as social welfare, schooling, the right to own property, to bring their spouses or children with them, or even any right to residency.[11] Once their labor is no longer required, they are supposed to go back to their place of origin.[12] Socially they are discriminated against by local residents, as illustrated by case 10.[13]

The migrants are subject to tight "immigration" controls under China's household registration (*hukou*) system. In order to leave their village, peasants have to apply for a permit from their local government. To stay in any city, they have to apply to the local police for a temporary residential permit. To work in the cities, they need to secure a contract with an employer, and then their stay needs to be approved by the local labor bureau, which issues a work permit.[14] Periodically, the police carry out raids to round up those who do not possess a permit. Those caught are harassed, humiliated, and mistreated, thrown into detention centers where the conditions are sometimes worse than state prisons, and then sent back to the countryside.[15] The temporary residence permit is therefore extremely important to migrant workers. The permit system controls them in a similar way to the passbook system under apartheid. Most migrant workers live in crowded dormitories provided by the factories or in shanties. Their transient existence is precarious and exploitative.[16] The discrimination against migrant workers in the Chinese case is not racial, but the control mechanisms set in place in the so-called free labor market to regulate the supply of cheap labor, the underlying economic logic of the system, and the abusive consequences suffered by the migrant workers, share many of the characteristics of the apartheid system.

The household registration system provides the perfect conditions for forced and bonded labor. The Zhaojie workers' letter provides an idea of how this works. Workers are required to pay for the temporary residence permit and the work permit in one lump sum. Often, when the cost of the permit is too high for the migrants to afford, the factory pays on behalf of the worker and then deducts a sum from each month's wages, trapping the worker in a bonded relationship.[17]

In a buyers' labor market, factories can dictate terms of employment and often charge "deposits" of between half a month to a month's wages, further bonding the workers.[18] Workers forfeit the "deposit" if they quit without the permission of management before the contract expires, or if they are fired. In many other cases, the factory simply keeps part of the workers' wages each month, promising to return the money at the end of the year.[19] Even if working conditions at these factories are truly terrible, migrant workers cannot afford to lose the "deposit" and other sums of money that are owed to them, and have to continue to work there until their contracts expire. In some cases, the factory management collects the workers' residential permits and identity papers for "safekeeping," as in the Zhaojie case—a practice that is illegal. Without the permit, workers cannot go out into the streets, becoming vulnerable to being caught by a police identity check, still less quit to seek another job. With the support of this system, the factories can be assured of a low labor turnover rate and a stable workforce (cases 2 and 6).[20] Western criticism of China's forced labor system usually focuses on prison labor, but China's household registration system to all intents and purposes leads to a situation of forced bonded labor for millions of "free" workers.

The hiring of private security guards in factory and dormitory compounds is very common in China. The Zhaojie case is extreme in that more than one hundred guards were hired for a factory of 2,700 workers.[21] Companies that supply private security guards are often connected to the police or the armed police (*wujing*); in fact, in their spare time, police officers sometimes work as security guards. They often carry electric batons and handcuffs, which are freely available in China's domestic arms market. This internal security system set up behind factory walls is extremely effective in intimidating and controlling workers, especially since it often is augmented by off-duty police who simply switch uniforms.

Under this atmosphere of intimidation, some factories can get away with imposing strict rules to control the workers. One commonly used restriction is to drastically limit the number of times workers are allowed to drink water (as in Zhaojie Company) or go to the toilet. In an extreme case, workers at one factory who went to the toilet more than twice a day were fined 60 yuan, more than two days' wages.[22] Some other factories conduct body searches whenever workers leave the factory compound.

These sorts of controls are most prevalent in the Korean and Taiwan-invested firms, and to a lesser extent, in firms with owners from Hong Kong. This is borne out by a survey that I conducted in 1996 of 1,530 workers in fifty-four footwear factories of all types of ownership. For example, among workers at enterprises with owners from Taiwan and Hong Kong, 81 percent reported there were restrictions on going to the bathroom, and 70 percent said they needed to obtain permission to go to the toilet. No restrictions were reported in enterprises under PRC Chinese managers. When workers break factory rules, they are often fined, and some factories even get away with disciplining them physically (again, see the Zhaojie workers case). Corporal punishment occurs in all kinds of enterprises, but is highest in the foreign Asian-invested factories. Nearly a third of the workers at the factories surveyed reported that their factories had used physical punishment.[23]

The millions of peasants roaming the country desperately looking for work to earn a hand-to-mouth living make up an almost inexhaustible pool of human machines. They can be worked to the breaking point, and when they flee these dreadful factories, they are simply replaced by fresh, vulnerable batches of workers.

The Myth Surrounding Migrant Workers' Wages

Despite the large of amount of evidence from China's own media that migrant workers are an exploited class, there exists a belief that work in foreign-funded enterprises earns high wages. This myth is built on several misrepresentations. First, the characterization does not distinguish between the investors from the West (including Japan) and from Asia. The Western enterprises generally are larger and more capital intensive, and the wages they pay to production-line workers are comparatively high. For example, the Siemens joint venture in Beijing paid its workers on average 700 yuan a month in 1995 (the average monthly income of state workers was 686 yuan),[24] plus other benefits and subsidized housing, and Siemen's management considered this wage to be lower than in other large Western joint ventures.[25] Western firms do not have the reputation for mistreating and disciplining workers that Asian firms have. Not one case of a Western-owned enterprise surfaced in my collection of documentation. In contrast, many workers at Asian-owned, labor-intensive enterprises are paid below the local legal minimum wage, as can be seen in the cases collected in this volume, and experience harsh discipline and abuse.

It is difficult to gauge what a "fair" international minimum wage would be, as each nation's cost of living and level of development varies. In fact, that is one of the arguments against including any specific amount in international labor standards. We must rely on China's own minimum wage standards, which have been computed by local governments down to the level of districts in cities based on the local cost of living, to judge whether Chinese workers are paid fairly.

In recent years, the Chinese government has introduced such standards for its urban workforce[26] and has made paying minimum wages mandatory in the Labor Law.[27] In 1997, for a forty-four-hour week,[28] the minimum monthly wage was set at 420 yuan (U.S.$54.00) for the Shenzhen Special Economic Zone, 290 yuan ($36.00) for Beijing, and 315 yuan ($45.00) for Shanghai.[29] These standards compare poorly with the minimum wage of $45.00 for Ho Chi Minh City in Vietnam in 1997,[30] given that the cost of living in these Chinese cities is much higher.

Despite this very low minimum wage, managers engage in a wide variety of manipulations to avoid paying it. For example, according to a survey carried out by the Guangdong trade union, 35 percent of the workers interviewed were not paid a higher rate for overtime work as stipulated by law, and when the numbers of hours worked were calculated, it was revealed that 32 percent of the workers were paid below the legal minimum wage. A monthly pay that is higher than the minimum is usually earned by a large amount of enforced overtime. Working two or three hours of overtime seven days a week, with only one or two days off every month, is not uncommon. In fact, in 1996, local trade-union officials in Putian, in Fujian province, told me with some pride that they finally had been able to get the foreign-funded shoe factories (mainly Taiwanese) based there to grant workers at least two days off a month.[31] This regulation still breaches the Labor Law, which stipulates at least one day off a week. If workers are lucky, the enforced overtime is paid at the normal wage rate or a slightly higher rate. In some cases, workers are not paid at all for the overtime.[32] The pay is inadequate even at the best of the Taiwanese- , Hong Kong- , and South Korean–owned factories in China. Take for example, a modern Taiwanese-run enterprise that I visited in Dongguan city, Guangdong province. It is the world's largest footwear factory, employing 40,000 workers and producing running shoes for Adidas, Nike, Reebok, and other major brand names. On average, the workers there made 600 yuan to 700 yuan a month, which is almost double the local minimum wage of 350 yuan. But this seemingly high wage is attained by working about eighty hours of overtime a month (the Labor Law stipulates a maximum overtime of thirty-six hours a month). If the pay is computed based on the legal overtime rate, when averaged out, the entire pay rate is barely above the legal minimum wage.[33] Two rights are being violated here: the right to a fair wage, and the right to rest.

It is clear that the legal minimum-wage standards set by labor-intensive, export-oriented Asian countries such as China, Vietnam, and Indonesia[34] are the lowest possible price at which a government can sell their workers' labor in the international labor market while maintaining their workers' physical survival. This often becomes the maximum price international investors are willing to pay, or not pay, if they can get away with it.

A further problem for workers is that factories often operate a rigid system of discipline, with deductions and fines if factory rules are broken. These rules are often arbitrary in breach of the Labor Law. Fines for violating the rules can be heavy. Fines are meted out for being late, for not turning up for work even if due to illness, or for negligence at work. But the penalties can also be for behavior not related to production: fines for talking and laughing at work, for littering outside work hours, for forgetting to turn off lights, untidy dormitories, and so on.[35] That is to say, workers' wages are eroded by a multitude of deductions. Only if substantial overtime is worked can workers earn above the minimum-wage levels.

Although the two kinds of foreign-invested enterprises (*waizi qiye*)—the Western and Japanese firms on the one side and the Taiwanese, Korean, and Hong Kong firms on the other—treat and pay workers quite differently, no clear distinction is made in Chinese reports. Chinese readers have the impression that Chinese workers are being exploited by Western factory managers because the Chinese character *"wai,"* meaning foreign, invariably conjures up a vision of white-skinned, high-nosed Westerners.[36] The majority of foreign investors are actually ethnically Chinese and they are largely the ones who mistreat mainland Chinese workers.

The Plight of Urban State- and Collective-Sector Workers

The migrant workers from the countryside are not the only ones to face poor working conditions and mistreatment in Chinese factories. For many formerly privileged workers in the state-owned industrial sector (as will be seen in some of the cases contained in this book), working conditions, benefits, and job security have declined precipitously over the past fifteen years. Millions of workers in these state factories are now encountering some of the same conditions that migrant workers face. Before reforms began in China, all regular state-enterprise employees enjoyed lifetime employment and benefits provided by their work unit. But as a market economy emerges, these conditions drastically decline. The decline accelerated during the second half of the 1990s after the Fifteenth Party Congress of September 1997, as state enterprises began to restructure and privatize. Redundancies are reaching unprecedented proportions. According to one estimate, between 20 and 25 million people were laid off in 1996 and 1997, and another 23 to 31 million lost their jobs in 1998 and 1999.[37] In the first half of 1998 alone, 400,000 textile workers were laid off.[38] On average, the families of laid-off workers live on less than 300 yuan ($40.00) a month, and almost half of these people received no money from their work unit and were not entitled to medical benefits.[39]

The number of laid-off workers is not easy to ascertain, and figures vary enormously depending on whether "off-post workers" (*xiagang*) are included. *Xiagang* workers are those who no longer have any work due to closure of production lines or entire factories. But the central government has instituted policies to cushion the shock of state-enterprise restructuring by allowing them to remain employees of their work units, from which they are entitled to draw a survival stipend for a couple of years. This system exists because China does not have an adequate government unemployment system. *Xiagang* workers are not immediately thrown out of their enterprise housing, although their situation is precarious due to the housing reform, and they are also entitled to continue to enjoy some form of health subsidies and pension, provided the enterprise can afford it. The enterprise will also try to find them alternative work or may provide retraining. With such a large number of people out of work though, reemployment is not easy and a stratum of urban poor has emerged in China.[40] After two years of being laid off, employment with their work units is officially terminated. They can then register as unemployed and collect meager unemployment benefits. When benefits expire, they are eligible for other forms of welfare. These urban workers are better off than migrant workers. Above all, they have the security of urban residency.

For urban workers who are able to keep their jobs, conditions have been deteriorating. Pressure from cheap and abundant migrant labor forces employees to accept worsening work conditions. They can be made to work very long hours (case 5), sometimes suffer physical mistreatment (case 9), are owed wages in arrears, or are threatened with redundancy. If their enterprise restructures into a share-holding kind of ownership, they may have to buy shares in the enterprise to keep their jobs, using their lifelong savings even if the enterprise is clearly not viable. In areas of high unemployment, parents are likely to have to pay a high price for a good state job, of up to a year's salary, to ensure that their children enter the job market (cases 14 and 15).[41]

State enterprise employees are more aware than the migrant workers of government rules and regulations and their legal rights. They have better support systems, and because of this, they have the courage and confidence to sometimes fight back collectively, as can be seen in some of these selected cases (cases 16 and 22). In fact, all workers in China, represented by their workplace trade union, are legally entitled to collective consultation (*jiti xieshang*), a euphemism for collective bargaining.[42] The workplace trade-union branch or the higher level trade union and/or local government may support their actions. If they're aggressive and/or lucky enough, they may even be able to democratically elect their workplace trade-union chair (case 15). But holding a line of defense in face of macroeconomic and labor-market changes is not easy. With massive downsizing and the privatization of small and medium-sized state and collective enterprises steaming ahead since the Fifteenth Communist Party Congress of 1997, for many workers the best option is to stage open protests. The threat of social instability is, for the time being, practically all that is stopping the authorities and the free marketeers in government think tanks from sacrificing workers in a headlong rush to capitalism.

The Machinery of Suppression

As noted above, the state is not monolithic. Although some bureaucracies are pro-labor or at least neutral in their attitudes, some offer support and even connive with management to exploit labor. Whereas the central state—

the Ministry of Labor, which enforces labor laws, and the All-China Federation of Trade Unions (ACFTU), which represents the workers vis à vis employers,[43]—may sometimes try to uphold the law, the situation is very different in the counties, townships (former communes), and villages. The lower the level, it seems, the tighter the collusion between officials and management. For example, after the national government mandated that, as of May 1997, the entire country should implement a forty-hour week, the Shenzhen city government appealed to the State Council to delay implementing the new work hours. It argued that foreign investors were complaining that this regulation only allowed an average maximum of one hour of overtime a day, and that this would be impossible to implement because of the frequent necessity to fulfill rush export orders. The State Council did not grant the request, but did compromise by allowing flexible overtime, so long as permission is received from the local labor bureau, and the workers agree. But the total amount of overtime per month should still be within the maximum limit of thirty-six hours, as stipulated by the Labor Law.[44] While the central government is more willing to enforce the law than local governments, in practice, it has allowed the law to be eroded. Because workers must consent to work overtime, this provides management with a loophole, as several of these cases reveal—migrant workers have neither the power nor real representation to negotiate with management. In Shenzhen city today, many of the workers labor ten to twelve hours a day, six or seven days a week.

The local governments' partiality toward management is quite obvious. Corporate tax is a main source of local revenue, and local governments compete to attract foreign investors. The more relaxed the enforcement of labor standards, the more likely that investors will come. Moreover, many local governments and bureaucracies are themselves partners of the joint ventures (see cases 1, 3, and 21). The Chinese side usually provides the land and the factory building, and seeks to ensure the docility of the workers. In such circumstances, government and management stand together against labor. This is quintessentially "bureaucratic capitalism," where power and money fuse into one. The consequences are harsh and exploitative labor regimes. The fact that the workers are mostly migrants, not constituents of these local governments, make them all the more vulnerable to exploitation.

When bureaucracies involved are all pro-management, a willingness to overlook fire, labor, and health and safety regulations is commonplace. The local government does not need to be a partner in business for this to happen, especially since bribery has become an expected component of an official's income. The long investigative report on the Zhili Toy Factory fire (case 13), in which more than eighty workers died, provides a detailed example of a network of bribery.

This book is organized into chapters in accordance with the various kinds of labor-rights violations suffered by the workers, violations that impinge directly on their well-being. While some of the cases collected here are extreme, the very fact that such serious violations exist shows that China's regulatory system has gone awry. The information provided in these reports helps us to comprehend the mechanisms that have allowed such incidents to arise. They may also help to explain the protests that have been breaking out with increasing frequency. At a certain point, workers' docility becomes transformed into collective protest and violence. Workers in several of these selected cases stood together in protest and even went on strike (cases 8, 15, 16, 20, and 22). Others exploded into violent mobs (cases 10 and 21), while yet others tried to resolve their problems through legal avenues (cases 16, 18, and 23).

The authorities prefer workers to take the last course of action, but at the same time, as shall be seen, the legal system is infested with corruption and is beginning to be used by the powerful as a tool to legalize their illegal activities (cases 18, 19, and 20).

Notes

1. Another example is Wang Ningde, "Fifteen-Day Diary of a Journalist as a Worker," *Chinese Sociology and Anthropology*, Vol. 30, No. 4, 1998, pp. 47–74. (Translated from the Chinese text "Yiming jizhe de shiwu tian dagong riji, Gongren ribao xinwen zhoumo," April 27, 1996.)

2. The main exception is that a few of the big subcontractors of famous brand-name apparel companies have instituted some improvements within the past couple of years due to the intense international campaign organized by labor unions and non-government organizations in industrialized countries. But this is not at all the norm. On the improvements, see Steven Greenhouse, "Anti-Sweatshop Movement Is Achieving Gains Overseas," *New York Times,* January 26, 2000. My field interviews in August 1999 in Longgang, near Shenzhen, with several workers at a factory that makes sneakers for one of the big brand names, indicated there have been some reforms for the better—a psychological counsellor has been hired for the workers' benefit, the expression "human rights" has been mentioned, and work hours have been shortened (though this could be due to a decrease in orders).

3. Asia Monitor Resource Center (ed.), "Labour Rights Report on Hong Kong Invested Toy Factories in China," January 1996 and April 1997; "Conditions of Workers in the Shoe Industry of China," November 1995; Hong Kong Christian Industrial Committee & Asia Monitor Resource Center, "Working Conditions in the Sports Shoe Industry in China," October 1997; Hong Kong Christian Industrial Committee, "Nike, Show Workers That Your Commitment to Human Rights Is Genuine," *Exchange*, February 2000, pp. 1–6.

4. *Zhonghua gongshang shibao* (Chinese Industry and Trade News), July 5, 1996. See also Zhuhai City General Trade Union, "Guanyu Zhuhaishi waishang touzi qiye laozi guanxi zhuangkuang de diaocha baogao " (Investigative Report of the Industrial

Relations of Foreign-funded Enterprises in Zhuhai City", *Guangdong gongyun* (Guangdong Labor Movement), No. 12, 1999, pp. 21–23.

5. Zhou Shan, "Laodongfa: taping kanke cheng dalu*"* (The Labor Law: Smoothing out the Bumps to Form a Thoroughfare), *Canyezhe* (Founding Fathers), No. 7, 1999, pp. 4–6.

6. ACFTU Policy Research Department, *1997 Zhongguo zhigong zhuangkuan diaocha: shujuquan* (Survey of the Status of Chinese Staff and Workers in 1997: Volume on Statistics), Beijing: Xiyuan Publishing House, 1999, pp.1346–1349.

7. A recent study of the situation of migrant workers is Dorothy J. Solinger, *Contesting Citizenship in Urban China: Peasants Migrants, the State, and the Logic of the Market,* Berkeley, CA: University of California Press, 1999.

8. Zhang Xi, "Liudong renkou guanli fazhihua*"* (Legalization of the Management of the Floating Population), *People's Daily*, January 27, 1999.

9. Examples of abuses in state-owned enterprises are described by Zhao Minghua and Theo Nichols, "Management Control of Labour in State-Owned Enterprises: Cases from the Textile Industry," *The China Journal*, No. 36 (July 1996), pp. 1–21.

10. See Dorothy Solinger, "Human Rights Issues in China's Internal Migration: Insights from Comparisons with Germany and Japan," in Joanne R. Bauer and Daniel A. Bell (eds.), *East Asian Challenge for Human Rights,* New York: Cambridge University Press, 1999, pp. 285–312.

11. These rules and regulations vary slightly from place to place in accordance with local government policies. In some places, an urban registration can be bought for several thousand to 10,000 yuan, at least about seven times a peasant's annual income. Details of the control system can be found in "Reform of the *Hukou* System," *Chinese Sociology and Anthropology*, Vol. 20, No. 1 (Fall 1996), entire issue.

12. The "International Convention on the Protection of the Rights of All Migrant Workers" refers only to cross-national labor migrants, but it could have applied equally well here, as these people are trapped in analogous circumstances. See the "International Convention on the Protection of the Rights of All Migrant Workers and Members of Their Families," A/RES/45/158, December 18, 1990 (*The United Nations and Human Rights, 1945–1995*, New York: United Nations, Blue Books Series, volume VII, 1995), pp. 383–402.

13. For a description of the economic and social relationship between peasant migrant workers and local residents in a village near Shenzhen, see Anita Chan, Richard Madsen, and Jonathan Unger, *Chen Village Under Mao and Deng*, Berkeley: University of California Press, 1992, pp. 299–308.

14. Since labor contracts are stipulated by law to provide some sort of job security for workers, requiring approval of contracts from the local labor bureau is not necessarily disadvantageous to the worker. An officially approved labor contract entitles the worker to legal protection when a dispute with management arises.

15. Zhao Shukai, "Criminality and the Policing of Migrant Workers," *The China Journal,* No. 43 (January 2000), pp. 101–110; Human Rights in China report, *Not Welcome at the Party; Behind the "Clean-up" of China's Cities—a Report on Administrative Detention Under "Custody and Repatriation,"* HRIC Arbitrary Dentention Series, No. 2, September 1999.

16. Mobo Gao, "Migrant Workers From Rural China: Their Conditions and Some Social Implications for Economic Development in South China," in David Schak (ed.), *Entrepreneurship, Economic Growth and Social Change: The Transformation of Southern China*, Brisbane: Griffith University, Centre for the Study of Australia-Asia Rela-

tions, Paper no. 71, pp. 21–38. Also see Dorothy Solinger, "Employment Channels and Job Categories Among the 'Floating Population,'" in Greg O'Leary (ed.), *Adjusting to Capitalism: Chinese Workers and Their State*, Armonk, NY: M.E. Sharpe, 1998, pp. 3–47.

17. The cost of the work permit varies from place to place, ranging from 20 yuan to several hundred yuan in the Shenzhen region. See Zhao Shukai, *Nongmin liudong de jizhi yu zuzhi (jianjiu baogao)* (The Mechanism and Organization of the Movement of Peasants), Beijing: State Council Development Research Centre, Village Section, 1996, p. 35.

18. Anita Chan, "Chinese Factories and Two Kinds of Free Market (Read Bonded) Workforce," *Asia Pacific Business Review*, special issue on "Globalization and Labour Market Deregulation: Trade Unions in the Asia Pacific Region," Vol. 6, Nos. 3 and 4 (Spring/Summer 2000), pp. 260–281.

19. *Zhujiang sanjiaozhou gongren quanyi zhuangkuang* (The Situation of Workers' Rights in the Pearl River Delta Region), Hong Kong: Asia Monitor Resource Center, 1995, p. 14. My own fieldwork in April 1997 in a township in Guangdong, where most manufacturing enterprises are domestic and privately owned, showed the payment of wages seems to be even more irregular than in the foreign-funded enterprises.

20. For an excellent example of how this system was able to bond workers under horrific conditions, see *Workers' Daily*, April 17, 1994. This practice is in blatant violation of ILO Convention 105 concerning the abolition of forced labor, which China has not ratified. One of the core standards proposed for inclusion of the social clause in the WTO negotiations is the prevention of forced or slave labor.

21. Examples of this kind of intimidation and the violence inflicted on workers can be found in *Zhuhai laodong bao* (Zhuhai Labor News), October 24, 1994; *South China Morning Post*, December 6, 1995; *Fujian tongxun* (Fujian Bulletin), No. 2, 1994, pp. 21–23.

22. *Nanfang ribao* (Southern News), January 24, 2000. In the factory described in this article, workers are only allowed to go to the toilet two times a day. But because there were not enough toilets, one worker was not able to have his turn. When he went a third time, he was fired.

23. Chan, "Chinese Factories."

24. *Chinese Statistical Yearbook, 1995*, Beijing: State Statistical Bureau, 1995, p. 117.

25. Based on my field research in Beijing in 1995.

26. The rationale and motivation behind the Chinese government's introduction of the minimum wage and poverty line in the 1990s need further research. For example, it is not clear to what extent the government found the minimum wage necessary to prevent exploitation of labor, especially in foreign-funded enterprises, or to what extent it was set with the intent of arriving at the lowest possible minimum wage for Chinese labor so that Chinese wages are still competitive in the world labor market. For minimum-wage standards set for different parts of China in 1995, see *China Labour Bulletin*, No. 18 (October 1995), p. 6.

27. Chinese Labor Law, Chapter 5, Articles 48 and 49. *Workers' Daily*, July 6, 1994. China has ratified ILO Convention No. 26 regarding the setting of a minimum-wage standard. ACFTU, Legal Work Department, *Waiguo laodongfa yu guoji laodong gongyue he jianyishu xuanbiao* (Collection of other Countries' Labor Laws and International Labor Conventions and Recommendations), Beijing: Chinese Workers' Press, 1994, pp. 580–585.

28. As of May 1, 1997, the legal work week has been shortened to forty hours for the entire nation. *Zhongguo laodong bao* (China Labor News), July 28, 1997.

29. Ibid.

30. *Nike Labor Practices in Vietnam,* an unpublished report distributed by Vietnam Labor Watch in New York, January 30, 1997.

31. Based on June 1996 field interview.

32. Based on a survey of twenty foreign-funded enterprises carried out in 1993 by the Guangdong Provincial General Trade Union. *Zhujiang sanjiaozhou gongren,* Hong Kong: Asia Monitor Resource Center, 1995, p. 19.

33. Anita Chan, "Boot Camp at the Shoe Factory: Where Taiwanese Bosses Drill Chinese Workers to Make Sneakers for American Joggers," *Washington Post,* November 3, 1996. A general picture of the problem of violation of labor standards in China is summarized in a Chinese Communist Party document issued in February 1994, "Yixie waishang touzi qiye yanzhong qinfan shigong hefa quanyi" (Some Foreign-funded Enterprises Seriously Violate Workers' Legal Rights), *Jiushi niandai* (The Nineties), April 1994, pp. 53–55.

34. "Minimum Wage Set to Rise 15 to 55 Percent," *Jakarta Post,* February 22, 2000; "Workers Demand Higher Minimum Wages," *Jakarta Post,* April 7, 2000.

35. See *Jiushi niandai* (The Nineties), April 1994, pp. 53–55, for a good example of such a list of fines. Monetary penalties have also become very prevalent in state enterprises. My survey of fifty-four footwear factories mentioned earlier also shows widespread monetary penalties across all kinds of enterprises.

36. Yet between 1979 and 1995, 67 percent of foreign direct investment in China came from Hong Kong, Macau, and Taiwan. The other two main foreign investors were Japan and the United States, each making up 8 percent. South Korean investment only constituted 1.3 percent of the total. *The Economist,* March 8, 1997, p. 12.

37. Antoine Kernen and Jean-Louis Rocca, "Social Responses to Unemployment and the 'New Urban Poor'—Case Study in Shenyang City and Liaoning Province," *China Perspectives,* No. 27 (January–February 2000), pp. 35–51.

38. *China Daily,* July 22, 1998.

39. Ding Yang, "Xiagang—jintian Zhongguo de remen huati " (Being Laid Off—A Hot Topic in Today's China), *Dangdai Zhongguo yanjiu* (Contemporary China Research), No. 1, 1998, p. 113.

40. Kernen and Rocca, "Social Responses to Unemployment."

41. Chan, "Chinese Factories."

42. The expression "collective bargaining" is not used because it suggests an industrial relationship that is too confrontational for China's current ideology. For details of the history and legal framework of China's collective consultative system, see Ngok Kinglun, "New Collective Labor Relation Mechanisms in the Workplace: The Collective Contract System in Mainland China," *Issues and Studies,* Vol. 35, No. 6 (November/December 1999), pp. 119–143.

43. Anita Chan, "Chinese Trade Unions and Workplace Relations in the State-Owned and Joint-Venture Enterprises," in Malcolm Warner (ed.), *Changing Workplace Relations in the Chinese Economy,* London: Macmillan, 2000, pp. 34–56.

44. Li Guiru, "Laodongfa zai zheli xingtong xushe—yige dagongzai zhi si yinqi chu fazhi huati" (The Labor Law Here Is an Empty Shell—Discussion of the Legality Question After the Death of a *Dagongzai*), *Zhongguo qingnian bao* (China Youth Daily), January 5, 1999.

Chapter 2

Forced Labor and Violations of Shop-Floor Labor Standards

The five newspaper articles selected for this chapter are intended to give readers a picture of the forms of exploitation faced by many migrant workers and an increasingly large number of state enterprise workers. The first selection describes the findings of the investigations by officials of Guangdong province in the letter by the Zhaojie workers (the letter itself appeared in the previous chapter). The next two newspaper articles about other factories provide graphic details of migrant workers' exhaustion from long work hours and their struggle to survive on extremely low, or worse, unpaid wages. For these workers, there is no exit option because they are "bonded." Management has withheld their ID cards, or refused to return their deposits and unpaid wages. Many find themselves trapped in a Catch-22 situation. The longer they have worked, the more their unpaid wages accumulate, and the more difficult they find it to leave. That explains why some workers continue to tolerate abusive conditions. These cases are worse than most, so they have elicited outrage and exposure by investigative journalists. But the mechanisms through which management can pay migrant workers below the free-market rate exists to one degree or another in many other factories.

In the most extreme circumstances, even bonds and unpaid wages become insufficient means to retain workers, and workers are literally held captive. Such a situation was mentioned in the Zhaojie letter, and case 4 provides a second example, this time involving two murders. Unlike the first four cases, which are about migrant workers, the chapter's final case is about urban workers and their offspring who, used to the regulated labor standards of the state sector, have recently begun working in joint-venture firms. It will be seen in this article how the entry of large numbers of migrants into the labor market has been driving down labor standards throughout China.

CASE 1

The use of security guards and corporal punishment at the Zhaojie Footwear Company in Guangdong province was described in the previous chapter. Workers secretly sent a joint letter to the Workers' Daily, *the national union newspaper located in Beijing. The workers were aware that the higher the level of authority they approached, the more likely it would be that their complaints would attract attention. They were right. The provincial government intervened.*

The Zhaojie factory is a joint venture established by three partners: a local city-owned enterprise, China Travels; a Hong Kong firm; and a Taiwanese footwear factory. The Taiwanese partner was the main owner and was solely in charge of the day-to-day management of the factory. Rather than acting as a moderating influence to ensure that management did not excessively exploit the workers, the Chinese partner ignored the abuses, and may even have acted in complicity.

A close reading of this article, based on the workers' letter, and of another article published five months earlier in December in the local Guangdong Labor News *(Guangdong laodong bao)[1] suggests serious disagreements among the various bureaucracies involved in handling the case. This case reveals important dynamics of Chinese bureaucratic politics toward labor. The workers' letter, which they had titled "Zhaojie Footwear Company Is a Living Hell," had originally been sent to the* Workers' Daily *in November 1995. But the* Workers' Daily *did not immediately publish it. Instead it was included in an internal classified news bulletin, indicating the sensitivity of the case. In response to the letter's appearance in this bulletin, the Guangdong provincial government asked the provincial labor bureau and the provincial trade union to each set up separate investigations. Based on the labor bureau's investigation, the* Guangdong Labor News *published an article accusing the workers of exaggerating their conditions, accompanied by a mild reproach to management. For a while it looked like the workers had lost.*

But two months later, the provincial trade union and the provincial government produced reports that confirmed the workers' complaints. As a result, the Workers' Daily *published this article a full five months after it received the letter. Without saying as much, the story challenged the "facts" presented in the* Guangdong Labor News *article. Exactly what bureaucratic maneuverings occurred during that five-month period is unclear. What is obvious, though, is that the* Workers Daily, *being a central-level newspaper, did have some influence in spurring the Guangdong provincial government to investigate. It appears also that Guangdong's provincial labor bureau preferred to tread very softly when the mistreatment of factory workers was raised, while the provincial trade union, in producing an investigative report that exposed the factory management's practices, undercut that strategy by taking a pro-labor stance.*

ZHAOJIE FOOTWEAR COMPANY: MISTREATMENT OF WORKERS UNDER INVESTIGATION—OVERTIME, EXTRA SHIFTS, AND ARBITRARY PHYSICAL PUNISHMENT—WE CAN'T TAKE IT ANYMORE*

After being published in the "Selected Letters to the Editor" column of our newspaper's classified publication for officials, the letter from Yang Shuangqi, Li Xiaohua, and twenty other staff and workers of the Zhaoqing city's Zhaojie Footwear Company drew the attention of the Guangdong provincial leadership. Provincial Governor Zhu Senlin instructed the Guangdong labor bureau, "please send someone to this factory to investigate." Provincial Party Secretary Xie Fei also instructed, "provincial trade union, please send someone to investigate and also discuss with the local leadership how to handle the matter." In November and December 1995, the provincial labor bureau and trade union both sent investigators to Zhaoqing city to look into the Zhaojie incident. This was followed by months of close contact with the factory to ensure that the footwear company implements rectification measures. This February and March, the *Workers' Daily* separately received copies of the reports written by the provincial labor bureau and trade union for the provincial Party and provincial government.

The reports confirm the validity of the workers' letter of complaint, reflecting in various degrees that the Zhaojie Footwear Company collects deposits, recruits child labor, confiscates personal documents, physically punishes staff and workers, and imposes excessive overtime and shifts. Of all these violations, excessive overtime is the most serious. Staff and workers must work overtime shifts five nights a week, from 6:00 P.M. to 10:00 P.M.; the less dexterous workers sometimes have to work until midnight. Sometimes, to finish a rush order, workers are made to work all through the night. The length of working hours far exceeds the maximum stipulated by China's labor laws.

---

*Translation from the Chinese text: Liu Xinhua, "Zhaojie xieye gongsi kedai yuangong shou chachu," *Gongren ribao* (Workers' Daily), April 17, 1996. Translated by Anita Chan.

The company has 2,700 staff and workers, 90 percent of whom are from outside the province, and 85 percent are women. All new employees have to pay a deposit of 500 yuan for men and 150 yuan for women. If for any reason the employee leaves the job or is dismissed before the end of two years, the deposit is not returned and the last month's pay is docked.

As for the problem of child labor, because the company is not rigorous in examining identity documents, it has hired five children under sixteen years of age (now they have been allowed to go).

The workers' temporary work permits were collected by the company and kept locked up. Management practices include physical punishments. The most commonly used method was to make the worker run laps in the factory grounds while carrying shoe tops or other manufactured parts, make them hop like a frog, stand on a high stool, or spin on the spot in a bent-over position with one hand and both feet touching the ground.

The investigative report confirms that a Henan employee was indeed run over by a train. Before this incident he had applied to quit his job, but had been refused. The company has now paid a certain amount of compensation to his family.

The report also points out that staff and workers were not compensated for work injuries. In the first half of 1995, those who were injured had to pay their own medical bills. In the second half of the year (after official investigations), the policy was changed: the company paid the medical bills, but not wage nor living costs. The problem of overtime work not being properly compensated is a serious one. Overtime wage rates at the factory are paid at normal wage rates: that is, there are no overtime penalty rates. This does not comply with labor laws.

Zhaojie Footwear Company is a joint venture set up in 1991 by the Zhonglu (China Travels) Corporation from Zhaoqing city, the Taiwan Zhongjie Footwear Company Ltd., and the Hong Kong Chonghuang Company Ltd. The general manager was brought in by the Taiwanese partner. After the letter of complaint appeared in our internal publication, it caused a big stir in both the Zhonglu Corporation and the Zhaojie Footwear Company. The leadership of these companies immediately reported to the authorities that they were rectifying the problems.

To prevent the recruitment of child labor, management stated that the recruitment procedures would be strictly observed and that documents would be sent to the labor bureau for approval. There were other promises: if management personnel violated regulations by using physical punishments, they would be penalized; shop-floor ventilation and meals would be improved; 500 new workers would be recruited; proper training would be provided; the amount of overtime would be reduced; the wages of staff and workers would be gradually increased; and the functions of the company's trade union, youth league, and women's federation would be utilized to help cultivate staff and workers' feelings of identity with the company. The Guangdong Provincial

General Trade Union raised a few objections to these rectification measures. It objected to the company asking workers to pay the so-called property safeguard fees in lieu of what was previously called "guarantee fees." The union argued that both were deposits in disguise. It also expressed concern that the company continued to show a lack of interest in improving workers' occupational health and safety compensation and overtime wage rates. In response, the company indicated it accepted the criticisms and said that it would implement changes.

The investigative report fully supports the workers' complaints. It notes that under the conditions of today's market economy, supply of labor exceeds demand, thus placing laborers in a weak position and forcing them to tolerate any invasion of their legal rights. Very few dare to use the laws that endow them with rights to step forth to defend themselves. But only if people begin to act like Yang and his colleagues and bring the problem to the attention of the authorities can this kind of problem be speedily resolved. We hope that our brothers and sisters who have come to Guangdong to make a living will learn from this report, and that when they encounter similar situations in the future, they will not be intimidated, will not capitulate, and will step forward with courage and report the mistreatment to the authorities. The Party, the government, and the law will be there to support you.

CASE 2

After a local evening newspaper received letters from workers complaining about the work conditions in one factory, one of the newspaper's reporters volunteered to work in the factory disguised as a migrant to experience the working conditions herself. This article is a day-by-day report of what she witnessed. The factory's owners were not revealed, but from the context it was most likely a small urban collective or privately owned factory that only hired migrant laborers. As shall be seen, work conditions were unusually harsh, the pay incredibly low, and the length of bondage longer than the normal one or two years.

Although the reporter did not specify the gender ratio of workers in the factory, there seems to be quite a large number of men. These men seem to be doing the same tasks as women workers, earning the same wages. In my visit to the collective and private enterprises in Fujian, I generally found more men on the production lines doing the same work as women, as opposed to the foreign-funded enterprises in Guangdong province which tend to put only women on the production lines.

WORKING UNDERCOVER IN A FACTORY*

> In early March more than ten workers eagerly told their stories about the Hangzhou Tewaida Company to the complaint hotline set up by *Qianjiang Evening News*. To find out the full story, reporter Hong Xiaoyan, after much detailed and elaborate planning, disguised herself as a migrant, and arrived at the door of Tewaida with her bundle of bedding and belongings. The following is her record of her seven-day experience working at Tewaida.

As I Passed Through the Factory Gate in the Midst of a Heavy Downpour, the Security Guard Yelled: "Stop! What The Hell Are You Doing Here?"

On March 30 it was pouring. After a half-hour bus ride, I arrived with my bedding at No. 984, Xiqi Street, Hangzhou city—Tewaida Company. Outside the security guard kiosk at the factory gate hung a noticeboard that read, "Recruiting eighteen to twenty skilled machinists." As I walked through the gate, suddenly I heard a piercing yell: "Stop! What the hell are you doing here?"

I turned to encounter a fierce-looking uniformed security guard. "I have come to be a machinist."

"Take out your ID card!" I handed over my ID clumsily because of the big bundle I was holding. He looked at me and then at the card to make sure I was the right person, and then concluded with: "It is tough working here. You have to be prepared." Then he waved, indicating I could go in.

After asking a few people I came to shop-floor manager Li Qiangding on the third floor. Li said: "Since you are eager to work, I'll give you a chance. But mind you, it is real tough. You have to work overtime all the time."

"Is it okay not to work overtime?"

"No, it is not up to you. If I want you to work overtime, then you work overtime. Now, you go to the finance department to pay a 200 yuan deposit."

"When can I get the deposit back?"

"If you resign, you don't get back the deposit."

"What if I am fired?"

"We'll talk about it when the time comes."

Because it was already 4:00 P.M., there was no one in the finance department. The light was still on in the general manager's room, so I knocked before entering. A small, middle-aged woman took my deposit and told me to report to the production manager, Zhang Jianxin.

---

*Translation from the Chinese text: Hong Xiaoyan, "Wodi dagong ji," *Guangdong laodong bao*, July 3, 1998, p. 1. Translated by Anita Chan.

Zhang scanned me up and down, and said: "You don't look like a migrant looking for a job. What did you do before?"

"Oh, I was . . ."

"Okay, you go start working. I'll talk to you some other time." As I left the office, I heaved a sigh of relief—I had finally become an "employee" of Tewaida.

Packed Dormitory Covered with Spiderwebs, Rickety Beds, Smelly Toilets, and Two Queues of Women Workers

Huge drops of rain continued to pound on my belongings as I went around the factory wall as directed by the security guards, and came to a gray, three-story, dilapidated building.

The corridors were dimly lit. On both sides the windows were pasted with yellowing newspapers, with window frames covered with grime and dust. The foul smell almost knocked me over. The person in charge of the dorm showed me to Room No. 8 on the third floor, "Here it is."

It was a room about ten square meters. The ceiling and walls were covered with black spiderwebs. More than half the room was taken up with four bunk beds. One only had to touch the beds and they creaked. It took me some ten buckets of water before I had somewhat cleaned up my space. As I climbed up to put on the sheets, the bed planks suddenly gave way. I immediately went to the attendant to tell him the problem. He came back, adjusted the planks, and told me with confidence: "This is a good bed. No problem." But at night when I lay there I slept in fear that the bed would collapse at any time.

March 31, Tuesday. I was awakened by the shaking of the bed. The women workers were all getting up. I hurried to the washroom with my toothbrush and towel. The smell was unbearable. I was confronted by two queues, one for the toilet and one for a sink, which had two faucets. The sink was also for laundry. Because there was no drainage pipe for the dirty water, water was swishing around the workers' feet. The toilet no longer flushed. In this dormitory housing over one hundred workers, the toilet was cleaned only once a day. After ten minutes, I considered myself washed.

A Male Worker Earning Only 5 Yuan a Day

As of March 31, I began working as a trainee on team 6. I worked on the third floor, which had sixty to seventy sewing machines lined in rows, along which the floor manager walked up and down. My responsibility was to sew up the shoulder straps and then attach them onto the knapsacks. Compared to other tasks, this was relatively simple. After I had sewed thirty straps, my neck began to ache and my eyes turned red. As I was resting my hands on the sewing machine, the shop-floor manager came over to hurry me, "How come you are not working? Just that little bit of work and you are already tired. How will you work overtime all through the night?"

I did 100 straps that day. My arms and legs were sore all over. A few women workers next to me told me quietly, "This is nothing. It is now the slow season. During the busy season working overtime all through the night is normal." Exhaustion and hardship were not what the workers were most scared of. What scared them the most was working for an entire month and still not making enough money to feed themselves. Little Y was in charge of quality control. Next to her there was always a mound of leather bags. Her task was to examine the bags, snip off the threads, and put on the labels. The whole day she could not even stop for a minute. Sometimes I went over to help her. It never occurred to me that such simple tasks could be so tiring. My shoulders were aching after I had examined only a few dozen bags. Looking at me she said in her Hunanese accent: "You are tired already? Last month I examined several thousand bags, my shoulders hurt so much that I could not sleep well."

"You must have made a lot of money then?"

"No way. After paying for meals, buying toothpaste and soap, I made 90 yuan last month. Look, I came from my home wearing this pair of shoes. They are now in tatters and I have no money to buy a new pair."

Just at that moment a male worker, Little B, who had brought over a box of bags for her, chimed in: "She is in better shape, getting 90 yuan. The team leader just told me that this month I have only some 40 yuan, not enough to fill my tummy." B was a twenty-year-old from Inner Mongolia. His task was to clean up the zippers and to turn them over; for doing the former he got 0.8 of a cent, for the latter, one to two cents.

That night when I got off work, I could not describe how exhausted I was.

April 1, evening. A male worker from Jiangsu whose surname was Li came to our dormitory. When he saw me lying in bed he remarked with sympathy: "For a new worker like you, to be able to make 40 to 50 yuan a month is considered not bad. An 'old worker' like me made only five cents today."

"Not possible. How can it be so little?"

He went through it carefully with me gesticulating with his fingers: "I made 2.05 yuan today. Breakfast was fifty cents, lunch fifty cents, dinner 1 yuan. What's left is five cents, right?"

I asked, "In Hangzhou, isn't the minimum wage 270 yuan?"

"Ha!" The veteran workers nearby all chimed in, "Two-hundred-seventy yuan? This is considered a high wage here. Fortunately, at least now, no matter how low the wage, there is still some wage. Last year, a bunch of skilled workers worked for three months and did not get a cent. When they quit they did not get back their 200 yuan deposit either."

Because the wages were so low, the workers tried hard to "punish" themselves—in the canteen many workers often only bought twenty cents worth of plain rice, which they gulped down with pickles.

April 2, Thursday. While lining up in the canteen I asked a male worker behind me, "How much did you make last month?"

"Forty-five yuan."

"That's too little, isn't it?"

"But what can I do?"

I started asking him for his name and where he came from. A male worker sensing something, asked, "Could you be a reporter?"

"What makes you think I am a reporter?"

"We wrote a lot of letters of complaint to the *Qianjiang News*, and you are asking so many detailed questions as if you are a reporter." Then he continued, filled with disappointment: "No, you could not be. If you were a reporter, you could not have lasted half a day. You could not have been with us for so many days."

For the sake of my safety, the newspaper had been sending someone to the factory to "visit" me in the last few days, pretending that he was my relative. Probably because I looked like a "city person," my fellow workers were suspicious of my migrant background. Anyway, they did not report me to the factory authorities.

Security Guards on Patrol on the Shop Floors. One of Them Pointed at a Worker and Told Him, "You're Fined!"

April 4, Saturday. At about 12:10 P.M., after lunch, the workers had resumed work. A security guard appeared quietly on the shop floor and began patrolling up and down the aisles. Suddenly, he spotted one worker talking to another, "What the hell are you up to?"

The worker timidly explained: "He does not know how to sew properly. I am just teaching him."

The guard pointed his finger right at the nose of the worker: "This is unauthorized movement between work stations. You are fined ten yuan!"

A male worker next to me uttered under his breath, "This security guard likes fining people for nothing."

I asked softly, "How come a security guard has the authority to impose a fine?"

"Who knows? He punishes whomever he wants."

In the factory, penalty warning signs are pasted up all over—relatives who come visiting without registering—fine 10 yuan, unauthorized use of the elevator—50 yuan; "fine" seems to be management's most beloved expression. At the door of the canteen there was even a silly sign that read, "Violation, beware of being fined." It made no sense; it was not even specified what the fine was for.

During work hours, workers generally were not allowed to leave the factory grounds. One day, I wanted to go out to buy something. The moment I got to the gate, the security guard demanded to see a leave permit. So I went back to the shop-floor manager to see whether I could get a permit. Some workers seeing this advised me to forget it, "Unless you are sick, the shop-floor manager is not going to give you a leave permit."

It had been three days, but the factory still had not brought up the question of signing a labor contract with me. Workers who have been working there for three years told me that they had never seen a contract. So I went to ask the shop-floor manager whether I would be signing a labor contract. His reply was, "Wait and we'll see." I thought it was about time to quit.

April 5, Sunday. It should be a day off. But most workers were at work as usual. I wanted to ask the shop-floor manager the procedures for handing in a resignation. It turned out he had gone home for the weekend. So I went to the finance department where I found a woman sitting at a desk. "I want to resign. How much deposit do I get back?"

Without even looking up, she blurted out, "No refund!"

"Why no refund?"

"No refund until after three years of work. It is specified in the contract."

"But I have signed no contract."

"I don't care. Whatever, no refund."

There was nothing I could do. "Please give me back my ID card."

She showed her irritation, "The person who keeps ID cards is not here." She proceeded to ignore me completely.

In order to get back my ID card that the factory took away, I had to postpone my plan to quit for three more days.

April 6, Monday. As I passed through the gate of Tewaida I took a few deep breaths of free air. As scenes of my last few days' experiences flashed through my mind, my eyes began to water—not for myself but for the fellow workers whom I had lived with for seven days. . . . I got what I wanted; I had quit Tewaida.

Comments

According to an epilogue that appeared alongside this report, two days after Hong Xiaoyan accomplished her mission, the Hangzhou City Labor Inspection Team undertook an investigation. It fined the factory management and ordered that workers' deposits be returned to them and that their wages be raised to the level of the minimum legal wage. The factory was also told to stop employing children, sign labor contracts, and to take out insurance for its workers. In addition, it was discovered that the factory's three security guards were wearing police uniforms illegally bought by the factory (details on how police uniforms could be purchased were not provided). Under regulations, the three should have passed a police training course after which they would have been issued security guard permits. The three were told they could no longer continue to be security guards.

This all sounds very good on paper. Justice has been restored. But reading between the lines and analyzing carefully, there are a few caveats. The most puzzling is why it took four months for the reporter's exposé and the labor inspection team's investigations to be published? Was there pressure on the newspaper not to carry the article? Moreover, even after the labor inspection team and the public security bureau confronted the factory management with the factory's many labor law violations, the penalties were modest, probably not enough to deter other factories. The factory was only asked to pay the legal minimum wage. No penalty at all was imposed on the factory for dressing its security guards in police uniforms. Donning of police uniforms by imposters has become a serious problem in China.

CASE 3

Again, the ownership of this factory was unclear. But because the factory was located in a village in Guangdong province, and because there was no mention of a foreign investor or foreign manager, it was likely to be either a rural collective or a kind of joint venture that had minimal foreign involvement. Again, only migrants worked on the production line. The labor and living conditions seemed to be even worse than those described in the previous case. Workers here were owed several months' wages and the security guards were more apt to use violence, hitting workers and even literally shooting from the hip at the slightest commotion, reminiscent of America's Wild West. In this kind of village-turned-industrial park in Guangdong province, power comes from the barrel of a gun.

BLOOD AND TEARS OF THE SOUL—THE STORY OF A GROUP OF WORKERS GOING ON STRIKE*

Dozens of Workers Gather in Appeal at the Doors of the Labor Bureau

It is a balmy sunny day, September 12, 1994. At nine-thirty in the morning, a group of young laborers from Sichuan, men and women, are squatting, sit-

---

*Translation from the Chinese text: Liu Yuanyuan and Zhou Shan, "Qixue de lingyun: yiqi wailaigong jiti bagong shangfang shimo," *Zhuhai laodong bao* (Zhuhai Labor News), October 24, 1994. Translated by Kevin McCready.

ting, or standing at the doors of the provincial labor bureau on Guangzhou's Education Road. They look serious and angry, as if taking this action is their last resort.

Today will perhaps be the most unforgettable day of their whole working careers. This is the first time they have come with such courage, on such a scale, and with such acute awareness, to the doors of the provincial labor bureau. They have come to a place they can trust to seek justice, to seek redress.

In order to fully understand the whole story behind the strike and the visit to appeal to higher authorities, so as to write an objective investigative report, we decided to gather some information at Baitang Textile Manufacturing Plant in Guangzhou's White Cloud district that afternoon.

Outraged Male Migrant Workers Explain Their Story

At two in the afternoon, in the company of reporters Li Mengning of the *Modernist* and Shao Ming of the *Morning Times*, four of us entered the Baitang Textile Manufacturing Factory. We had a good look around and discovered that the factory buildings were old and dilapidated, and that the equipment was rudimentary.

Factory Manager Shen Jinpei, Longgui Township Economic Committee Member Hu Hanzhong, Baitang Village Party Branch Secretary Shen Bochang, and Village Security Chief Su Zhixian welcomed us into an old factory office. They gave us a rundown of their side of the story.

Professional sensibility told us that we had to interview the migrant workers as well, otherwise we would have no way of obtaining an accurate picture. So the two of us spread our forces: one took responsibility for talking to management, and the other stole into the dormitory to collect information. When I stepped into the dormitory, the migrant workers immediately surrounded me, all speaking at once with great animation.

Sitting in front of me was Zhang Qingguo, a twenty-eight-year-old worker from Mianyang in Sichuan. He has a middle school education and was one of the elected representatives. At his side sat another representative, Ou Qijun. They explained in detail the whole history of the incident:

Baitang Textile Manufacturing Factory has a rule of paying wages on the twenty-fifth of each month. But it only pays the previous month's salary. That is to say, no matter what, the factory owes us a month's wages.

August 25 was payday for July's wages. But we waited from daylight to dusk and did not see a cent of it. The factory continued to make us work as hard but did not say a single word about the delayed payment.

We continued working as we always do: normal hours plus overtime. We worked overtime almost every day until twelve midnight and we have never received any allowance from the factory for overtime, not even for the times when we worked all through the night.

On September 2 we had still not seen a cent, and the factory had not provided any explanation. We could not stand it anymore, so we went to ask the factory manager when we would actually be paid. The factory manager said, "I don't know, you'll get paid when you get paid."

By September 5, the mood of the workers was getting more and more dejected and they started complaining louder and louder. They demanded that the factory provide an explanation. From that day on, quite a few staff members and workers began to refuse to work overtime.

Already quite a few workers did not have enough money to buy food and had no choice but to borrow money from the factory manager. In the beginning, the factory allowed us to borrow a little money. Under normal circumstances, each person could borrow only once, about 10 or 20 yuan, and, at the most, 50 yuan. Later, when too many people had to borrow, the factory absolutely refused to lend any more.

On September 6, the factory still had not paid. That day all the workers decided on their own to stop work. And it was on that day that the factory transported truckloads of goods to the Qinglong Woolen Knitwear Factory in Huadou city. It looked like the factory was going to stop production for some time. The factory manager let it be known that, "Now even if you want to work I won't let you. Unless you beg me I won't let you work."

The next day, all of the factory's eighty-plus workers unanimously selected Zhang Qingguo, Ding Qiang, and Ou Qijun as their representatives. Some workers accompanied the three to the Longgui Township Labor Services Company and the White Cloud District Labor Bureau. We told them that we wanted to return to our hometowns, and requested that the factory return our deposits and identity cards, and the wages for July and August.

We gave three main reasons for wanting to go home: First we do not feel safe working here. We often suffer sexual harassment by local hoodlums. Women workers were even afraid to go out during the day. Second, the factory owes us wages, even for as long as four months. Third, living conditions are horrible and the food at every meal is inedible—moldy potatoes and pumpkin. Furthermore, the factory does not care whether the workers live or die. When a worker gets sick, the factory does not give a cent for medical expenses. One only lies in bed waiting for death.

On the afternoon of September 11, a security officer from Baitang Village suddenly charged into our dormitory and roared: "Who's the trouble-making representative? Who is Ou Qijun?" When he found out who Ou Qijun was, he said ferociously: "Damn it, what the hell are you lodging a report about? Why have you said that security here is bad? If you go to make a complaint again I'll beat you to death and when you're dead you won't know where to buy a coffin." He went on and on, and then he took off his shoe and began beating Ou Qijun. He pressed Ou Qijun to point out who the other representatives were, "If you don't tell, I'll take out my gun and kill you." He then left the dormitory, and we saw the factory manager standing at the factory gate, smiling.

At 10:00 P.M., the gatekeeper brought in three village security officers, who came bursting into the dormitory. Among them was the officer who had done the beating during the day. As soon as they entered, they yelled: "Who is Ding Qiang? Why did you say that our security here is bad?" Having asked that, they wanted to take us representatives away.

Zhang Qingguo said: "What power does the village security and safety committee have to look into our problem? We're not hoodlums robbing and stealing." We insisted that the factory manager come out.

Then one of the village security officials barked furiously, "I'll count to three and if you don't come with me obediently I'll open fire."

We knew that if we went with them we'd be mincemeat, perhaps tortured, and savagely beaten. So we insisted that we would not go. Then the one that had done the beating during the day just opened fire. It frightened us to death and several women ran out shrieking. We had no choice, and the three of us representatives went downstairs with them. We still insisted on seeing the factory manager and refused to leave the factory with them. The one that had done the beating was furious and fired again, pointing at Ding Qiang.

At the sound of the gunshots, all the migrant workers in the building came out and shouted in unison that they wanted to see the factory manager. The manager finally emerged. We crowded around him and asked him to take responsibility for our safety. On the spot we wrote on a scrap of paper and gave it to him requesting that he sign his name to certify that we had been beaten. After he took the piece of paper he just ripped it up, saying, "I know nothing and it is none of my business." It was clear he would not take responsibility for our safety.

The next day, about a dozen of us went to the provincial labor bureau. We believed that under the Communist Party this type of despotism should not be permitted.

Factory Management and the Village Security Team Have Their Spiels

During the interview, Baitang Village Security Chief Su Zhixian said:

> I heard some people in the factory had said that security around here is bad. Therefore, I came over to investigate. They now accuse me of having

beaten someone during the day. That is absolutely false. I merely came over to ask some questions.

In the evening, we did indeed enter their dormitory. We only wanted a few of the representatives to come with us to the village office to check out the situation. We didn't go there to arrest people.

When we entered the dormitory we said: "You say that we've handled security poorly. Who in here has been bashed? Whoever has been bashed please raise your hand." But nobody raised their hand.

I've been the security chief for many years and obviously know how to handle this type of problem. I often catch thieves and never beat or abuse workers. How could I have beaten them?

You've asked me whether or not I opened fire. I acknowledge I fired two shots. One was in the dormitory and one was downstairs. They say I aimed at their eyes and this is completely false. If I had, wouldn't the eye be hurt? When I opened fire it was at the sky. When this type of tear-gas gun goes off, even people 50 meters away can feel the sting. They say that I aimed at them, how could that be possible?

The four of us journalists then went to the factory office. Factory Manager Shen Jinpei tried to explain to us the reasons for the wage arrears and subsequent incidents. But before he had spoken a couple of sentences, he was interrupted by Hu Hanzhong of the Longgui Township Economic Committee. Hu Hanzhong said: "You're not telling it clearly. Let me speak."

Hu Hanzhong is about forty-five years old, wears glasses, and appears to be capable and shrewd. Obviously, he is an important person who is not willing to play second fiddle. When we asked why Su Zhixian opened fire, Hu Hanzhong immediately took control of the conversation and said, "With so many people surrounding them, how could he not fire in such a dangerous situation?" When Su Zhixian tried to explain himself, Hu Hanzhong again hogged the conversation, "You can just simply say it was in self-defense."

From beginning to end, Hu Hanzhong was always very lively. He said this factory had been going for many years and there had never been any problems. This year, after several Sichuan laborers came from Taihu, Guangzhou, they started trouble and turned things into a total mess.

As for the deteriorating security situation in the village, Baitang Village Party Branch secretary Shen Bochang said: "Everywhere these days security is less than desirable. So I can't really guarantee that the waters are unrippled here. But nobody has ever come to the village committee to report security problems. Nobody has ever reported being beaten or being robbed."

In the end, the Party branch secretary said the economy in their village really was not developed and there have been very few outsiders coming to invest in and establish factories. They have always placed great importance on this problem of outside investors.

Not the Last Word by Any Means

After the Sichuanese migrant laborers went on strike and went to appeal to higher authorities, all levels of the Department of Labor took the incident very seriously, and repeatedly ordered the factory to solve the problem. Baitang District Labor Services Company's Xie Guachang told me over the phone that the Department of Labor had already made the following decision. Before September 15, the factory must: (1) pay in full all wages owed and return all deposits docked; (2) return workers' identity cards; and (3) allow those who do not wish to stay to return home, and sign new contracts with those who are willing to stay.

By the time I filed this report, a Sichuanese worker told me over the phone that the factory was still withholding wages, and I could hear a female worker sobbing in the background. We believe that with the active intervention of the Ministry of Labor, the "Baitang Incident" will reach a satisfactory resolution.

Perhaps this report should come to an end at this point. But we have all thought long and hard about the many problematic legacies of this unhappy incident.

The Baitang Textile Manufacturing Plant actually has been using factory regulations as a kind of work agreement when staff and workers enter the factory, instead of signing contracts according to labor legislation and regulations. Obviously, this is absolutely outrageous. When the factory owes workers wages for such a long time, workers have no choice but to "create trouble."

While gathering material for this story, we discovered that conditions in the workers' dormitories were appalling. The door on the women's dormitory was wrecked and just about falling off its hinges. Anyone could simply walk in. I am wondering who is there to take responsibility for women workers' security. There was a wall in the workers' living quarters that wobbled with just a slight push of the hand. If such a wall collapses and someone gets hurt, again who is responsible? Factory Manager Shen Jinpei said the factory had already been renovated many times. We could imagine the dilapidated state it was in before.

Workers stopping work is plainly wrong. But looking at it both subjectively and objectively, the workers actually had no choice. If they had not adopted strike measures, could the problems have been solved?

The job of the village security and safety committee is to maintain village public order. But when several security personnel charge into a factory and start grabbing and beating people up, and even using firearms, what legal basis do they have for doing so? Citizens have the right to freedom of speech and when a few citizens say a few words about the lack of local public order, how can security officials respond with such audacity?

Where Is the Respect for the Law?

In recent years the Guangdong economy has developed rapidly. It should be recognized that 10 million male and female migrant workers are the backbone of Guangdong's speedy progress. For a long time, some officials have overemphasized local economic development and have been far too coddling and protective of investors. Many investors arbitrarily dock and delay paying workers' wages, force workers to work excessive overtime, and sacrifice their compatriots in a frenzy of primitive capital accumulation. Some foreign investors will stop at nothing to make money.

Cruel exploitation must of necessity lead to worker resistance. Don't the strikes and appeals to higher authorities one after another in recent years actually demonstrate a crisis in the conflict between labor and capital? Doesn't it actually demonstrate that our legal system is not completely healthy?

After much hard work, the Labor Law of the People's Republic of China was finally passed, and it will take effect on January 1, 1995. This is worth celebrating. We are confident that the Labor Law will bring tens of millions of migrant workers a bright and glorious future.

Comments

One irony about this case is that although the workers were owed several months of wages, when they went to management to ask for some money, the article described them as going to "borrow" money. The reporters surprisingly did not put "borrow" in quotes. Far from being an accidental omission, this is surely the result of the power of management's hegemonic discourse over the monetary relationship between workers and management. To call this "borrowing" is to consign the workers to a weak position, robbing them of moral authority over the situation. Both workers and reporters have succumbed to this hegemonic power.

Many local bureaucrats and grass-roots institutions joined forces against the migrant workers: the factory manager, the township economic committee member, the village Party branch secretary, and the village security chief all gained enormously from the labor of the migrants. The lawlessness of the place has to do with the fact that, not many years ago, these industrial dis-

tricts were agricultural villages. Most of these officials, who are today over forty years old, grew up in rural environments where law and order barely existed. Party fiat and violence against the weak were the order of the day. In the Maoist period, these villages had their own militia known as the security protection committee (zibaohui), which was under the command of the village Party secretary and was a law unto itself.[2] This was particularly the case in the heyday of the Cultural Revolution when China's legal system broke down.[3] The violence that is the legacy of the Maoist kangaroo courts and class-struggle campaigns still leaves its mark on these villages, which are now undergoing rapid industrialization.

When the entire indigenous village population was out to keep the migrant workers in their place, the only possible course of redress the workers had was to bypass the village or township authorities and bring their grievances to the provincial labor bureau. But, as was seen, the help the bureau gave the workers was minimal and halfhearted. Culprits were barely punished. Higher authorities usually only intervened to the extent of containing excessive social unrest, and the solution for the workers was usually only partial and temporary.

CASE 4

In the modern world, forced labor has not disappeared and is still common in the remote parts of poor countries such as Brazil and India.[4] Dongguan City in Guangdong province is a densely populated city surrounded by industrial districts that have been gobbling up farmland in the past two decades. That a group of migrant workers could be made to work like slaves at a brick kiln in broad daylight without nearby residents noticing is unthinkable, even though the location was somewhat isolated. The kiln was owned by a few peasants, although the village government and village public security were fully aware of what was going on. Only after two migrant workers were murdered did the public find out about the horror.

Incidents of migrant workers being enslaved have been uncovered in various places in China: in a township near Wuhan,[5] in Harbin City,[6] in a suburb near Suzhou,[7] and in another township in Guangdong province.[8] By no means is this list complete. The cases have tended to involve private individuals forcing the migrants to work long hours of grueling manual labor during the day and locking them up at night. It is the kind of work that only strong able-bodied men used to very heavy labor can do. Invariably, the laborers are migrants who have just arrived at some city or county town as strangers looking for work. They are usually lured to a work site with promises of food, shelter, and a wage. Once there, however, they'll be immedi-

ately isolated from the outside world and made to work like slaves or prisoners. All the cases indicated that there has to be some form of collusion with local residents in order for these prison-like factories and work sites to operate.

THE TWO WERE CHASED AND BEATEN TO DEATH IN THE RIVER*

> On January 18 of the lunar calendar, when people were reveling in Chinese New Year celebrations, in the warm climate of southern China, a shockingly brutal murder took place: in a brick factory in Dongguan City of Guangdong province, two out-of-province peasant workers were clubbed to death by gang bosses while trying to escape.

***Zhuhai Special Economic Zone News* Editor's note. This is a shocking murder: that in our socialist state, with an increasingly regularized legal system, there exists such lawless and unconscionable people intent on squeezing the last drop of blood and sweat from hired laborers. We should be angry. We should call for justice. We publish this article to appeal to your conscience. We should learn from this lesson so that such incidents will never happen again.**

At 6:30 A.M. on February 17 this year (January 18 lunar calendar), inside a brick factory about 1,000 meters south of Hongyuan Bridge in Huang Village of Dongguan City, two out-of-province peasant workers[9] who had come to Guangdong to work were chased and clubbed to death in the river while they were trying to escape mistreatment by the factory's gang boss and his accomplices.

Fierce and Sadistic Gang Boss

Four of us reporters rushed to the scene on March 3 to investigate the moment we learned what had happened. An old Hunanese peasant worker, Yang Huihou, who had been working in the factory for two years and had shared living quarters with the victims, told us that one of the victims was called Li Dayin. He was forty-one years old and was of Han extraction. The other, Huang Shande, was thirty-nine years old, of Yao minority. Both of them came from Bei township of Guangxi's Fuchuan Yao Minority Autonomous County. They arrived to work in the brick factory last November. They were quiet, honest, and hardworking people. Li was from a poor family. The reason why he came out to work as a laborer was to make money to pay for his son's university education.

---

*Translation from the Chinese text: Jiao Huidong, "Tamenliang bei zhuida sangming hezhong," *Zhuhai tequbao* (Zhuhai Special Economic Zone News), July 12, 1995. Translated by Anita Chan.

Because it was just after Spring Festival, there were not enough hands in the factory. So the gang boss, Li Meng, and his eight other thugs, posing as if they were from Hongyuan Corporation, went to Dongguan city to recruit laborers. They got hold of three peasant workers from Shaoguan prefecture in Guangdong and one from Hunan province. Early the next morning, they started to force the four peasant workers to labor. Before the day was over, the four of them were beaten four or five times simply for being slow. On the evening of February 16, the three Shaoguan peasant workers planned to escape. When the gang boss learned about the attempt, he had his boys furiously beat the three, and stripped them of two watches and 370 yuan. That evening, Li Dayin quietly said to them: "If you want to escape, remember, don't do it at night. In case you're caught they'll either beat you to death, or at least turn you into a cripple. Besides, they guard the site more closely at night. You don't stand a chance. If you try during the day, there might be some hope."

These words somehow got back to gang boss Li Meng. So Li gathered together eight to nine of his gang and began beating Li Dayin and Huang Shande until they were bloody and about to lose consciousness. Li Meng then threatened them, "You work here obediently for another year. You won't be paid a cent."

In the early morning of February 17, when the gang bosses opened the iron door of the little brick house where the peasant workers were locked up, Li and Huang tore their way through and ran for their lives. The pack of thugs chased after them, beating them, and forced them into the river. There in the river, Li and Huang were beaten to death.

We reporters had a look round the work site. The site is unusual: the north, east, and south sides are all surrounded by water, with only the west side accessible to the outside. To escape is not easy. Two Sichuan and one Guizhou peasant workers who did not want to give their names told us: "When Li Dayin and Huang Shande tried to flee toward the east, we saw the whole group of them descend upon them, cursing and hitting them with bricks. When they were pushed into the river, the thugs continued to smash their bodies and heads with bricks."

We asked, "When you saw them being beaten like this why didn't you go to help."

The Guizhou peasant worker replied, "While that was happening there were several others guarding us with iron rods. Who dared to go forward?"

On March 8, we went to interview the head of the public security bureau of Huang Village, Mr. Zhang. He confirmed what we had learned earlier. "Li and Huang died in the river around 6:00 A.M. By the time the factory bosses came to report the deaths, it was past 11:00 A.M. After that, every day we went to hurry the bosses to search for the bodies. But whether they tried or not we had no idea."

According to the peasant workers, Huang's body floated up six days after the incident. As for Li's body, it was discovered 8 km to 9 km downstream at Houjie township. Huang's body was cremated on February 23 at Dongguan Crematorium and Li's was cremated on February 25. Their relatives from Guangxi did not get to Dongguan until February 27 and March 1, respectively. So they did not have a chance to bid farewell before the cremation.

The peasant workers also told us that after the Li-Huang incident, the four factory bosses were detained for three days at the Huang Village Public Security Bureau and then released without explanation.

Prison Dormitory

A few of the factory's peasant workers took us reporters to have a look at Li Dayin and Huang Shande's "dormitory." It was a sight so shocking that it was beyond belief. Spread in front of us was a 6 meter by 3 meter, crude, dank, and dark one-story structure. This was where several dozen peasant workers slept at night. The floor was their bed, meaning a layer of flattened-out cardboard boxes spread over a redbrick floor. The floor level inside is about a meter lower than the ground outside. The smell was unbearable. The peasant workers told us that each day after the evening meal they were locked up in the dormitory. The gang boss and his boys would padlock the door and reinforce it with a iron bar. Just outside the door they would pull up an iron bed where one or two thugs armed with daggers and iron rods would take turns standing guard while the others slept. The peasant workers were not allowed to go outside to use the toilet. A hole in the ground in the north corner of the room was dug out for that purpose. To stop the peasant workers from running away, the boss had a huge dog which prowled around the site (the dog was destroyed by the Huang Village Public Security Bureau on March 3).

The peasant workers said that they had to do fourteen to fifteen hours of heavy labor each day. The longest they had worked was eighteen hours one day. While working they were guarded by the thugs. Even when they went to the toilet, one of the boys would follow closely behind. Every day they had to get out of bed at 6:00 A.M. But they were not allowed to eat. They had to work until 10:00 A.M. before they were given food. Except for mealtime, which was only fifteen minutes, every single minute was spent working. There was no rest on Sunday. If they had not finished eating when the fifteen minutes was up, the thugs would snatch away the bowl, pour all the rice out, and make them start working immediately. Anyone who was a bit slow would invite a shower of punches and kicks. A peasant worker from Shanxi and another from Guizhou told us, "We have worked here for more than a year, but the 'wages' the gang boss has paid us are less than 200 yuan each."

We were told that several Dongguan peasants had bought the brick factory, known as He An Brick Factory, from Humen township's Zhenkang Company for 2,180,000 yuan. The four factory bosses contracted out the work to the gang boss at a piece-rate. For every 10,000 bricks, the bosses paid the gang boss 50 yuan. Later the price was increased to 80 yuan per 10,000 bricks and Sunday was counted as overtime. So every batch of 10,000 bricks was paid at 96 yuan. As to whether the workers got paid or were mistreated, the factory bosses did not care. The peasant workers said that the gang boss and the factory bosses played mahjong and drank together every day. The bosses had never intervened when they saw the gang boss bullying the workers. On the morning of the tragedy, although the bosses' residences were only 20 meters from the scene, they claimed that they had heard nothing. Even an hour after the incident they had not opened their doors.

The Case Is Still Pending

After the case was publicized by the mass media, there was a strong reaction from the public. As a reporter I received a lot of letters, faxes, and telephone calls from readers expressing their anger at the brutality of the murderers and their sympathy for the victims. One Chinese student studying in the United States telephoned me long distance and said that after he read the report he was not only angry, but shocked and deeply disturbed. He said: "When some American friends asked me to lend them the newspaper, I hid it away not wanting them to read it because it was too shameful. I was afraid people will look down on us . . . I hope this case will be dealt with justly by our legal system."

But no one related to the case was dealt with, as many had hoped and expected. The only thing that has happened so far was that the Huang Village Public Security Bureau has given evidence, and that each of the victim's families, after negotiation with the factory bosses, was compensated 22,000 yuan.

I put the question to the head of the public security bureau, Mr. Zhang, "Should the factory bosses share some responsibility in the case?"

Mr. Zhang snapped without hesitation: "No, not at all! This is because they (the bosses) did not instruct them (the murderers) to do it!" But at 3:00 P.M. on May 5, when the same question was asked in an interview, Mr. Zhang answered: "Yes, the bosses definitely should be responsible too. They were negligent in educating, supervising, and investigating."

Then I followed up with the question: "For such a serious criminal case why did you not bring it up to the procurator's office and the court?" Mr. Zhang replied, "because of insufficient evidence."

I continued: "I recall that when we interviewed you on March 8 about the case, you said that there were altogether nine people involved in the beating of Huang and Li. Later, six were arrested. Could I ask what's happened to these six people?"

Mr. Zhang said: "Released! Except for one by the name of Chen who is still under investigation, the rest were all released on March 30."

I was flabbergasted. "Why were they released?"

Zhang replied calmly: "After our bureau's investigation, we found they were innocent. So of course we released them without charges."

On the morning of May 18, I received a phone call from Huang Shande's family in Guangxi and was told that they had support from their local Party and government which encouraged them to press charges against the brick factory. They were in the midst of looking for a lawyer to help resolve the case through legal channels.

No matter how the case will turn out in the end, we should be glad about one unexpected development—that the victims' relatives have chosen to seek the legal channel to resolve the case. It looks like a real court case is just about to begin.

Comments

At least one positive outcome came from this horrible story. The two victims' families from far away Guangxi province took steps to take the murderers to court. This is indeed a big step forward—simple folks with little education and resources seeking justice through the legal system, as opposed to the highly educated Chinese student studying in the United States who said he was too embarrassed to let his foreign friends know that such things happen in his own country. The much less-educated peasants can be a lot more "modern" than educated Chinese.

CASE 5

Although not clearly specified, from the context it can be seen that the three letters to the editor of a Shanghai trade-union magazine included in this article were written by local state enterprise workers. Being state workers they were accustomed to regulated labor regimes. But in the past few years, more and more state enterprises have become joint ventures, either fully or partially (where only a section of the enterprise becomes a joint venture).

In either case, in the course of transformation, it is normal practice that the new management employs at least some of the parent company's workers.

In joint ventures that originate from state enterprises, as opposed to joint ventures that originate from township and village enterprises (case 3), the workers are aware of their rights. Unlike migrant workers, urban workers do not have residency problems and are not as vulnerable to exploitation. As is obvious from this article, the labor regimes in these more regulated joint ventures are not as harsh as those found in cases 1, 2, and 3. On the other hand, the article was published in 1991, showing that the incursions on labor rights of urban workers began a decade ago. As cheaper and more subservient migrant laborers started to flood into the cities to replace the urban workforce, labor standards in state enterprises and in joint ventures derived from state enterprises further eroded. By the late 1990s, amid massive layoffs of state enterprise workers, the Beijing government, for instance, set a new policy penalizing employers for hiring non-Beijing residents instead of locals.[10]

GIVE ME BACK MY EIGHT-HOUR WORKDAY SYSTEM, CRIED SOME EMPLOYEES FROM "THREE CAPITAL" ENTERPRISES*

The Shanghai Municipal Trade Union Council has been receiving quite a lot of letters from employees working in "three capital" enterprises[11] who complain that they have been subjected to relentless overtime. Below are excerpts from three such letters:

1. A letter dated October 22, 1990, and signed by "an employee of Daweili Company." "I want to tell you about our miserable situation in this joint venture that I am an employee of. But please excuse us for not giving you my name because I am afraid of being fired. I am terribly angry with my work unit, the Shanghai Daweili Footwear Company. To fulfill rush orders we have been forced to work overtime every day since August. This was particularly bad in September and October when there were almost no Sundays off. Each night we, including management personnel, cannot go home until eight or nine o'clock. If you dare raise an objection, you run the risk of being sacked. There is no trade union in our factory and every day the workers come into contact with toxic gases, with no health and safety protection. I want to jump out of this "tiger trench," but realize that finding a job is not easy, so I have to tolerate the intoler-

---

*Translation from the Chinese text: Wei Ran, "Yige sanzi qiye zhigong zhihu: huan wo ba xiaoshi gongzuozhi," *Shanghai gongyun* (Shanghai Labor Movement), No. 1, 1991, pp. 30–31. Translated by Anita Chan.

able. Could the city trade union come to the factory to carry out an investigation and speak up on behalf of the workers, and return to us our eight-hour workday system? I beg of you."

2. A letter from an employee. "I am an employee of the Chinese–foreign joint venture, Shanghai Aisi Travel Goods Company. We were psychologically prepared for the company's tighter labor discipline. But we truly cannot take the unlimited imposition of over-time anymore. In August, the temperature was unrelentingly hot. By the time we got home we were totally exhausted. We could not eat and could not sleep. As a result, industrial accidents have been mounting. There was a case of one female worker who literally collapsed and passed out on the shop floor. This month, the amount of overtime is even more unbearable. It has been day after day. We have even worked all through the night. No wonder everyone wants to quit, but no one dares to utter a word of complaint. With no way out, all we can do is plead that our *niangjia* [our own families] can help to get our eight-hour workday system back.[12]

3. A letter from a factory intern's parent. "I have a child who gradu-ated in 1989 and was then assigned to Aisi Factory. The factory does not care about the workers' health, making them work twelve hours a day without even a day off on Sunday. This is detrimental to the health of sixteen-year-olds. Now several kids have fallen sick from exhaustion, but they dare not complain because they are so worried to be thrown out of work. Please do something to save our children."

Comments

A point to note is the relationship between state workers and the official trade union. The three letters were written to the Shanghai trade union's official magazine. The way these female state workers refer to the official trade union as "niangjia," is very interesting. A woman is always closer to her own family than her husband's family. The fact that the woman calls the trade union niangjia shows she sees the trade union as her protector and supporter. This trust in the union may be misplaced, but for state workers, the trade union is quite possibly the only institution that they can go to for help.

Notes

1. Wu Hui and Ouyang Guanghua, "*Toushuzhe kuadaqizhi, bigaofang yiyou guocuo* " (Complainants Exaggerated While the Accused Party Also Made Some Mistakes), *Guangdong laodong bao* (Guangdong Labor News), December 31, 1995.

2. See Zhao Shukai, "Criminality and the Policing of Migrant Workers," *The China Journal*, No. 43 (January 2000), pp. 101–110; "China's Public Security Control in the Local Level," *Change*, December 1998, p. 2. For details of the structure and function of the village security committee in this part of Guangdong province, see Anita Chan, Richard Madsen, and Jonathan Unger, *Chen Village Under Mao and Deng*, Berkeley, CA: University of California Press, 1992, pp. 58–59.

3. Ibid., pp. 103–140.

4. Matt Moffett, "Work Against Their Will: Slavery Has Been with Us for a Very Long Time. Some Forms Are Just More Obvious Than Others," *Wall Street Journal*, January 11, 1999, p. R28; Kevin Bales, "Modern Trade in Disposable People," *Guardian Weekly*, June 20, 1999, p. 25.

5. *Workers' Daily*, March 27, 1996, p. 1.

6. *Liaoning zhigong bao* (Liaoning Employees News), August 12, 1998, p. 2.

7. *Suzhou gongren bao* (Suzhou Workers' Daily), September 24, 1998.

8. *Pingguo ribao* (Apple Daily), June 21, 1995.

9. The term "peasant worker," *nongmin gong*, or *nonggong*, is commonly used to refer to rural migrants who do not work in a factory. They usually work outdoors as construction workers in heavy labor jobs. The nature of the job relegates them to an even more lowly status than factory workers. The word "peasant" has connotations of uncouthness.

10. Based on my field interviews in Bejing, 1998.

11. "Three capital" enterprises (*sanzi qiye*) is a collective term for the existence of foreign capital in China in three different forms: equity joint ventures, contractual joint ventures, and fully funded joint ventures.

12. *Niangjia* refers to a woman's side of the family after marrying out to her husband's family. Here she is likening the trade union to her parents. Now that the state factory has been married to a foreign investor, she hopes her "parents" can come to save her from being mistreated.

Chapter 3

Corporal Punishment and Physical Assaults

Five articles have been selected for this chapter to illustrate violence against workers. Chinese media reports show that a militaristic management style tends to be most often found in Taiwanese-managed factories. Korean managers are also notorious for imposing a very harsh labor regime. Though less blatant, the Chinese themselves are also known to commit violence against workers. Based on my own survey of fifty-four Chinese factories of all ownership types, 27 percent of workers in overseas Chinese-funded joint ventures reported that corporal punishment existed in their factories, compared with 17 percent for state and collective enterprises.[1]

Assaults on Chinese workers take a variety of forms. Discipline at the workplace is sometimes institutionalized, with bosses meting out regimented and militaristic penalties, the kind normally found in army boot camps. The regimentation controls the workers down to even the most minute details of bodily functions (case 6). A second kind of violence occurs in fits of rage (cases 7 and 8). A third type is meted out by enterprise internal security departments charged with maintaining discipline at the workplace (case 9). A fourth type is armed suppression of workers taking part in collective protests (case 10).

CASE 6a

This case concerns a Taiwanese footwear factory in Guangzhou (Canton), the capital of Guangdong province. Of all the documented cases that I have come across in which management uses militaristic disciplinary techniques and corporal punishment, the Yixin Footwear Factory has the harshest regime. I have collected six articles on Yixin, two of which are included here. The first is an article written by two reporters of the Yangcheng Evening News, *one of Guangzhou's main newspapers, after they had worked in the factory for a week disguised as migrant workers. The day after the reporters left the factory, they brought officials from the labor bureau to the enterprise to conduct an unannounced inspection.[2] The second translation is an article that argues in defense of Yixin's harsh management practices. It was published in Taiwan by the* Taiwan Footwear Industry Bulletin, *representing the views of Taiwanese shoe manufacturers. It portrays the mentality and rationale the Taiwanese management have for mistreating mainland workers.*

WAILS FROM BEHIND A HIGH WALL*

Two male reporters of the *Yangcheng Evening News* went undercover as migrant workers at Yixin Footwear Factory and obtained a firsthand account of Taiwanese bosses' unlawful use of corporal punishment, beatings, and humiliation of workers.

"You Can Run, but I'll Beat You Until You Can't Even Get Up!"

Jiang Wenqing, a migrant worker from Liangping county, Sichuan, came to our office one day to file complaints. With bruises all over his body, he revealed what he encountered inside the Taiwanese-funded Yixin Footwear Industry Company Ltd. in Guangzhou.

He started working at the factory, located in Zhongluotan in Guangzhou, at the end of March this year, and was later promoted to be the chief of the sewing department. There, he witnessed how workers were physically punished, beaten up, and humiliated. He was unable to tender a resignation but chose to leave voluntarily on July 7. In the afternoon of July 23, the Taiwanese boss, surnamed Wang, sent his driver, surnamed Kuang, to invite Jiang to go back "to have a talk" and took him back to the factory. Once there, Wang summoned Assistant Manager Jiang to bring with him six security guards and they detained Jiang Wenqing in the conference room. They pinned Jiang's hands and feet to a chair, and Assistant Manager Jiang began hitting him with a plastic rod while howling, "You can run, but I'll beat you until you can't even get up!" Assistant Manager Jiang then ordered the security guards to take turns to have a go at Jiang Wenqing. That went on for more than an hour. Afterward four security guards carried a battered Jiang outside the factory gate and dumped him on the road.

Jiang Wenqing and other male migrant workers who escaped from the

---

* Translation from the Chinese text: Cheng Xiaoqi, "Laozi gaoqing de kusu," *Yangcheng wanbao* (Yangcheng Evening News), August 30, 1997. Translated by Eva Hung.

factory also revealed that Boss Wang had breached the Labor Law by compelling workers to work overtime. He physically punished workers at will and would sometimes brutally beat them. Inside Yixin, they suffered the most inhuman treatment.

In order to get to the truth and obtain firsthand materials, we reporters embarked on a discreet investigation by working in Yixin as male migrant workers. At the same time, we also tracked down and interviewed some workers who had run away from Yixin.

"It's No Use Kneeling Down! Keep Doing Push-ups!"

On August 23, we were granted the "qualification" of migrant workers by the Yixin production management department and were assigned to work in the lasting department. We then became eyewitnesses of how workers were physically abused.

At around 2:20 P.M. that day, we saw a worker from the cutting section being dragged to the open ground of the factory area. He was then ordered to stay in a push-up position in the scorching sun. Lying on his stomach, propped up with both hands, he was sweating under the burning sun. After several tens of minutes, someone went out and shouted, "Order released!" Only then was the worker taken back to the building.

On August 27, at around 8:00 A.M. or 9:00 A.M., two workers, a man and a woman, were punished by being exposed to the sun on the open ground near the entrance of the workshop. And at around 5:00 P.M. that same day, another thirteen workers, lined up in two rows, were also punished in a similar manner.

At 4:00 P.M. two days ago, four workers from sewing department team A and one woman worker from team G were physically punished. They were ordered to stand in the sun alongside the flowerbed, each holding a plastic box filled with shoes. It was not until 5:10 P.M. that they were released, during which time we saw Boss Wang pass by without so much as noting their presence, as if it was a common occurrence.

Prior to these five workers, more than ten workers had also been ordered to stand beside the flowerbed for more than twenty minutes.

Two nights ago, we reporters had to work overtime in lasting department team B. Since we were not able to meet the production quota of that day, the team leader got hit by Boss Wang on the head three times with a shoe brush. Yesterday morning just when we got to work, Boss Wang blew the whistle to assemble all the lasting department's team leaders. He first lectured them and then instructed them to split into two groups to do push-ups. Three of them could not keep up and knelt down on the ground. But when Boss Wang stared at them, these three team leaders resumed their push-ups. When it was over, Boss Wang raised his arm and yelled, "Back to work!"

We would have stepped forward to stop this kind of inhuman practice were we not charged with this special mission. This is what we saw yesterday at 11:00 a.m.: thirty-three workers were penalized by being exposed to the fierce sun on the open ground when the outside temperature was 34 degrees Celsius. They were not allowed to leave until noon.

Yesterday afternoon at two, the team leader of sewing team F, Song Yuangang, rushed into Wang's office requesting him to sign some documents that involved some overdue payments. But Wang just yelled and threw the documents on the floor. Song picked them up and quickly left the office, but Boss Wang ran after him, snatched the documents, threw them at Song's head, cursing and screaming, "Get out of here!"

Window Five: "Special Window for Pig Feed"

Hanging iron lasts (iron molds for shaping shoes) around the neck was a common way Boss Wang used to penalize his staff. Those who had been punished in this way described an incident on May 19 this year. Because Boss Wang was dissatisfied with the production output of the sewing and lasting departments, at around four in the afternoon he summoned their managerial staff, a total of more than forty people, to gather on the open ground. He then made them hang iron lasts on their bodies. The number of iron lasts was the same as the number of shoes that missed the quota. Some of them therefore had several tens of kilograms of iron lasts hanging around their necks. Moreover, they were ordered to run around the factory ground, while Wang himself rode a bicycle chasing and cursing them from behind. When he discovered that Li Shenglin, from lasting department team C, had only thirty-five iron lasts in his bag, he slapped Li on the face twice, had his bag increased to ninety, and ordered him to continue running.

We were also told that Boss Wang had once gathered some forty workers from the sewing section on the open ground. He then punished the workers by having them hung upside down from the three-foot-high retaining wall of the flowerbed, with their hands propped on the ground. They were made to maintain that posture for more than an hour.

Other workers said that they had once been forced to place plastic buckets filled with water on their heads and leap like frogs back and forth along the corridor of the workshop. When water splashed out onto the workers, Boss Wang and company would burst into laughter. Workers said this method of punishment had been used several times.

Some workers from Jiangxi told us of an incident that happened two years ago. In July that year, Boss Wang received some letters from families in one of the villages saying that the meals provided in the factory were too poor and that they hoped for an improvement. Wang then gathered all the workers and announced, "You people said that the meals are worse than pig feed. From now on, I will ask the kitchen to prepare pig feed for you!" A public notice appeared in the factory the next day. It read: "As of today, workers from Village X will be getting special treatment. The factory is reserving window five especially for them." At lunchtime, Boss Wang assembled all the workers to visit the canteen. Only then did the workers see the sign on window five, "Special window for pig feed. Reserved for workers from Village X."

We were told that there were three big basins of pig feed. One was soup made up of husked rice and rice bran, one was wild grass, and the other one was swill mixed with cooked rice. Boss Wang and Manager Jiang ordered the fifty workers from Village X to each eat a bowl. Many refused to eat, and several female workers cried. Most of them went hungry for three days and some of them bought instant noodles with their own money.

"The Black Season": Never-ending Overtime Work

In the week that we were there, apart from one public holiday, every night each shop floor was brightly lit with machines running nonstop. Workers were compelled to work overtime for at least three hours every day, and this was actually the slack season for shoe manufacturing.

We were able to get hold of an overtime record and discovered the following: between August 1 and August 27, 80 percent of the sixty-nine workers from the storage, washing, and rubber-smelting sections worked thirty-six hours of overtime more than the legal maximum. The longest overtime worked was eighty-nine hours. This is in absolute violation of the Labor Law, which stipulates that overtime must not exceed thirty-six hours a month.

Given that there was overtime work during the slack season, one can imagine that the situation would be much worse in the peak season. Workers do not have one day off a week and it is common for them to work overtime until midnight or even later. Workers call this the "black season." According to the managerial staff from sewing department teams F and G, between May and July this year, workers were kept on the production line for sixteen hours every day. The boss demanded normal output to be doubled without adding even one more machine or worker. Workers from the sewing department also said that during the peak season in mid-May this year, they had to work until three in the morning almost every day. And even though the workers were working until late into the night, the kitchen did not provide any refreshments for them. Moreover, because the wage in the sewing department is calculated on a piece-rate basis, there was no overtime pay. The workers could do nothing about it.

As we walked out of the factory gate with a heavy heart yesterday evening, we looked back at the iron fence and the video camera mounted on top of the enclosing wall. For those male and female migrant workers inside, can you take up the law to defend your legitimate right as laborers?

CASE 6b

It might be expected that other Taiwanese investors would want to distance themselves from Yixin's kind of management, but two months after the exposé, the Taiwan Footwear Industry Bulletin, *a magazine for Taiwanese footwear manufacturers, carried an article vehemently defending Yixin's management. This "collective voice" of Taiwanese footwear investors openly claims that for the sake of production efficiency, violations of China's labor laws and inhumane treatment of workers are necessary: "The more direct and primitive the method, the more effective it is." It is not possible to know the percentage of Taiwanese investors who condone or practice this kind of management, but this article suggests that abuses of labor in Taiwanese-managed factories in China are commonplace.*

WHAT IS THE MOST APPROPRIATE WAY TO MANAGE MAINLAND-
CHINESE WORKERS?—A HEADACHE FACING TAIWANESE
INVESTORS THAT NEEDS TO BE DISCUSSED*

A while ago, the exposé of the mismanagement of a Taiwanese-funded footwear factory became a hot topic for the media in Hong Kong and China. It is a well-known fact that mainland Chinese workers are difficult to manage: how to increase their productivity without breaching the stringent local labor laws has therefore become the most difficult dilemma facing every Taiwanese investor in their daily management of mainland enterprises.

According to media reports, numerous incidents of corporal punishment had occurred at a Taiwanese-funded enterprise, Yixin Footwear Industry Company Limited, located in Baiyun district in Guangzhou. Some workers would not accept being physically punished and had filed complaints to the local public security bureau as well as the media. This blew the case out of proportion. After the incident was made public, the Guangzhou City Labor Inspection Team made an unannounced inspection of the factory and revealed that apart from corporal punishment, the Yixin Footwear Industry Company had also breached several other articles stipulated in the Labor Law. For example, the factory required a deposit of 500 yuan from each worker it hired; and some new workers received wages of only 20 yuan after having fees for

*Translation from the Chinese text: Chen Meijun, "Dalu yuangong gai ruhe guanli zui hedang? Dalu Taishang jingying guanli touteng wenti fantao," *Taiwan xiexun* (Taiwan Footwear Industry Bulletin), October 1997, pp. 62–64. Translated by Eva Hung.

meals and accommodation deducted, thus violating the legal minimum wage of 380 yuan as specified by the Guangzhou city government.

Moreover, Yixin also breached the law by inserting a rule in the labor contracts it signed with employees, "Those who apply to resign before having finished working in the factory for one month are required to pay 10 yuan a day for meals, and also for accommodation, before they can leave." Furthermore, in terms of the actual working hours, the factory made frequent demands for overtime work, which again were illegal.

Actually, these various violations of the Labor Law by the Yixin Footwear Industry Company are very common among foreign-invested enterprises in China, in particular in the more labor-intensive manufacturing industries. For example, it is common practice to require those who have worked in a factory for less than a month to pay for accommodation and an extra 10 yuan a day for meals in order to be allowed to leave. Most Taiwanese businessmen are aware that this violates the Labor Law. But if they do not impose this rule, workers will quit after working just for a couple of days, and labor turnover will be totally out of control. In this case, how is it possible to maintain and increase production efficiency? Has the mainland authority ever thought about this from the vantage point of the Taiwanese investors?

Moreover, the accusation that workers received a mere wage of 20 yuan is not correct. The author has checked with the Yixin Footwear Industry Company, and was told that this particular worker had been with the factory for just a week. After deducting the several kinds of fees, the actual wage he received was, of course, minimal. In fact, to induce motivation among workers, many Taiwanese investors in the footwear industry have adopted a piece-rate wage scale. As long as they are hardworking, it is not uncommon for workers in foreign-invested enterprises to earn over 1,000 yuan a month. In this Yixin incident, it would be somewhat unjust and one-sided to conclude that Taiwanese investors are entirely responsible for wrongdoing. But it is hoped that this case can serve some kind of communicative purpose to induce the mainland authority and Taiwanese investors to arrive at the establishment of more reasonable laws and regulations.

Skirting the Edges of the Labor Law—Not Easy for Taiwanese Investors

The difficulty in managing mainland workers has always been one of the headaches reported in surveys of Taiwanese businesspeople who invest in China. One businessman stated, "Why do most foreign-invested enterprises think that mainland employees are hard to manage? You have to realize that these employees all come from places several thousand miles away. Under a situation in which you cannot place any trust in them, is there any other better way but to resort to a militaristic style of management?"

Herein lies the crux of the problem—this so-called militaristic style of management. This kind of management means that the freedom and rights of employees to a certain extent have to be restricted and confined, and inevitably it contravenes mainland labor laws. This is how the Yixin incident became a problem.

True, the Labor Law in mainland China can be said to be well-intentioned, aiming to provide the best possible protection for a vulnerable laboring class. But the point is, in view of the unequal quality of Chinese workers at present, this kind of comprehensive protection for laborers has become a hindrance for capital to increase production efficiency.

Mainland workers and employees' lack of self-motivation, and the historical remnants of the "big rice bowl" work ethic are the core of the problem. Many Taiwanese investors in China indicate that they really want to be more humane to Chinese employees but find this unfeasible: "Once you are humane, productivity would immediately drop."

One Taiwanese businessman says that commending workers in order to induce self-respect in them is not a useful means to increase productivity. It seems that the more direct and primitive the method, the more effective it is. But to adopt such a method sometimes results in Taiwanese businessmen harboring serious doubts about their own conscience and humanity.

How to increase production efficiency under the combined conditions of passive employees and a stringent Labor Law is not a problem that can be easily solved. Unlawful use of corporal punishment is, of course, not practical, and to skirt around the edges of the Labor Law is also risky. So what can be done?

Labor Contracts Should Include a Clause to Safeguard Companies' Interests

Since Chinese employees' turnover rates are high, foreign-invested enterprises should include some clauses to safeguard the company's interests when signing labor contracts. Employers should also delineate in the labor contract what constitutes a serious violation of labor discipline, of rules and regulations of the enterprise, so that employees can have a clear idea of what their obligations and responsibilities are. In case they breach the rules, employers will then have sufficient reasons to terminate the contract.

However, when signing labor contracts, employers should also pay attention to the fact that different cities in China have different regulations. For instance, in Beijing, labor contracts have a standard format, but they are for reference only. In Shanghai, there is no such standard format, and it is up to individual enterprises to design their own. In Guangzhou, however, the prescribed format must be adopted, but conditions can be modified with the attachment of an appendix.

Items often overlooked by employers when signing labor contracts are:

1. requiring that employees be responsible for keeping the enterprise's business secrets;
2. demanding that employees compensate the company for training costs when they leave;
3. defining very clearly what constitutes a "serious violation of labor discipline, rules, and regulations," so that employees will know what their obligations and responsibilities are; and
4. listing rules and regulations on occupational health and safety.

In fact, to include rules and regulations on occupational health and safety in the labor contract is to the advantage of both parties. On the one hand, this can avoid or reduce casualties arising from industrial accidents. On the other hand, these can provide some guidelines of how to penalize employees when they breach rules and regulations.

In theory, education is the most fundamental way to alter the employees' work attitudes. In practice, however, in view of the fact that most Taiwanese enterprises in China are of small or medium size, how many enterprises can afford the time to carry it out? We can only hope that Taiwanese investors can build up some kind of mutual trust and understanding with their mainland employees. Only then can the problems be fundamentally solved.

Comments

Readers should note that the article is misleading on one point. In my eight years of research on Chinese workers, I have never heard of a migrant worker on a production line in any Taiwanese-invested labor-intensive factory making 1,000 yuan a month, as claimed by the author. Only staff at mid-management level can earn more than 1,000 yuan. The author argues that one Yixin worker found to be making less than 20 yuan a month was a special case, but glosses over exactly how much Yixin workers were paid on average. Had Yixin been paying workers 1,000 yuan a month, the author certainly would have boasted about it. To put Yixin's wages into perspective, Yu Yuan, a Taiwanese-owned and managed shoe factory that manufactures for Nike, Reebok, and Adidas, the biggest shoe factory in the world, paid workers on average 600 yuan a month in 1996, which is considered high.[3] To earn this amount, workers have to work long stretches of mandatory overtime.

The article displays a twisted logic on another point. According to the author, a high turnover rate among migrant workers is due to a lack of gratitude and the disloyalty of workers, who change jobs incessantly. Under such circumstances, the author argues, it is understandable that management has to put in place all sorts of measures, even illegal ones, to prevent them from leaving. It is true that migrant workers are always on the lookout for a better job. But this is because they want desperately to escape from low wages, long hours, mistreatment, fines, and unpaid wages. One can imagine migrant workers who have just entered Yixin on probation. Once they realize that corporal punishment is the order of the day, would they not want to pack up and leave immediately? But they cannot, because when they passed into the factory gates, they paid a 500 yuan deposit, amounting to more than a month's pay. That is, even before they start working, the factory owes them money. Once they begin to work, they are already accumulating "debts" for room and board. It is not discussed in the article, but apparently those who cannot tolerate the conditions and insist on leaving while on probation will have these debts[4] deducted from the 500 yuan deposit, and will not be paid for the days they have worked. It is also likely that the workers will lose the entire 500 yuan.

In addition, the author displays contempt for China's labor laws. She openly advises Taiwanese investors to defy the laws and take advantage of loopholes. She reminds her readers to note the degree of laxity with regard to the drawing up of labor contracts in different Chinese cities. In Beijing, the city regulations are only guidelines; in Shanghai, management decides what is included in the contracts; and in Guangzhou, even though there is a printed form, it is possible to add extra clauses, which include rules and regulations that place all the burden on the workers. In addition, make sure to include in the labor contract that the so-called training fee must be paid back when they quit. This last piece of advice openly encourages investors to engage in illegal practices.

If such contempt for China's labor laws and Chinese workers is widely held by Taiwanese investors, and even publicly defended by management, it is unlikely that Yixin would have mended its ways after the exposé. True enough, only two months after this damning article was published, while official investigations into Yixin's mistreatment of workers were still going on, Yixin was in the news again, this time for industrial safety violations.[5] A worker's thumb was severed by an unguarded cutting machine (an unguarded machine is a violation of industrial safety standards), but the factory management refused to take him to the hospital to reattach the finger. As Yixin had not bought labor insurance for its workers, the workers launched an instant collection drive, and raised 5,000 yuan in pledges. But they still needed immediate cash because hospitals demanded payment before they would operate. So they negotiated with management to sign pledges authorizing contributions to be taken from their next paychecks. Only then did Yixin management give them the cash. The worker's thumb was successfully reattached.

The injured worker, aware of the power of the previous exposé about the factory published two months earlier, approached reporters with his story. Their report prompted the labor bureau to berate Yixin's management for violating occupational safety and health regulations, and for not taking out industrial accident insurance. Management was made to pay back the 5,000 yuan to the workers, to cover the hospitalization bill, and to pay the victim's wages over the duration of the hospital stay and the rehabilitation. But as in the previous cases, no fines were imposed nor was the worker compensated for the injury. Except for some bad publicity, there was no deterrent to keep Yixin from continuing to flout Chinese laws.

CASE 7

Korean managers have gained a notorious reputation as being among the harshest and most abusive foreign investors in the world (although reports of Korean managers abusing Chinese workers are relatively few because there are fewer Korean firms in China than firms from Taiwan and Hong Kong).[6] South Korean and other observers have used the term "military culture" to characterize Korean management practices. Back in the 1960s and 1970s in Korea, before the union movement became a force to be reckoned with, beating female workers on the shop floor was part and parcel of the Korean labor scene.[7] Today, such abuses have been transplanted to Korean-managed factories in China, Vietnam, Indonesia, and elsewhere. The case selected here is about a Korean manager in northeast China, who made an entire shop floor of Chinese workers kneel down in front of her when she lost her temper. This particular incident was reported in many of China's newspapers and magazines and provoked national outrage— how can Chinese workers be humiliated and mistreated like this by foreigners?

KOREAN WOMAN BOSS FORCES 120 WORKERS TO KNEEL DOWN*

Workers Kneel in Panic

March 7, 1995 was a day of unforgettable humiliation for 120 Chinese workers on the shop floor of building six at Zhuhai Ruijin Electrical Goods Company Ltd.

At 3:00 P.M., workers were overjoyed to receive the unexpected "benevolence" of a ten-minute rest. Some rushed off to the bathroom while others, tired after working extra shifts, rested their heads on the assembly line for a snooze. But they forgot the "iron rule" stipulated by the Korean woman boss,

*Translation from the Chinese text: Liu Yuanyuan, "Hanguo nülaoban fagui 120 ming gongren de qianqian houhou," *Laodong bao* (Labor News), April 14, 1995. Translated by Kevin McCready.

Jin Zhenxian: At rest times—without exception—they must leave the workshop in rows of four.

When Jin Zhenxian arrived in building six "on patrol" at 3:05 P.M., she immediately bawled, "Assembly line supervisors, put your hands up and get over here."

Four supervisors slowly emerged from behind the machinery with both hands raised. They looked like soldiers surrendering and laying down their weapons. They walked over to Jin Zhenxian with their heads drooping. "Everyone kneel down! Kneel down!" Jin Zhenxian roared.

The woman interpreter, imitating Jin Zhenxian, shrieked: "Kneel down! Everyone kneel down!"

At first the workers looked blankly at the Korean woman boss, not knowing if they had misheard. Most workers sat still at the assembly line. Jin Zhenxian flew into a rage and rushed over to a worker, dragging her off her stool, knocking it over. "Kneel down!" she thundered, "If one of you does not kneel down, I'll make everybody in the workshop kneel down here all day."

First the worker who was pushed knelt down, next came those sitting near her, then one by one all the rest of the workers.

A twenty-three-year-old man from Henan, Ji Xuesheng, seeing that the workers all around him had knelt, quickly crouched down. "I hoped the boss wouldn't see me hiding. I wanted to avoid kneeling."

But Ji Xuesheng's hope quickly gave way to despair when the fierce eyes of Jin Zhenxian fell upon him. She pointed at him and roared "Kneel down!" This young man, who had never knelt to anyone in his life, flopped to his knees.

"I was really afraid I'd get the sack and not get paid," Ji Xuesheng said when he was interviewed, "Now I really regret having knelt."

An eighteen-year-old woman worker, Lu Chengtao, from Mashan in Sichuan, hesitated for a moment when she saw her sisters kneeling.[8] "I was confused; I felt afraid," Lu Chengtao said. "I burst into tears as soon as I knelt down."

Initially, Hu Fengwu, a twenty-one-year-old worker from Shaoyang county in Hunan province, was determined not to kneel. She just kept standing there. But when she saw a row of workers in front of her get fired on the spot by Jin Zhenxian for not kneeling, she was frightened that Jin Zhenxian would dock her two months' worth of hard-earned money, and that the blood and sweat of days and nights of overtime would be wasted. She capitulated and knelt.

"Thinking back over it now, it was really a huge insult, just as if a public sign of humiliation had been hung on my chest. I couldn't leave the factory without ripping it up or pasting something over it," said Hu Fengwu.

Probably the only woman worker who crouched down but was not discovered was Zhao Hongbo from Hunan, because she happened to occupy the last station on an assembly line and Jin missed seeing her. This seventeen-year-old was educated in a technical middle school and had arrived in Zhuhai six months ago with a dream. "When I saw my sisters kneeling there, I was incredibly upset. I just wanted to stand up, rip up the factory sign, and avoid the insult by walking away. But as soon as I thought about my bread and butter, I chickened out."

For the entire ten-minute kneeling episode, the workers wailed aloud in unison. Only about ten workers escaped Jin Zhenxian's punishment because they were sleeping in the warehouse at the time.

The Man Who Refused to Kneel

While workers all around knelt down, twenty-two-year-old Sun Tianshi from Nanyang in Henan remained standing. Among over one-hundred-twenty workers, he was the only one who refused to kneel to Jin Zhenxian.

When Jin Zhenxian saw Sun Tianshi standing, she flew into a rage and ordered him repeatedly to kneel down, but this indomitable youngster just would not give in.

"Kneel down!" shouted Jin Zhenxian fiercely.

"Why should I kneel down?" Sun Tianshi shouted back.

"If you don't kneel you can piss off," Jin Zhenxian's eyes were popping.

"Well, just kneel, eh?" one of Jin Zhenxian's trusted personnel managers urged.

"What reason have you got for telling me to kneel down?" Sun Tianshi was almost screaming. He turned around and asked the kneeling workers, "Are you Chinese or not? What are you kneeling for?"

When interviewed by a journalist from the *Zhuhai Labor News* on April 10, Sun Tianshi was indignant: "The kneeling workers looked at me blankly. Some of my good friends were kneeling there. I felt hurt and angry. Angry that they could be so gutless. Why couldn't they just take the sack?"

"Jin Zhenxian ordered me to leave. I left the seat and stomped out," Sun Tianshi recollected. "I had only one thing in mind; even if I died I wouldn't kneel! I'm Chinese!"

As soon as he left Ruijin, Sun Tianshi phoned the Zhuhai Labor Inspectorate and then went straight over to make a report.

The next day, Sun Tianshi went again to the labor inspectorate with more than ten indignant dismissed workers to inform them of what had happened. Sun Tianshi then disclosed the news to several media outlets in Zhuhai.

Sun Tianshi said there were two main reasons for his not kneeling down.

First, his education in patriotism from primary school to high school made him believe that to kneel to Jin Zhenxian not only insulted him personally, but also insulted the national character of the Chinese people. The second reason was his father's influence. Sun Tianshi's father is a cadre in the trade department of a government bureaucracy who is the kind of person who refuses to capitulate.

The Boss Apologizes: "Punishing Workers by Making Them Kneel" Is an Act Of Love

At 9:00 A.M. on March 24, I accompanied four labor inspectorate officials to Ruijin to ascertain the progress of the company's rectification program. A woman interpreter tried to detain us in the reception room at the entrance to building five saying, "The boss has no free time." From where we were, we saw another Korean-national interpreter sitting and chatting away at the boss's desk.

"We are labor inspectorate officials. Your boss has five minutes to come out here to talk with us," Wu Shaoqiang said sternly to the interpreter. Soon the interpreter led us into Jin Zhenxian's office. When Jin Zhenxian saw me taking pictures with my camera, she stretched out a hand saying, "No pictures."

After sitting down, Jin Zhenxian stressed repeatedly that we could not take pictures. She answered all the questions of the labor inspectorate officials through the two female interpreters.

On the problem of arbitrary docking of pay, arbitrary punishments, and arbitrary firings, Jin Zhenxian said that more than twenty old factory regulations and disciplinary measures had been torn off the wall and new ones had been sent to the Ministry of Labor for examination and approval. On the issue of not having signed labor contracts, she said she had agreed to give contracts to the 120 workers and had already sent the contracts to the labor bureau. In relation to excessive overtime, she took out a list of signatures of workers who had agreed to work overtime. She said that workers' monthly income would only be 380 yuan if they did not work overtime.[9] "Workers should earn extra money when they are young," Jin Zhenxian said, trying to make a joke. In relation to paying the wages owed and one month's wage in compensation to the twelve workers who had resigned, she indicated she would comply. As for making a public apology to workers for punishing them by making them kneel, Jin Zhenxian felt truly wronged. She said that to punish children by making them kneel was "purely an expression of love." "For more than a year I've been so kind to the workers, I didn't expect that they would treat me like this for making them kneel. I'm really deeply hurt." Jin Zhenxian tried to show some emotion.

When the labor inspectorate officials requested that she make a public apology to all workers, she was extremely reluctant and would only agree to provide an explanation while the workers were eating dinner. Section Head Wu Shaoqiang immediately pointed out that Jin Zhenxian's behavior in making the workers kneel had already violated Clause 2 of Section 96 of the Labor Law of the People's Republic of China, and that she could be detained, fined, and charged by the public security. He insisted Jin Zhenxian had to assemble all the workers before 10:00 A.M. to make a public apology. Jin Zhenxian nodded, looking painfully hurt.

At 10:00 A.M., more than two hundred workers gathered in the meeting hall. Ashen-faced and with a raised voice, Jin Zhenxian began her Korean-style apology. She said that punishing children who had done wrong by making them kneel was perhaps understood differently in China and Korea. In Korea it was "simply an expression of love" to smack the hand or bottom of someone who had done wrong, or to punish them by making them kneel. She had "acted out of love" in punishing the workers.

As soon as she said this, there were hisses all around the room. Huang Xiaoqin, a nineteen-year-old worker from Jiangxi province, sitting in the front row, said, "Making us kneel is love? Bullshit!"

When Section Head Wu Shaoqiang saw the workers becoming agitated, he immediately said, "Anyone who feels in any way dissatisfied, please speak up."

The first to stand up and query Jin Zhenxian was Huang Xiaoqin. She said that workers often did overtime until midnight or 2:00 A.M. But why did workers, who were hungry while working overtime, not receive overtime pay, as stipulated by the Labor Law? She said the number of rules, regulations, and fines set by the factory was uncountable. There was a 50 yuan fine for losing a plastic bag. For being one minute late the fine was 10 yuan, and the fine for taking a day off was 300 yuan.

The second person to stand up was Liu Zhixun, from Anhui province. He said that in his repair workshop they had worked overtime all through the night four nights in a row. Workers had not slept in a bed for four days and four nights. Jin Zhenxian replied that this must be because the workers in the repair workshop were inefficient, otherwise there would be no need to do overtime like that. Liu Zhixun asked Jin Zhenxian to leave the room because they had many things to say. During the "apology" session, Jin Zhenxian did not utter the word "apology." She did not say anything like "I hope the workers can forgive me." In fact, she used the word "explanation." A male worker said: "What sort of apology is that? It's a lecture."

Due to a lack of time, the labor inspectors had no choice but to interrupt the workers' speeches. Wu Shaoqiang made a concluding remark that he hoped the workers would study, understand, and abide by the law. He guaranteed, "This type of punishment of workers by making them kneel will not happen again, and you need not work additional shifts throughout the night again." He then told the workers the telephone number of the Zhuhai Labor Inspectorate complaint hotline. The whole place immediately burst into loud applause.

The Boss Plays Another Dirty Trick

On the very afternoon that the labor inspectors left, Jin Zhenxian played some devious tricks. She quietly transferred Huang Xiaoqin to another task. Jin Zhenxian had not "forgotten" the labor inspector's parting words, "Do not undertake attacks or reprisals against workers who have expressed opinions."

Huang Xiaoqin asked Jin Zhenxian, "Why have you changed my task?"

The female boss's excuse was very simple: "It's a work necessity. If you don't like it, you can resign."

Huang Xiaoqin glared with hatred at the boss. She fought to hold back tears and warned herself, "Whatever you do, don't cry in front of her. You must show that you are a woman with a backbone."

"Well, then, I resign." Huang Xiaoqin was extraordinarily cool. "I was forced to resign, but I walked out of the Ruijin Electrical Goods Company Ltd. with my head held high. This time I did not lose face."

But on March 25, when this puny little girl from Jiangsu province walked into the office of the manager of the Zhuhai People's Broadcasting Station's citizens' hotline to complain, she broke down and wept.

When I interviewed her, Huang Xiaoqin said, "Don't blame us for our weakness. We really couldn't weather the pressure." She sighed sadly and said, "Who will be the guardian angel of us workers?"

After leaving Ruijin, Huang Xiaoqin was out of work and in dire straits. "To bid farewell to Zhuhai and return to my home village was perhaps the best thing I could choose." She really had no choice.

Liu Zhixun suffered a reprisal at the same time as Huang Xiaoqin. This time, Jin Zhenxian did not have to lift a finger. A subforeman with the family name of Lin did a beautiful job.

On the afternoon of March 24, the subforeman came looking for Liu Zhixun and roughed him up. The subforeman threatened: "Hey, good-looking, I'm going to get a few people to kill you. If you don't piss off out of here, you'll be dead in no time."

Liu Zhixun was under no illusions; the subforeman had the numbers and could do anything he wanted. Moreover, with the boss behind him, he would not have a single good day at Ruijin.

Liu Zhixun and his wife were forced to leave as well. The workers said Jin Zhenxian was much "milder" than before and did not scream and shout. She did a beautiful job of firing Huang Xiaoqin, Liu Zhixun, and three others.

The People's Wrath

The news media in Zhuhai reacted swiftly to the kneeling incident. The Zhuhai People's Broadcasting Station, in particular, carried a big story calling for social justice for the workers.

On March 21, the Zhuhai People's Broadcasting Station opened a citizens' hotline for the "March 7 kneeling incident." The line was flooded with calls condemning the vicious behavior of Jin Zhenxian. The hotline ran for a week and had a profound influence on popular sentiment. According to the program manager, they had gotten calls from comrades in the public security department, the trade unions, industrial associations, and other organizations, offering to assist in carrying out a full investigation. Some people even sat by the phone trying to get through while missing their lunch. People were outraged and quite a few demanded that Jin Zhenxian "piss off."

Many of those who could not get through by phone wrote to the station. One letter signed, "A Chinese," thought "an apology is too lenient." Another "faithful listener" wrote that "his wrath would not subside" and that "the violator should not be spared."

Many others held the opinion that, though we now have the Labor Law, such incidents still happen. This is no coincidence. It is the inevitable result of some foreign businesses' complete disregard for the law and the connivance of some bureaucracies. At the same time though, the incident points to one pressing issue—the urgent necessity for migrant workers to improve their own quality of life (*suzhi*).

Comments

As we have seen, the workers in this factory were subject to an iron discipline. On the other hand, compared with the kind of violence imposed on the workers at Yixin (Case 6) and Zhaojie (Case 1), kneeling down was a very mild form of punishment, and long work hours and fines are commonplace. So what caused this national outrage in China?

My interpretation is that the symbolism rather than the degree of abusiveness instigated Chinese anger. To make Chinese kneel en masse in front of a foreigner represented a national humiliation. The affront to national pride, rather than the violation of Chinese labor laws (or the violation of their human dignity as laborers) was the issue here. Most of the workers under-

stood the practical consequences of resistance and succumbed to the command to kneel. Only one worker refused to kneel down and he drew his courage from national pride, "I had only one thing in mind; even if I died I wouldn't kneel. I'm Chinese!" Nationalism superseded proletarian consciousness.

Interestingly, the Korean manager, in her defense, deployed a relativist cultural argument—that she acted in accordance with Korean "enterprise culture," and therefore the incident was a misunderstanding. This same defense has been used by many Asian governments, including the Chinese government, when criticized by the West for violations of labor standards. Taiwanese investors, in contrast, cannot use the cultural argument when caught mistreating mainland workers. So often, as in the Yixin case, they resort to a straightforward classical economics argument—punishing workers is the only way to raise productivity.

Readers may want to note that despite the public outrage and vast amount of publicity stirred up by the incident, all that the Korean manager offered to rectify in terms of wage rates was to pay exactly the minimum wage set by the Zhuhai government. No one, neither the local officials nor the workers, raised any objection to this pathetic improvement. After all, this is legal. This is an excellent example of how minimum wage standards in reality have become maximum wage rates for workers.

CASE 8

Dogs, or references to dogs, appear repeatedly in a number of the articles collected in this volume. Dogs are used to guard work sites and to scare workers. Their effectiveness in this regard was fully demonstrated in case 4, in which migrant construction workers were imprisoned like slaves. Another reference is by management, comparing their workers to dogs. Workers complain that they are being treated worse than dogs, and demand to be treated as humans. In this article about a Taiwanese factory, dogs appear in several forms. A worker was punished by being locked up with two huge wolfhounds, a punishment that is frightening and immensely humiliating. Later, when the workers went on strike in protest, the manager humiliated the workers, calling them dogs and making them pass through a side gate that was normally reserved for dogs.

WHY DO FEMALE MIGRANT WORKERS GO ON STRIKE?*

The mainland has established a fairly good legal and human resource environment for Taiwanese capital, which has been developing rapidly. Statistics

---

* Translation from the Chinese text: Gan Jingshan, "Dagongmei weihe nao bagong?" *Fazhi ribao* (Legal System Daily), February 21–23, 1994. Translated by Kevin McCready.

show that Taiwanese business investment in the mainland already exceeds 10 billion yuan; Taiwanese-funded enterprises account for over 40 percent of some 4,000 foreign enterprises in Fujian.

But some foreign businesses regard themselves as saviors—allowing mainlanders to work in their enterprises is an act of benevolence. They think they can order the mainlanders about and insult them as they please.

On November 4, 1993, at the Taiwanese Yongqi Shoe Factory in Fujian province, an extraordinary event took place when a hired female laborer was locked up with wolfhounds. In the small hours of the morning, as she was finishing her shift, Yu, a female migrant worker from Jiangxi province, tossed a roll of sticky tape over the wall onto the lawn outside. But when she went to pick it up, she was grabbed by security guards who were hiding there. On the lawn were also two pairs of shoes. She explained in her defense, "I was only picking up the sticky tape, not the shoes."

The security guards took Yu to the police station. The comrade at the police station, taking it as a case of pilfering, thought that the amount involved was too petty to be dealt with by the law. It could be handled according to factory rules. So the security guards took Yu back to the factory security office. When factory manager Chen Muquan heard what happened, he was furious. He grabbed Yu, ripping her clothes. He yelled at her and smashed her head against a wall, causing a large lump to appear on her head.

It so happened that Pan (the business representative of the Taiwanese Ding Li Company), a client of the Yongqi Company, was at Yongqi on business. Although he had nothing to do with the affair, in trying to ingratiate himself to Yongqi Company, he too stepped forward and slapped Yu on the face several times. He then tied a pair of shoes together with their laces, forcibly tried to hang them around Yu's neck, and was prepared to "parade" her for all to see. Yu, seeing this as a personal humiliation, struggled violently.

Yu was locked up until 8:00 A.M. and then was taken back to the office. Yongqi's company director, Zhang Longrong, asked sarcastically, "What do you reckon, eh?"

"The sack?" Yu knew the penalty was dismissal under the factory rules.

"The sack? That lets you off too lightly! I'm going to lock you up with the dogs! You can spend three days in the dog cage and then you can go!"

As soon as Yu heard this, she was terrified and pleaded: "I beg you. Just sack me. Whatever you do, don't lock me in the dog cage."

Zhang Longrong looked at her fiercely, ignoring her pleas.

Yongqi Company keeps two large wolfhounds and has a dog shed and a dog cage. The dog shed was constructed out of a narrow enclosed space between the walls of the toilet and another room.

Acting under orders, a security guard, Chen Linzhuang, pushed Yu into the shed. When the two wolfhounds saw a stranger come in they barked and lunged toward Yu. One of them put its two front legs on Yu's shoulders, and she screamed and backed into the corner. Luckily the dogs did not bite. They were accustomed to the women workers passing back and forth on their way to the toilet. But Yu was shaking from head to foot, her face ashen white.

When workers going to the toilet saw this, they became furious. They talked among themselves and were extremely upset with the bosses. When they thought about how the factory director and manager arbitrarily fired staff and workers at will and abused and swore at them, they got even angrier.

About twenty minutes later, the security guard moved Yu into the dog cage. It was a special contraption made of iron sheets and bars welded together, and at the bottom was fitted four wheels so that it could be pushed around.

Several workers crowded around and pretended to be having a closer look, but actually they had come to help Yu climb out of the cage.

Yu was able to climb out, but except for slipping out through the main gate, there was nowhere to escape. But before she got to the gate, she was discovered by Chen Linzhuang and the others. Yu quickly turned on her heels and darted into the women's toilet to hide.

When Zhang Longrong found out what had happened, he was beside himself with anger: "Lock her up in the dog cage! When everyone's finished their shift roll out the dog cage so that everyone can see her."

Yu was dragged out of the women's toilet and again locked up in the dog cage.

After 10:00 A.M., Mao Zhongbing, a worker brave enough to step forward, untwisted the wire that fastened the iron gate to let Yu out. Then he sneaked over with an electrician's ladder and helped her climb over the wall and flee.

In a little while, the security guard came over to check and discovered Yu had escaped. He immediately informed manager Chen. When he found out that it was Mao Zhongbing who had released Yu, he bellowed: "You're fired! This month's wage, overtime pay, all your deposit monies will be docked!"

"But my family is a long way away in Jiangxi. If you dock all my money, I won't have traveling expenses to get home," said Mao Zhongbing.

"You're even worse than a dog. If you haven't got money to get home you can crawl back!" Chen jeered.

Mao Zhongbing retorted, "There are many dogs like me. When you leave, you'd better watch out!"

When Chen Linquan heard this he was livid and yelled, "You want revenge! Do you want to kill me?"

Chen Linquan immediately got on the phone to a nearby police station. The policeman on duty who took the call came around immediately to arrest Mao Zhongbing and take him to be locked up at the police station. No matter how Mao Zhongbing tried to explain himself, it was all to no avail. The policeman said: "If you want to go, pledge in writing to guarantee manager Chen Linquan's personal safety. If anything happens to him we'll come and get you for questioning."

After Mao Zhongbing complied, they still would not let him go. In the end, they released him after someone from the neighborhood committee who knew him agreed to be his guarantor.

But the incident was not over. Manager Chen added fuel to the fire. On November 5 he called a meeting of all of the more than six hundred men and women workers in the factory and said with a murderous look on his face: "I used to look on you as people, now I look on you as dogs."

Director Zhang Longrong was even more cutting: "From now on anyone found stealing will be beaten up and then locked in the dog cage!"

In this "fortified village," the words of Zhang, Chen, and other Taiwanese businessmen are holy writ. As a result, a few days later when a worker, Wu, was discovered stealing a pair of shoes, the security guards kicked and beat him on the spot. They then tied both his hands behind him with a rope and fettered him to the main gate, putting him on display from 2:00 A.M. until 6:00 A.M. (the factory has a night shift). Wu couldn't bear it and begged the security guards crying, "I really can't stand it; if you let me go I promise to give you a good reward. Please do a good turn."

Two of the guards felt sorry for him, and also wanted the money, so they released him.

That day, Zhang Longrong conducted an investigation into how Wu had got away. The two security guards had no choice but to own up. They were sacked and fined 90 yuan each.

The bosses beat, swore at, and mistreated the staff and workers again and again. The migrant workers' dissatisfaction turned to antagonism and resistance. On November 24, some thirty female migrant workers refused to work in protest of the bosses' inhumane treatment.

When manager Chen went to the dormitory to make them go to work, they were unanimous, "If the bosses won't treat us as human we won't work!"

Manager Chen threatened, "If you don't go to work today, you're fired!"

The women workers would not back down and tendered Chen a reasonable proposal: they would work if they were treated as humans, not as dogs. They demanded two rest days a month, no overtime two evenings a week, an increase in meal subsidies, and an increase in overtime wage rates.

The factory manager rejected the demands outright. "If you don't work, there are other people who will. I have no authority to approve your demands."

The women workers got even more outraged. By the morning of November 17, more than three hundred of the women migrant workers had joined in the "strike."

Manager Chen Linquan flew into a rage. He threatened the workers who had gathered outside the main gate, saying: "If you don't go to work, I'll fire all of you! If you go to work right now you can still make it! The side gate is for dogs. If anyone wants to go to work, enter the factory by the side gate!"

The women workers shouted back: "If you don't agree to the conditions we've proposed, we won't go to work! And when we go to work we go through the main gate, not through the dog's entrance!"

The women negotiated for some time, but with absolutely no result. Then someone had the idea of going to the media to complain. Some started making phone calls while others began writing publicity material. One piece read:

> People need a spirit of mutual respect and love. But the sinister and perverse cunning of people like director Zhang Longrong of Yongqi factory sends you shivering. Every time a staff member or worker gets sick and thinks about applying for a day off, he/she is subject to his sarcastic and derisive abuse. Last time, when a woman worker from the stitching department approached manager Zhang for a sick day, he scolded her, "Why do you need a day off? You're not dying, are you?"
>
> Once a transport worker had his toe broken while on duty. Because it was only twenty minutes before the shift finished, he asked manager Zhang for time off to go to the hospital to get it bound. Zhang not only refused permission, but sarcastically said, "You're a doctor, aren't you?" When some workers overheard this they began to weep . . . Foreign businessmen investing in mainland China must respect the mainland's laws. But the Yongqi factory has contravened the law in many ways, such as violating the personal freedom of staff and workers, tying them up, beating them, secretly setting up a dog cage as a prison, and so on . . . We request the government and news media come and conduct an investigation.

On November 27 at about 3:00 P.M., several Fuzhou city government officers and several reporters arrived at Lian Jiang Road. As soon as they got out of the car, a crowd of migrant workers surged forth, all trying to speak at once in their own dialect. They spoke emotionally of their miseries and mistreatment as the reporters captured them on their video cameras, cameras, and notebooks.

- "Putting a female worker into a dog cage for pilfering is too cruel."
- "The bosses bodysearch everyone. As soon as the female workers start work, the main gate is locked and they are not allowed out even when there is no work during a power cut. When work is over, everyone has to line up in a long queue to be bodysearched before they can leave the factory."
- "The wages are really low. For three months after starting, you only get 90 yuan a month, after that you get 140 yuan a month. If you leave the factory midway, you don't get the 130 yuan deposit you've paid or the monthly 10 yuan deposit that's been deducted."
- "Regulations in the 'Staff Manual' are already unreasonable, but the behavior of the bosses is far worse than the regulations. Female workers asking for an hour's sick leave have to pay 2 yuan; anything over an hour is counted as being absent without leave for a day, and an additional three days' pay and 30 yuan of full-attendance bonus will be deducted."
- "We're forced to work overtime and the overtime rate is extremely low. The hourly overtime rate for new workers is only 0.38 yuan; experienced workers get 0.58 yuan. The amount we get from working overtime until daybreak is not enough to pay for a snack."

In the last few months, there has been no let up in compulsory overtime. Many female workers start overtime at 4:30 P.M. and go straight through until midnight without a bite to eat or anything to drink. Many women collapse from fatigue. Sometimes the section head will suddenly shout an order, and everyone is forced to run two laps around the factory yard to "freshen up." Then they work the overtime shift straight through until daylight. This type of overtime goes on for more than two weeks running. According to a conservative estimate, in the last two weeks the shoe-soles section has worked eighty-six hours overtime, the shoe-making section seventy-five hours, and the handwork section sixty-seven hours. Many women workers were fired after they had collapsed from exhaustion.

So this is the story of how over three hundred women migrant workers at the Yongqi Company went on strike.

This incident shocked all government departments. For a few days in succession, they sent people to examine the situation. Relevant departments did ideological work on the bosses of Yongqi Company, assisting them to improve factory rules and raising their awareness of relevant legislation and regulations.

Fuzhou city Party committee and city-government officials have direct management responsibility over the factory, and Party Secretary Xi Jinping was the first to issue some guidelines. He pointed out that foreigners must conduct their business within the law and are absolutely forbidden to detain people unlawfully. He ordered immediate investigations in order to apply legal procedures.

Even before they had received orders from the city committee and city government, the reaction of the Fuzhou City and District People's Procuratorate, as the political-legal organ, had begun an investigation. When Wang Xianyao, the chief procurator, read in the *Legal System Daily* that a woman migrant worker had been locked up with wolfhounds, he immediately sent Chen Longliang and other case officers to Yongqi Company to undertake a legal examination of those directly responsible for the illegal detention of Yu. The investigation revealed a prima facie case against director Zhang Longrong and the security guard, Chen Linzhuang, for the crime of illegal detention. The case was immediately taken up for investigation. Chen Linzhuang was arrested and brought to justice. But Zhang Longrong, having been suddenly "dismissed" by the general manager, fled back to Taiwan.

While the incident was under investigation, the general manager in Taiwan came to Fuzhou to make enquiries. He presented a "statement of self-examination" to the Fuzhou City People's Government that read:

An incident occurred at this factory on November 27 and 28. The majority of staff and workers went on a collective strike, instigating great concern from many government departments and work units. Assistance came from many quarters, for which we are extremely grateful. The factory is deeply hurt by the occurrence of this incident and has paid a bitter price. When I heard in Taiwan that the woman worker, Yu, was locked in a dog cage for stealing shoes, I felt personally guilty and responsible. I came as quickly as possible from Taiwan to Fuzhou to attend to the issue, and have severely criticized the personnel who are responsible for this dereliction of duty. With the agreement of the board of directors, I have sacked Director Zhang. At the same time, I have tried to locate Yu so that I could extend my deepest apologies to her personally and also to apologize on behalf of my Taiwanese friends. From now on, we will strictly forbid a recurrence of this type of incident. We will also strengthen our Taiwanese managers' understanding of the legal system. We make the following guarantees:

1. The company will not seek to lay responsibility on those who participated in the strike, including the leaders. At the same time, we will also strictly forbid managers at all levels from seeking revenge. We should adopt a magnanimous attitude toward the strikers.

2. Not only will we not hold anyone responsible for this strike, it will not be counted as absence without leave. Their bonuses will not be affected.

3. We guarantee that each month there will be at least two days off. If there are power blackouts or water shortages, the company can make appropriate adjustments and do its best to aim for one day off per week.

4. From January 1994, wages will be increased by about 15 percent. Overtime loadings will have a corresponding increase as of December 1993. If normal shifts are extended by an hour, a snack allowance will be paid. The food allowance will be increased by 20 percent.

Chen Jing, who was sent by Fuzhou city government to deal with this case, then said to General Manager Lin: "The critical point is to implement these as quickly as possible. I hope that your company will prosper even more after these changes have been made."

In addition to the Fuzhou city government, the provincial and city-level trade unions, and the Department of Labor, all wrote investigative reports and submitted their opinions and recommendations.

The provincial general trade union regards locking someone up with dogs and conducting regular body searches as violations of Sections 37 and 38 of the Constitution and Section 131 of the Criminal Code. Victims should be compensated for defamation and economic loss. In addition, a guarantee should be given that such a mistake will not be committed again. Factories established on Chinese mainland soil should respect China's constitution and other relevant laws and regulations. The factory's own rule for body searching should be abolished, and guarantees should be given to staff and workers on wages, working hours, labor safety, special safety measures for women, and so on. Yongqi Company should immediately organize a trade union to safeguard the legal rights and interests of staff and workers, to mediate management–labor relationships, and to work together toward the enterprise's development. During this incident, the "X" police station did not uphold justice or protect the legal rights and interests of staff and workers. On the contrary, they arbitrarily imprisoned staff and workers, intensifying the conflict. Relevant departments should criticize and educate them.

The provincial labor bureau's investigative report is of the opinion that to lock a women worker in a dog cage is illegal, and that many of the demands of those who went on strike are reasonable.

A prominent lawyer, Zou Zhiming, declares that to lock a person in a dog cage is a criminal act. The circumstances under which Yu stole the shoes were petty in nature, did not constitute a crime, and should have been dealt with according to the factory regulations. But the factory had no right to make an illegal arrest. Director Zhang has run off, but to absolve him of legal responsibility by "dismissing" him is not right. The monk can run away, but not the temple.

An article by the *Legal System Daily's* commentator points out that the roots of foreign businesses' "transgressions" lie with us. Taxes have undergone repeated reduction, land prices have kept coming down, and local officials' bowing to foreign businesses has gotten lower and lower.

The media and many government departments have received a huge number of letters expressing sympathy for the workers from the countryside, cities, factories, and schools.

At a press conference, the Fuzhou City People's Government emphasized yet again that foreign investors must strictly abide by China's relevant regulations, conduct business legally, and they are not permitted to violate the legal rights and interests of the employees and workers of the PRC partner. Otherwise, they will be dealt with according to the law. The city government requested Yongqi Company to draw lessons from this incident.

Yongqi Company has now made concessions to the women migrant workers who went on strike by raising their wages and overtime pay. For new workers, the hourly rate for overtime has gone from 0.38 yuan to 0.50 yuan. Experienced workers receive an increase from 0.58 to 0.80 yuan. The mood of the workers is basically stable and production is back to normal.

On the afternoon of December 20, Mr. Lin, the head of the Yongqi Company's board of directors, arrived at the Fuzhou district procuratorate and made a personal apology to Yu. He also presented her with 1,000 yuan as defamation compensation. He invited Yu to return to Yongqi Company but she declined. Two days later, she returned to her hometown in Jiangxi.

Comments

The workers' protest here was quite unusual in that it was initially over an issue of human dignity, rather than simply over pay or working conditions. When the workers finally went on strike, their demands were extremely modest—two nights a week without overtime and only two rest days a month. Even when granted, these were still below the standards set by Chinese labor regulations. Worthy of note is the cozy relationship between Taiwanese investors and the local police. The manager only had to pick up the phone and the police would come to put a worker in detention without going through any due process. This is also a case in which the bondage of workers was progressively increased by withholding 10 yuan from the workers' wage every month.

CASE 9

As we have seen, the private security guards in foreign-funded enterprises sometimes have immense power over the workers both on and off the shop floor. A parallel parapolice force exists inside state enterprises. These are the "internal security departments" (neibaochu), which are carry-overs from the security control system of the Maoist period, staffed mostly by demobilized soldiers or former public-security personnel. Up until 1995, as in the Maoist days, these were extensions of the police force stationed at work units, where they simultaneously came under enterprise-level Party leadership. For example, their personnel were recruited by factory management, not sent by the bureau of police. In the Maoist era, when "politics was in command," they enjoyed a good deal of discretionary power over the workers and staff, investigated people's work and private lives, and were in charge of surveillance and interrogation. They were allowed to "enact a wide range of administrative punishments for which there are no trials or legal appeals, ranging from putting workers under a form of control similar to parole to sending them to prison or labor reform camps."[10] In fact, looking back at the violent history that pervaded many state factories in the days of the Cultural Revolution, this historical past sets the norm that accepts using paramilitaristic personnel to impose workplace discipline of staff and workers.

Since Mao's death, the internal security department's function has been limited to handling criminal activities at the workplace. The department has the power to interrogate suspects, but no power to arrest. Their parasecurity status, however, allows them to abuse their power without much upper-level oversight. In 1995, the government severed its ties to the police bureaus on the grounds that problems in the workplace are "contradictions among the people," and it is the management's responsibility to handle these, not the business of a public-security unit.[11]

Whether deregulation of the enterprise internal security department has lessened its power is something that needs research. In the following case, the department had retained a lot of control over factory staff and workers. In this particular case, the internal security department was allowed to discipline workers on both work-related and non-work–related infractions. The internal security staff demanded a fine of 2,000 yuan from a worker who had done nothing wrong, but had simply refused to assume a submissive attitude. They threatened to fire him if he did not hand over the money, which was probably equivalent to three or four times his monthly salary. The security department's responsibility for dealing with criminal activities was ill defined and all encompassing, and included dismissal. These staff members behaved more like thugs than law-enforcement personnel.

Workers in this particular factory had complained in the past about the internal security staff. But nothing was done to curtail their power because they enjoyed the protection of the manager, the enterprise Party committee, and the trade union. The factory had been making a substantial profit, which was unusual among Chinese state enterprises by the 1990s. It seems that management had purposely condoned the internal security staff to infuse an environment of intimidation and suppression at the workplace and keep staff and workers in line. Management saw this kind of "enterprise culture" as necessary for maintaining high productivity. Authorities outside the enterprise had ignored the various violations such as the internal security department's possession of handcuffs, electric batons, and equipment for torture. Moreover, as underlined in the editor's note, the Workers' Daily *receives a lot of letters from workers complaining about the kangaroo courts set up by the internal security departments and the beatings that are carried out. This case was by no means an isolated incident. Understandably, the Chinese press underreports violence against workers in state enterprises.*

ENTERPRISE "INTERNAL SECURITY DEPARTMENT" SETS UP A KANGAROO COURT: WORKER BEATEN UNTIL CRIPPLED FOR BREAKING RULES *

Recently, *Workers' Daily* has been receiving a lot of letters from staff and workers reporting that personnel of internal security departments inside enterprises have been setting up kangaroo courts and arbitrarily beating up employees. The case of the staff and workers of the Shang Qiu Textile Factory in Henan province being beaten after breaking factory rules is one of the most serious of such incidents. To find out what happened, one of our reporters carried out an in-depth investigation. We hope that this will attract the attention of the relevant authorities, and that they will seriously take steps to deal with incidents of a similar nature.

On November 18, 1995, at 2:20 P.M., electrician Wang Bao'an of Shang Qiu Textile Factory in Henan province had just finished repairing a machine and was heading toward the washroom to wash his hands. As he walked down the corridor, he casually tapped a sign on the wall that read "Preparatory Work Shop-Floor Office." It so happened that the factory manager, Mo Kemao, had just come from outside and saw Wang doing it. Manager Mo asked, "Why did you tap on the sign?"

Wang Bao'an retorted, "What's wrong with tapping the sign a bit." Some heated words were exchanged, and at that point the manager discovered that Wang Bao'an "reeked of alcohol."

Half an hour later, after Wang Bao'an had already begun work on the shop floor for some time, the shop-floor manager beckoned him to leave his workstation. He was then told to go with the head of the internal security

---

*Translation from the Chinese text: Tian Jie, "Qiye 'neibao' sishe gongtang weiji zhigong jingbei da can," *Workers' Daily*, March 27, 1996, p. 7. Translated by Anita Chan.

department, Shao Hua, who had come to fetch him. Shao Hua summoned two other staff from the internal security department, Zhao Jingeng and Yuan Jie, to come along. The three "invited" Wang Bao'an to the internal security department office situated on the third floor of the factory administrative building. There he was brutally beaten up for breaking factory rules.

On February 8, 1996, at Shang Qiu City Hospital, Wang Bao'an, who had been staying there for over two months to recuperate, handed me a set of photographs and X-rays of his injuries that had been taken after the beatings. These were evidence that had been certified by both the city hospital and provincial hospital. The X-rays showed a crushed and splintered left humerus, two injured wrists, damaged soft tissues in the left leg and hip, and damaged nerves in the left armpit and central nervous system. Wang Bao'an then showed me his atrophied left arm and claw-like left hand, which he could no longer extend.

Wang Bao'an stated that after he was led into the internal security department office, they closed the door and the department head, Shao Hua, said to him, "Damn it! So you drank some alcohol and started making trouble! We need to wake you up a bit!"

"Just because of you, the manager bawled several of us out!" Zhao Jingeng and Yuan Jie then handcuffed Wang's hands behind his back, and began punching him on the chest and back with their fists, kicked him in the groin and stomach, and used instruments of torture such as electric batons on him. The interrogation and beatings lasted for four hours. While beating him, they also forced him to admit to having stolen a faucet from the second-floor toilet.

Several times, Wang collapsed on the floor and could not get up. He screamed in pain as the beatings got worse and worse. The political-work office of the Party branch was adjacent to the internal security department office, and although even the guard at the main gate could hear Wang's painful screams, not even one person came to mediate or try to put an end to this criminal behavior. Not able to take the torture further, Wang tried to commit suicide by climbing onto a desk near the window so that he could jump out. But they saw him and pulled him down for more beatings (since this incident, iron bars have been installed on the windows of the internal security department). It was not until around 6:00 p.m. that the three "internal security" staff members made preparations to call it a day. Shao Hua, who had been directing the entire interrogation, told Zhao Jingeng to go fetch a basin of water and have Wang Bao'an clean up his face. He then handed Wang over to the internal security staff who had arrived for the next shift, and told them to let Wang "rest" until 7:00 P.M. and then take him home.

Wang, by then barely conscious, was not sure how he got out of the internal security office. All he could vaguely recall was that someone carried him to the front office at the main gate, a comrade gave him two glasses of water, and another comrade called a paddle tricycle to get him home. That evening, he lost control of his urinary and bowel functions.

Shang Qiu Textile Factory is a state enterprise with nearly three thousand employees. According to the city's officials, the factory was important and influential—its annual contribution to the government from its profit tax reached almost 10 million yuan, one of the highest in the city. Because of this, the enterprise and its leadership were highly regarded by the authorities.

The factory's leadership cadres told me that because the factory was a special case, its regulations were [allowed to be] quite "comprehensive" and "strict." This has caused some staff and workers who do not comprehend the significance of this iron discipline to complain, even characterizing Shang Qiu Textile Factory as a "prison." This, they explained, has somewhat tarnished the image of the factory. The factory management is worried about fire, and strictly prohibits smoking at work. Because drinking could affect shop-floor safety or instigate quarrels, there are also strict rules at the factory against drinking. Anyone caught breaking these rules would be punished. The factory leadership took out two copies of the factory rules and regulations for me to see, and true enough, they were there in black and white. But according to some factory staff and workers, these "regulations" were not strictly enforced. When the factory leadership accompanied me to have a look at the canteen, I not only saw on display for sale the Beijing brand of spirit "ergoutou," I also noticed people eating there who were drinking beer sold by the canteen. On the day Wang was beaten, he had indeed shared one and a half catties of white spirits with five other workmates at a restaurant. But in another restaurant, Department Head Shao Hua, Zhao Jingeng, and Yuan Jie also shared one catty of spirits and four or five bottles of beer. Had the factory manager not contacted them through their pager at 2:30 P.M. telling them to come back to the factory to deal with a case of "drunken disturbance," they would still be at their lunch table drinking.

Based on the above, it is not unreasonable to believe enforcement of factory regulations was actually lax as reported to me by some employees.

The factory leadership also told me that the factory's internal security department was a very important department. Its staff was handpicked with great care. The department head was originally a police officer, and other staff members were all promising young people who were recently discharged from the army. The factory trade-union chair even told me that Zhao and Yuan (who by then had been arrested) were the factory's most "honest" young people. According to some factory employees, under the factory leadership's protection, the internal security staff had themselves repeatedly violated factory rules and regulations. It was not the first time that they had set up a kangaroo court and beat people. Buying handcuffs and using torture tools such as electric batons without permission had also occurred before. According to Wang Bao'an, that afternoon Zhao Jingeng told him, "According to regulations, you are fined 2,000 yuan—1,000 yuan for drinking at work, and another 1,000 yuan for drunken disturbance, that is, tapping on the sign."

Shao Hua, the department head, then told him: "Bring the money here on Monday morning, or else you'll be fired!" The three of them also took his hand and had him thumbprint the interrogation record.

If what Wang Bao'an said was true, then these internal security staff definitely were not the staff who were "handpicked with great care."

In two and half months, Wang Bao'an has spent almost 10,000 yuan on medical fees. The factory has given him 3,000 yuan (apparently for the Spring Festival, the factory gave him another 1,000 yuan). The rest of the expenses were borrowed from relatives and friends. Wang is now in deep financial trouble. Wang is twenty-eight years old. He has seventy-year-old parents and a one-year-old baby girl to take care of. Now that his arm is crippled, he will have difficulty getting by. He cannot understand why the enterprise is so unfair to him. He said: "Normally, when such a serious incident happened, we are all enterprise employees, right? Why does the enterprise leadership treat people differently?" He said that since he brought the case to court, not only did the enterprise stop paying his medical fees, it even treated his recuperation period as ordinary sick leave. Not only did it not assist the court with the case, it even allowed Department Head Shao Hua to take a long leave so that he could take care of his old mother. This way he could avoid the procurator's interrogation. Isn't it unfair to treat employees this way?

One positive development thus far is that the Shang Qiu City Party Committee has taken a firm stand on this case. A member of its leadership said: "Wang Bao'an did violate factory rules for drinking during work hours. It is necessary that he be disciplined accordingly. But it does not mean he should be beaten, and certainly not to the extent of being crippled. The three internal security staff members should be dealt with by the court as having committed a criminal offense. The enterprise should pay for Wang's medical expenses to ensure his recovery. As the city's leadership, we too should bear some responsibility. The city Party committee will ensure that those responsible for this case be dealt with according to law, in order that employees' legal rights can be protected."

CASE 10

Violence begets violence. This case is selected to show how bottled-up anger against the daily social discrimination suffered by migrant male workers in the Shenzhen area exploded into an armed battle, with several hundred mi-

grant construction workers pitted against the local authorities. The catalyst for the incident was a minor quarrel between the construction workers and a local man. Because a blackout of this incident was imposed on the local Chinese press, the incident was only reported in the Hong Kong press, and so the two reports here are taken from a Hong Kong newspaper. By the mid-1990s, Hong Kong reporters were regularly crossing the border into Guangdong to cover news stories. As can be seen from these two reports of the battle, both sides were brutal.

MOTORCYCLIST CRASHED INTO A FENCE AND REFUSED TO APOLOGIZE; VILLAGE "BIG SHOT" GATHERED THE TROOPS TO BATTLE MIGRANT WORKERS*

Armed violence exploded between several hundred out-of-province peasant workers (*mingong*)[12] and armed police in Longtian village in Shenzhen the day before yesterday. When firing into the air was useless, the police machine-gunned the workers. So far, at least two have been confirmed dead, with sixty injured. Five hospitals are involved in taking care of the casualties. The whereabouts of eighty others who have not returned to the construction site are still unknown after they fled from the scene.

Yesterday, all township government departments were on high alert, placing plainclothes police officers outside all their buildings. The Longtian village office and the township hospital were heavily guarded by uniformed police in case the peasant workers staged a counterattack. The police car that was overturned by the workers was still lying on the roadside.

Reports from the scene of the incident described the workers as mainly from Hunan province, with some from Hubei province. They belong to the No. 3 Branch of the Hunan Road and Bridge Company, which has a contract to construct the section of the highway between Danshui and Longgang. The day before yesterday at about 11:00 a.m., sixty to seventy peasant workers had just finished spreading tar in the fenced-off section of the highway. Suddenly, someone who was said to be one of the "big shots" from the village crashed through the fence and rode over the newly tarred surface. Several peasant workers came up and insisted that he mend the fence. When he refused, insults were exchanged, and the workers refused to give him back his motorcycle. He then called the local police using his mobile phone.

---

*Translation from the Chinese text: Reporter anonymous, "Tieqizhi chuangduan lanlutixian jujiebuo, longtiancun 'dakuan' banbing zhan mingong," *Dongfang ribao* (Orient News), December 5, 1995. Translated by Anita Chan.

Gun Aimed at the Supervisor's Forehead

Several security protection personnel arrived, but the peasant workers would still not give in. Half an hour later, more than fifty security personnel and riot police from several villages were called in as reinforcements. One of them reportedly pulled out a gun and pressed it against the forehead of one of the construction-site supervisors. Another hit him repeatedly on the back and on his head with an iron rod. This sparked a fierce battle between the two sides. Then, the workers lost out and began to flee. But several were grabbed and taken to the village committee office.

When the workers saw that several of their colleagues had been arrested, they phoned their construction headquarters for help. Under the leadership of a department head, more than five hundred workers soon arrived in some ten trucks. Armed with iron rods and other instruments, they surrounded the village office. At that time, there were only a few policemen and security-protection personnel guarding the place. When the department head went up to ask for the release of his workers, they put him under gunpoint. On seeing their "boss" attacked, the workers surged forth. In the chaotic violence, one policeman was beaten to death. The police and security-protection personnel finding themselves in an indefensible minority, retreated into the village office, but the workers tore their way in and rushed upstairs and badly beat up the village deputy Party secretary and village head. Only after the village officials, staff, and police barricaded themselves on the roof were they temporarily saved. The workers then proceeded to vent their anger by turning the entire office upside down. Even the iron bars of the security windows were bent out of shape.

One Beaten to Death and Five Shot

Around 5:00 P.M., police reinforcements arrived. The first police car that arrived on the scene was swamped by the workers, who, in a frenzy, battered the vehicle and the windshield with iron rods. The three police officers luckily escaped. The workers then climbed onto the vehicle, tore away the siren, and then turned the vehicle upside down. Soon, a large contingent of patrol police, riot police, and security personnel descended on the workers. The riot police fired the first warning shots into the air. But when the workers showed no signs of giving in, they began firing below waist level into the crowd. Eyewitnesses said that four or five of the workers immediately collapsed. One of them who was hit in the stomach was still in a critical condition as of last night.

According to some workers and eyewitnesses interviewed, once the police were in control of the situation, those police officers who had been beaten earlier took their revenge. They beat the workers until they were unconscious before throwing them into the police van. One of them died instantly after receiving a heavy blow to the head. The forty to fifty peasant workers together with the ten-plus police officers who were injured were taken to five separate hospitals. About ten in all were still in a critical condition last night.

Eighty Workers Still Missing

According to the Hunan construction company, more than eighty workers have not reported back to headquarters. The authorities would not let the company go looking for them in the hospitals, nor would it release the names of those under arrest, nor the precise number of casualties.

* * *

"HAVING FALLEN INTO THE HANDS OF PUBLIC SECURITY IS LIKE BEING TRAPPED IN THE TIGER'S DEN—WORKERS LAMENT THAT THEY ARE TREATED WORSE THAN DOGS"*

According to the Hunan Road and Bridge Construction Company, there are still fifty-four workers in the hospital. Those most seriously injured are at Longgang Hospital. But the hospital would not operate on them because the company has not put down the full deposit of 60,000 yuan per head. Because the company does not have so much ready cash, it looks like more of the critically injured will die in the next few days. The workers complain that the hospital did not give the wounded rice or dumplings to eat, and when colleagues brought them food, the hospital refused to allow them entry.

When we reporters went to the hospital to have a look, we saw that of the twenty-eight wounded, four or five had gunshot wounds in their stomachs; some had their limbs battered, some had wounds all over their backs with serious internal injuries. Some had died of gunshot wounds to their heads.

The authorities refused to comment on the incident.

When we went to interview the workers who had fled the construction site, we discovered that most of them had their backs lashed. Some backs were plastered up with bandages.

"In the eyes of public security, we are not even dogs," said a Hunanese worker who was slightly injured. He told us that he luckily escaped police suppression that day. But when he went to the hospital to visit his colleagues, he was arrested by the police and taken back to the police station, where they gave him a good lashing. They then ordered him to kneel head down on the concrete floor until 3:00 a.m., when they released him.

"After the riot police arrived at the scene, they assembled in formations of four in a row and cornered us, firing at our feet like the way the People's

---

*Translation from the Chinese text (excerpt): Reporter anonymous, "Luo gonganshou ru yu hulang, mingong zitang gou yeburu," *Dongfang ribao* (Orient News), December 5, 1995. Translated by Anita Chan.

Liberation Army did on June 4th [1989]. Five or six of us immediately collapsed and one died right there after taking one shot in the stomach and one in the chest."

Comments

From these two reports, it can be seen that the recruitment and employment situation of workers in the construction industry, particularly on large construction projects, is different from other industries. In manufacturing, the workers are usually recruited individually. Even when recruitment is through a labor service company or an agent, at the workplace workers are on their own. In the kind of construction team described here, the company is owned and managed by a local official in a poor inland county. It recruits peasants from that inland county, and the construction team, led by foremen, moves from project site to project site. As can be seen, these teams have a strong local identity. For example, the team "boss" (the person sent by the company to take charge of the entire team) identified his interests with his workers when it came to confrontation with the locals, despite conflicts of interest between the peasant workers and their boss.[13]

Another interesting point to note is that the Chinese local press usually writes sympathetically about abused factory workers, especially female workers, but not so when the cases involve migrant construction crews. The entire host community, including the hospitals, expressed little concern for them.

Notes

1. "Chinese Factories and Two Kinds of Free Market (Read Bonded) Workforce," *Asia Pacific Business Review*, special issue on "Globalization and Labor Market Deregulation: Trade Unions in the Asia Pacific Region," Vol. 6, Nos. 3 & 4 (Spring 2000), pp. 260-281.

2. This was reported in *Yangcheng Evening News*, August 31, 1997.

3. Anita Chan, "Boot Camp at the Shoe Factory: Where Taiwanese Bosses Drill Chinese Workers to Make Sneakers for American Joggers," *Washington Post*, November 3, 1996, pp. C1, C4.

4. It is quite common for workers to have to pay so-called training fees, buy uniforms and other kinds of supplies, and for these to be deducted from the deposit.

5. This second case on Yixin was reported in three articles in *Yangcheng Evening News*, October 4, 5, and 10, 1997.

6. Reginald Chua, Jonathan Friedland, and Kyung Kim, "Korea Exporting Tough Labor Practices—Some of the Country's Overseas Plants Abuse Their Workers, Critics Say," *Asian Wall Street Journal*, July 18, 1996, p. 1. For a general discussion of the Korean authoritarian management style, see Roger L. Janelli with Dawnhee Yim, *Making Capitalism: The Social and Cultural Construction of a South Korean Conglomerate*, Stanford: Stanford University Press, 1993, pp. 48–49.

7. Christian Conference of Asia—Urban Rural Mission, *From the Womb of Han: Stories of Korean Women Workers*, Hong Kong: Christian Conference of Asia Monograph, 1982.

8. It is common among Chinese women to address close friends as sisters.

9. The legal minimum wage set for Zhuhai in 1995 was 380 yuan a month. *Zhuhai laodong bao* (Zhuhai Labor News), May 19, 1995.

10. Andrew Walder, "Communist Social Structure and Workers' Politics," in Victor C. Falkenheim (ed.), *Citizens and Groups in Contemporary China*, Ann Arbor: Center for Chinese Studies Series, University of Michigan, 1987, p. 69. Also see Andrew Walder, *Communist Neo-Traditionalism: Work and Authority in Chinese Industry*, Berkeley: University of California Press, 1986, pp. 90–93.

11. *Zhonghua gongshang shibao* (China's Industrial and Commercial News), May 10, 1995. For more on the changing function of the internal security system, see Victor N. Shaw, *Social Control in China—A Study of Chinese Work Units*, Westport: Praeger, 1996, pp. 127–140.

12. "*Mingong*" literally peasant workers, generally refers to migrants who do not work in factories but in outdoor labor such as construction and agriculture.

13. For a study of construction migrant workers, see Dorothy J. Solinger, "Job Categories and Employment Channels Among the 'Floating' Population," in Greg O'Leary (ed.), *Adjusting to Capitalism: Chinese Workers and Their State*, Armonk, NY: M. E. Sharpe, 1997, pp. 3–47.

Chapter 4

Violations of Occupational Safety and Health

Management's violations of occupational safety and health (OSH) regulations sometimes have more serious effects on workers than the abuses discussed in previous chapters. The effects of toxic fumes, for instance, can diminish body weight and cause general ill health or even death, though sometimes the damage goes unnoticed since the severest symptoms of some of these ailments take months or years to develop. Maiming by machines, on the other hand, is instantaneously visible. In the Shenzhen region alone, 90 percent of some 12,000 hospital-certified industrial injuries in 1998 involved maiming.[1] Two of the cases in this chapter concern extraordinary instances of unnecessarily noxious and dangerous working conditions, caused by employers ignoring elementary safety precautions in the rush to profit.

A third case involves a fire in a toy factory that had built workshops, storage, and dormitories in one building, and had blocked exits and barred windows—all violations of workplace fire safety regulations. The fire claimed eighty-seven lives and aroused unprecedented public outrage in China. Those who survived suffered disfigurements and unrelenting pain. In addition to management's callousness, the root cause of these man-made disasters is corruption. The local authorities colluded with management to turn a blind eye to the safety hazards, and after the accidents, those responsible got away with paying little or no compensation.

CASE 11

This long report on the poisoning of workers and severe environmental pollution in Putian city, Fujian province, underscores the attitude of Taiwanese

*footwear manufacturers and the local government toward workers' health
and environmental degradation. Taiwan, the world's biggest exporter of footwear in the 1980s, had relocated to the mainland en masse by the early
1990s. Putian has become a major center for such investment.*

This article was published by Chinese Women's News, *the official publication
of the All-China Women's Federation (ACWF) after it began to regard women
workers' issues as part of its concern. As will be seen, the thoroughness and ag-
gressiveness with which the reporter probed and confronted the culprits is very
similar to a "60 Minutes" investigative report, except that this was not telecast.*

REPORT ON FOREIGN SHOE FACTORIES THAT ENDANGER WOMEN
WORKERS WITH HYDROCARBON POISONS IN PUTIAN, FUJIAN*

Part I: The Sea Goddess Is Crying

> Since 1984, Putian, the birthplace of Mazu, goddess of the sea,[2] has
> been inundated by a large number of foreign-invested shoe and
> leather enterprises.
>
> Every year, 2,500 tons of hydrocarbon fumes fill the shoe fac-
> tory workshops and disperse into the air over Putian, resulting in
> horrifying cases of poisoning. Seventy thousand young women from
> far and near have come to this "shoe city" to work for a pittance
> for ten hours or more a day, enveloped in high concentrations of
> toxic fumes. What awaits them is damaged health or even death.

Mention Putian city in Fujian province and Mazu, goddess of the sea, and
"shoe city" springs immediately to mind. Since 1984, a multitude of foreign-
invested enterprises, most of which are shoe factories, have flocked here.
The annual production of the city's factories is more than 100 million pairs
of shoes. There are more than one hundred fifty foreign shoe and leather
enterprises in all, of which seventy-four are sizeable, with total annual production more than 3.5 billion yuan. About 70,000 young women have come
from the surrounding villages of Putian, from the mountainous regions of
northern and eastern Fujian, and from the poor backwater villages of Jiangxi,
Sichuan, Anhui, and Shanxi. In exchange for a pitiful monthly wage of 300–
400 yuan, they labor for ten hours or more a day in workshops filled with the
poisonous fumes of the "three bens" [this is the Chinese collective term for
the three hydrocarbon chemicals—benzene, toluene, and xylene].

---

*Translation from the Chinese text: Chen Yonghui, "Fujian Putian bufen sanzi
xiechang bendu weihai nügong baogao: (I) Mazu you lei; (II) Chenmo de gaoyang;
(III) Qingxie de tianping," *Zhongguo funü bao* (Chinese Women's News), January
15–17, 1996. Translated by Kevin McCready.

These factories—numbering about one hundred—all generally use concentrated, volatile, adhesive glue containing benzene, toluene, and xylene. Adhesives containing excessive concentrations of the three hydrocarbons are extremely dangerous to the health.[3] They directly damage blood production and the central nervous system. Long-term contact can cause minor symptoms of dizziness, loss of appetite, loss of memory and mental capacity, and major symptoms of anemia leading to death. Most effects are gradual and may eventually lead to cancer and birth defects.

Even though there are national regulations stipulating that such enterprises must incorporate strict measures from the very beginning of the project, for prevention and control of pollution, and for protection and safety, in their hunger to attract foreign capital, the various levels of Putian government and functional departments turn a blind eye to violations. Most shoe factories begin operations without having installed sufficient facilities, but nonetheless still win the congratulatory applause of local leaders. Some leaders call this: "First catch the bus, then buy a ticket." But having caught the bus, such enterprises refuse to buy a ticket. In the eleven-year history of foreign shoe enterprises in Putian, up to 1995, only one has installed purification facilities. Even though some factories have installed exhaust fans, they are ineffective in getting rid of the toxins; and to save electricity, some factories are too miserly to turn them on.

Putian's Sanitation and Anti-Epidemic Station conducted a survey of the concentration levels of the three hydrocarbons on the shop floor of twelve large-scale shoe factories. The results showed that in the overwhelming majority of enterprises, concentrations exceeded national exposure standards. The concentration of toluene in the Dafu Shoe Company was the highest, at 486.6 mg per cubic meter, almost five times the national standard. Five of the twelve enterprises did not even have extraction facilities. Even though these are 1993 survey results, two years have passed and poisonous chemicals in the majority of shoe factories are still endangering the health and lives of women workers. Only the Jinxing (Golden Star) Shoe Company has attained the national standard for purification control.

In early January, I went to a large-scale, foreign shoe factory, and as soon as I stepped into the workshops, my nostrils were overcome by an acrid, choking stench that made me dizzy and weak in the legs. Inside those workshops, permeated by the toxic fumes, rows of eighteen- and nineteen-year-old women from the countryside were crowded along each side of the machinery, brushing poisonous glue on the soles of shoe after shoe. Incessantly, every minute of the day, they were inhaling this highly volatile, pungent glue into their young lungs. I struck up a conversation with them beside the machinery, but within a minute or two I was gasping and choking for breath. In the entire workshop, only a few electric fans were going. They were totally ineffective in expelling the poison. All they could do was to spread the highly concentrated fumes from the glue-brushing area to the entire workshop. The women workers were very young but there was not a single healthy, lively face among them. Their complexions were pasty and worn.

I interviewed a girl from Jiangxi. She had been brushing glue for more than a year and by now often felt dizzy and had no appetite. Originally, she had not known that the glue was poisonous—now she understood. But if the factory scheduled her to do the work, she had no choice. At least she could save a bit of extra money each month to give to her family. Other tasks bring in only some 300 yuan for more than ten hours of work, but for doing this, she earned 100 yuan more a month. Although it was only ten-thirty in the morning, she truly appeared haggard and exhausted beyond endurance. In this workshop, where I could not bear to stay for a couple of minutes, she would work until nine or ten o'clock at night.

I walked over to another woman worker who was absorbed in brushing glue. She looked only about fourteen or fifteen years old. I asked how old she was and at first she said sixteen but later corrected herself and said she was eighteen. She had just arrived in the factory and had been there a little over two months. She looked like she certainly had rosy and healthy cheeks before she came, but now her complexion was pallid and ashen. She was still not aware that the glue was poisonous, although after only two months she was feeling dizzy. Because other women workers were unwilling to do this work, management forced these new arrivals from the countryside to fill in the gaps. I discovered that the majority of women workers were assigned this task when they first arrived before they knew about the poison.

Thirty percent of women workers in the shoe factories engage in tasks that come into direct contact with toxins, while the rest of the workers breathe in the fumes that engulf the whole factory. The damage to their health is invisible and the harmful effects not immediately apparent. Nevertheless, you still hear of the tragedies caused by the hydrocarbons. In the mid-1980s, some women workers at a shoe factory in Putian died of poisoning. Last January, an eighteen-year-old Putian woman, Nai Hongyu, showed symptoms of poisoning after working at a shoe factory for only slightly more than a month. She is still being treated at the Fujian Provincial Staff Clinic. The factory completely denies responsibility, even refusing to pay treatment costs. A tragedy that happened in 1993, in Laidian township, Xianyou county of Putian city, still causes Putian residents to shudder at the mention of it. Several women who had been working at Jin Jiang Shoe Factory for a few months were hospitalized because of poisoning. Two contracted leukemia, and before they died their bodies rotted, becoming bloated and putrid. The stench was so overpowering that even their relatives would not dare to enter the ward. More tragic was the fact that when the two women workers died, they were carrying seven- and eight-month-old fetuses.

While I was investigating in shoe city, a comrade at the Sanitation and Anti-Epidemic Station told me that, although they conduct medical checkups every year, there is no way they can do follow-up examinations because workers move about so much. Sometimes they would detect symptoms, but when they came back a year later to do another examination, these workers were gone. Some bosses hire women workers to work at these hazardous tasks for several years and then get rid of them. The women come from all over the country, and do not understand that they should return and seek out the factory if any problems emerge. When medical checkups are scheduled, it is impossible to examine each worker because the factories usually select those women who are not working at hazardous tasks to undergo medical examination. Thus, it is very difficult to uncover problem cases in time. Even then the station continues to find during their annual medical checkups that many women workers have low counts of red and white blood cells. These are the two indicators for the onset of aplastic anemia. I have repeatedly requested to see the Sanitation and Anti-Epidemic Station's annual results of medical checkups but to no avail.

The large volume of fumes discharged daily from these shoe factories is not just endangering the health of women workers at the factories. Each year, the Putian shoe industry uses 3,000 tons of glue that contains the three toxins and 80 percent of this is released into the atmosphere. According to a Putian Environmental Monitoring Station survey, the pollution rate of these hydrocarbons in the city's residential areas exceeded the permitted rate by 30 percent. Therefore, in the past few years, the proud citizens of beautiful Putian's "shoe city" have become anxious and afraid. A journalist from the *Meizhou Daily* told me, "We in Putian all know what is in the air we breathe and there are many leaders and cadres in the city who are worried about the situation." One leader has publicly declared that if this goes on, "shoe city" will become "sick city."

When I interview people living near the shoe factories, they are full of apprehension because of the banana-water smell: "We're really scared of these waste fumes, even the mosquitoes are scared of them. What we fear most is their threat to the next generation."[4]

All the organic toxic fumes from the shoe and leather factories can be effectively controlled to minimize their threat to workers and the surrounding environment. But the bosses of most of the shoe factories will not take a paltry amount from their bulging wallets to install purification equipment. They use all sorts of excuses to procrastinate and avoid responsibility.

The goddess Mazu stands tall and upright on Meizhou Island, her benevolent eyes are set on the horizon of the Donghai Sea. Behind her, just a couple of kilometers away, are many girls suffering in a bitter sea. Good and merciful Mazu, had you known, would your heart not wept in grief?[5]

Part II: Lambs to the Slaughter

The "three bens" are dangerous, but they can be controlled. Their danger to people and the environment can be reduced to a minimum. Unfortunately, factory bosses use every excuse to procrastinate and shirk responsibility. They refuse to open their tight wallets and spend even 1 percent of their money to install the necessary purification and control equipment. Seventy thousand women workers of relatively "low quality"[6] accept their fate because they do not know how to protect themselves and do not know that working in a poisonous environment violates their rights. Some women workers are even unwilling to undergo medical checkups because they fear being fired if health problems are uncovered. They are meek sacrificial lambs.

Benzene, toluene, and xylene are fearsome chemicals, but there are ways to control them. The Chinese Academy of Preventive Medicine in Beijing long ago researched and manufactured a complete set of purification and preventive equipment and technology. Each production line needs an investment of only 120,000 yuan for workshops to reach the national exposure limits (for toluene it is less than 100 mg per cubic meter). With this investment, the toluene discharged to the atmosphere by the shoe and leather industry would also be able to fall within the standards set by Fujian province (50 mg per cubic meter).

Even though many foreign shoe factories declare a profit of 4 percent or less to the National Tax Department, everybody knows that the industry makes much higher profits. A pair of Nike shoes produced in Putian sells for U.S.$120 overseas. Personnel in the Environmental Protection Department told me that the profits of some shoe factories were as high as 50 percent. However, Deputy Factory Manager Zheng of the Dafu Shoe Company told me that profits were only 10 percent. Most foreign shoe factories have four production lines, each with an annual output valued at 25 million yuan. Even accepting Deputy Factory Manager Zheng's statement that profits are 10 percent indicates a profit of 2.5 million yuan. A shoe factory producing for five years on four production lines will make a profit of at least 50 million yuan. Spending 500,000 yuan of this to invest in a once-and-for-all solution of purification and preventive equipment would only increase the cost of production of a pair of shoes that sells for hundreds of yuan by 4 fen ($0.005). But to date, among the foreign shoe factories that have rushed into Putian since 1984 to make profits amounting to hundreds of millions, only the Jinxing (Golden Star) Shoe Company has invested money (500,000 yuan, at the end of 1995) to install purification and control equipment.

All of the bosses have their own reasons. Some say they are experiencing losses and don't have the money to control pollution. Some say they have installed exhaust fans, and isn't that enough? Some ask why Putian should take the lead in controlling pollution rather than big cities like Fuzhou or Quanzhou. Some hypocritically say that this is okay in Taiwan, so why not here? And the most irresponsible are those who simply express skepticism about the purification and control equipment recommended by the Environmental Protection Department, saying that if the results are no good, their few hundred yuan are just being thrown away. One boss who agreed to be interviewed had even more preposterous logic: "We did not manufacture the glue; go to the glue factories to get the problem solved."

If the major departments from above come for an inspection, most bosses bow and scrape and promise they will do something about the problem. But as soon as the officials leave, the bosses go back to their old ways. They all say it should be obvious that if you want to control pollution, you must do it one step at a time. Anyone with sense can clearly see that they will talk and talk but not spend the money. Moreover, some bosses who refuse to spend money installing pollution-discharge control equipment spend money like water in restaurants, bars, and music halls.

Thus, many bosses consider environmental law-enforcement officers a big nuisance and often complain to officials about the Environmental Protection Department. They blame Putian's "poor investment environment" and threaten to withdraw their businesses. The Health Inspection Department has also become a thorn in the side of certain bosses. According to regulations, women workers in the shoe industry must have an annual medical examination, but it is very difficult for the Health Department to perform them. Some enterprises say their staff and workers are unwilling to undergo medical exams, while some offer as an excuse that they must fill rush orders. One boss was even more barefaced, saying: "Medical examinations disrupt production. If you do not insist, we will just pay you whatever checkup fee you ask."

When it is time for the medical checkup, it is utterly perfunctory—women workers are brought in from a section of the factory where they are not exposed to the toxins. In 1995, the Sanitation and Anti-Epidemic Department arrived at Dafu Shoe Factory to conduct medical checkups, and among more than two thousand people only 200 to 300 staff and workers were brought in. The factory made the excuse that if workers are reluctant to go for the examination, the factory should not force them to do so. It is now 1996, and the 1995 checkup has not been undertaken.

On January 3, I accompanied Putian's environmental law enforcement and health inspection officers to the joint-venture Dafu Shoe Company Ltd. This factory has six production lines, and in 1995, the value of its output reached 220 million yuan, yielding almost 10 million yuan in taxes. But from the factory's completion and commissioning in 1991 to this day, it has not installed purification and control equipment. The factory's reason is that it is not happy about the control equipment recommended by the Environmental Protection Department. From the window of the reception room, I could see that the workshop where casting is done was filled with a huge amount of organic toxic fumes. The several exhaust fans were rusted and decrepit, and a couple were even left lying there as scrap iron. When he saw that we had taken note of this, Deputy Factory Manager Zheng, who had been accompanying us, left us for quite a while and the exhaust fans finally came on. But only two or three of the fans barely managed to wobble; of course, several crumbling, rusted ones did not move at all. I heard in Deputy Factory Manager Zheng's matter-of-fact introduction that the women in the factory worked twelve hours a day, did not get paid for overtime, did not get a day off, and that in summer, it became so unbearable that more than one hundred people quit every day.

We asked to go to the workshop to have a look. Deputy Factory Manager Zheng said there was nothing worth looking at. So I said we would just have a quick look around. Deputy Factory Manager Zheng was closemouthed, but when he saw that we insisted on a tour, he said he would request permission from the manager.[7] After a good while, he came back and said the manager had returned to Taiwan and he himself could not make the decision. I asked who was responsible for the factory at the moment, and he said a deputy manager from Taiwan. I asked that he go and request permission from the deputy manager. Deputy Factory Manager Zheng had no choice and went out again for some time. He came back and said there was a client present at the moment. The client was unwilling to allow us to look around.

I said that in that case we would like to see the deputy manager. Deputy Factory Manager Zheng left the room again. Deputy Manager He came in. He was an energetic and smart looking youth of twenty-five or twenty-six who had the flavor of a Taiwanese pop star about him. Deputy Manager He would not let us look around, either. The reason was that the factory was making a new style of shoe, so we could not look around for fear of leaking secrets. I said that we were three enforcement officials and one journalist, and only interested in news, not in shoe styles. Deputy Manager He was also closemouthed. We had reached a stalemate. I asked how many production lines were working on the new style, and Deputy Manager He said two. I said in that case we could look at the others. At that, Deputy Manager He did not utter a word. But then he insisted that we wait a few days until the manager returned.

I looked with questioning eyes to the three enforcement officers. They had the power to enter the workshop and did not need the permission of Deputy Manager He. But the three said nothing. Of course, they had been to this factory many times and did not need to enter because they knew very clearly what went on inside the workshops.

I could not enter the workshops of Dafu Shoe Company, but I got a Health Inspection Department monitoring report of the workshops, dated June 21, 1995, which proved that concentrations of toluene were seriously in excess of the standard. The gluing area of casting workshop A had a concentration of 148.6 mg per cubic meter, workshop B had a recording of 228.6 mg per cubic meter, workshop C had two instances of 210 mg per cubic meter, and workshop D had two instances of 189.4 mg per cubic meter. According to national regulations, the concentration should not be higher than 100 mg per cubic meter.

The majority of the 70,000 women workers of the foreign shoe factories only have primary or junior secondary education. They have little knowledge and lack information about how to protect themselves. Of all the women workers whom I met, not one knew that working in an environment of highly concentrated hydrocarbons was a violation of their rights. Many people still did not know that the glue was poisonous, and many women workers were definitely unwilling to undergo a medical checkup, fearing that if problems were found, they would be fired by the factory. The complaints most women workers had about the factory were only that wages were low, work hours too long, and they had to suffer abuse and swallow their anger.

They really are a group of lambs led to the slaughter.

Part III: Tipping the Balance

• **Bosses can ignore national rules and regulations and delay installing purification and control equipment because they have "direct access to the top."**
• **Local government does not adequately protect poor, uneducated women workers because certain leaders are concerned that tight control will cause foreign businesses to flee.**
• **When it comes to the rights of tens of thousands of women workers versus the interests of several bosses, certain leaders clearly tip the balance in favor of the latter.**

Seventy thousand girls from the countryside, inexperienced in the ways of the world, silently pay the cost, not knowing they have the right to rest and the right to breathe clean air. Their situation depends entirely on the good consciences of the bosses and managers.

They should have received adequate protection from mass organizations, including the All-China Federation of Trade Unions (ACFTU), the All-China Women's Federation (ACWF), and law enforcement agencies, such as the Ministries of Labor, Environmental Protection, and Health; and there are also the people's congresses and governments at all levels. But do the relevant leaders and departments of Putian city give adequate, sympathetic, and effective protection to the poor, uneducated women workers?

The All-China Women's Federation and the ACFTU's Committee for Women Workers serve as the women workers' natal family. But in Putian city, it is obvious that they are ineffective. The trade union has actively worked to overcome obstacles and establish unions and committees for women workers in foreign enterprises. But these enterprise-level trade unions cannot play a role. Most of the chairs of these trade unions and committees for women workers are highly paid white-collar workers in the employ of the bosses. It is very difficult for them not to do what the bosses want. Many bosses in the foreign enterprises even ignore the trade unions or the ACWF. The fact that three trade-union chairs from Xianyou county were once denied entry at the gate of a shoe factory is proof of this. Without the support and backing of Party and government leaders, the trade unions and the ACWF find it very hard to do their jobs inside foreign-invested enterprises.

The Departments of Environmental Protection and Health conduct their monitoring work according to relevant laws and regulations, but the problems are enormous. In spite of the fact that these are law enforcement agencies, some bosses continue to refuse to have anything to do with them. One shoe factory still does not even have ventilation equipment, and when the head of the Environmental Protection Department visited, the boss lied, saying he was in a meeting, and did not show his face. The Foreign Economic Relations and Trade Commission is the administrative organ in charge of all foreign-invested enterprises in the city, but it generally only reviews the applications of enterprises and approves them. After examination and approval, it is not concerned with whether the enterprises have installed safety equipment or pollution-control equipment. Section Head Huang of Putian's Foreign Capital Section of the Commission of Foreign Economic Relations and Trade told me jokingly, "It's like the railway police: each is in charge of only one section of the rail."

Of course, Putian's Foreign Economic Relations and Trade Commission also conducts annual checks and inspections. In 1995, 67 percent of foreign-invested enterprises in the city passed the annual inspection. But they basically use only one criterion: whether or not capital has been invested as agreed. Of the 67 percent of foreign enterprises that received an annual inspection certificate, only one shoe factory passed in the category of toxin purification and control equipment. Every level of Putian's Foreign Economic Relations and Trade Commission works hard to look after foreign businesses, doing its utmost to protect the viability of their investments. Even though it has the power to halt production and demand rectification in foreign-invested enterprises that are not obeying the law, it does not do so. A city-level leader of the Foreign Economic Relations and Trade Commission said something very significant in my presence, "If it were not for the foreign enterprises, there would be no women workers."

All of the above departments are responsible for monitoring toxin purification and control equipment, but nobody effectively takes charge. The bosses do as they please and no one can do anything about it. Why is this? All departmental cadres who agreed to be interviewed spoke with one voice, saying that the bosses all had direct access to the top.

An example will clearly show what type of "direct access to the top" these bosses possess. A large shoe factory had not installed pollution controls for many years, and the Environmental Protection Department had imposed pollution discharge fines according to the regulations. But the boss simply refused to pay up. The Environmental Protection Department had no choice but to take them to court to request that they be compelled to comply. However, in the end, the department failed because someone interceded on behalf of the boss. A deputy mayor of the city denounced the Environmental Protection Department for scaring away foreign business.

It must be said that, after all, the Putian Party committee secretary, the mayor, and other important leaders still strongly support environmental protection and the rights of women workers. The present Putian mayor, Wu Jianhua, was transferred here when he was head of the Fujian Provincial Legal Bureau. He knows the relevant laws and regulations like the back of his hand. The first meeting in which he participated after taking office was a working meeting on the city's environmental protection. At the meeting, he stressed that economic development should not be at the expense of environmental protection, that one should not only seek short-term profit, and that local governments that did not properly protect the environment were committing a crime against the people. He personally convened a meeting of some bosses of shoe factories, and spelled out that waste fumes of toxins were already a serious environmental pollutant that threatened the health of workers and local residents. If shoe factories continued to delay taking measures, the government would use the law to halt production and compel the factories to meet the standards. On one occasion, the city's Environmental Protection Department had used the law to fine five foreign shoe factories that were not controlling pollution. The factories lobbied some leading cadres to intervene and have the decision to impose fines reversed. After Mayor Wu heard of this he resolutely supported the Environmental Protection Department and went to talk to these officials himself.

Of course, not every leader has shown such concern about controlling toxic fumes. When it comes to the interests of dozens of shoe-factory bosses, the health of tens of thousands of women workers, or the living environment of 2.76 million local residents, certain leading cadres clearly tip the balance in favor of the bosses.

First, let us not talk about these biased words and deeds, but simply take a look at the two documents drawn up by the Putian city government in September 1995, concerning protection of the interests of foreign business by taking measures to "clean up" [a euphemism for eliminating] excessive fees that are collected on top of taxes, because they are a burden for the foreign enterprises. We should protect their legitimate interests, it says. But some clauses in the documents reveal an inherent bias on the part of the policymakers when it comes to the rights of women workers over the interests of foreign business, or the protection of the environment over the protection of foreign business. Controlling toxins is a long-standing and difficult problem for Putian. Some clauses actually run counter to the Environmental Protection Law, which stipulates that pollution must be controlled and that fees must be paid for exceeding pollution-discharge standards. Despite the large numbers of shoe factories in the city, Putian's annual levies of pollution-discharge fees are still the second lowest in the province. Naturally, if the Environmental Protection Department levied excess pollution-discharge fees in accordance with the law in a place like Putian, it would be an incentive for foreign businesses to install purification and control equipment as quickly as possible.

Moreover, the document actually stipulates, "During the period when rectification of the problem is in process, fees for excess pollution discharge may be reduced or exempted." But why should excess pollution-discharge fees not be charged when rectification has not yet been approved? Based on what criteria are the fees reduced or exempted? This obviously reduces the pressure on certain enterprises that are unwilling to spend the money on controls. The Environmental Protection Law stipulates that whoever causes pollution shall be responsible for controlling it. But the city's document again stipulates that fees or reduced fees collected for excessive pollution by factories "should be regarded as these factories' capital investment funds in environmental pollution control." This is tantamount to saying that the

Environmental Protection Department should give money to foreign enterprises to control pollution. The bosses can go make their money while you have to clean up their mess.

Relevant staff-protection and labor-protection legislation requires enterprise staff and workers to undergo an annual medical checkup. The women shoe-factory workers who are in contact with poisonous and dangerous substances have even more reason for a medical examination, so that cases of poisoning may be quickly discovered.

The fee charged by the Health Department for an occupational disease medical checkup covering six major items for women staff and workers is 18 yuan. A large shoe factory of 2,000 employees makes annual profits of hundreds of millions of yuan, while medical checkup fees for staff and workers would cost some 30,000 yuan. (Some factories even have the women workers pay half this fee.) But the city's document actually "cleans up" the fee by reducing it from 18.5 yuan to 4.5 yuan. In other words, workers may receive only an x-ray, a heart examination, and a quick general examination. The most important health check for workers in shoe factories is a blood test. But the fee for blood tests has been "cleaned up" as an "unreasonable fee."

On the morning of January 8, a Putian city deputy mayor in charge of foreign economic relations agreed to be interviewed. This deputy mayor thought that government leaders at all levels were generally willing to have a relaxed investment climate so as to attract foreign capital, and feared that tight controls would have the opposite effect, driving away foreign business and adversely influencing the outward-looking local economy. They were actually unclear with regard to the effects of the pollution from shoe factories.

The deputy mayor spoke with pride about the role of foreign enterprises in the development of the Putian economy. When it came to the issue of controlling toxins in shoe factories, he frankly said that opinions differed among the city leaders. He believed that, at present, it was not easy to attract business and capital and that if environmental protection was too strict, business would be driven out. The deputy mayor said:

> Putian's environment has a good foundation and is large in area [presumably this helps to dilute the pollutants]. Although there are currently many shoe factories, they are not creating serious pollution. The Environmental Protection Department has its job to do—of course, it tends to exaggerate the seriousness of the situation. (Survey results of the Putian Environmental Protection Bureau are gathered by highly precise instruments under rigorous scientific procedures. In addition, they are examined and verified at a higher level of the Environmental Protection Department.)[8] Perhaps

some exceed the standards, but overall they do not. (Since the conclusions of the Environmental Protection Department are doubtful, what evidence does he have to say they are not exceeding the standards?) Perhaps toxins have affected women workers, but in recent years, Putian has had no deaths from poisoning. There were two deaths in a shoe factory in Jin Jiang. Putian is fairly backward, and backward places must suffer a bit. Yes, the Environmental Protection Law is a national policy that must be honored. But now we have to attract foreign capital, and if everything is done rigidly following the law, foreign business will flee, and this is no good for the economy.

I cut in, "But it costs the factory owner no more than an additional 4 fen [0.04 yuan] per pair of shoes."

The deputy mayor replied, "For bosses, it is always the more money they can make, the better."

I asked, "Can the city government carry out monitoring?"

He replied, "The Environmental Protection Department is the functional department in charge of collecting pollution-discharge fees."

I then said, "The Environmental Protection Department often cannot enforce its regulations. The pollution-discharge fees collected in Putian were the second lowest in the whole province."

He replied, "I don't know how the Environmental Protection Department collects fees. The fees are low, but just the same, the bosses are already making a fuss. Since 1995, the whole shoe and leather industry has been in a recession, and in the first half of 1995, many have lost money. To impose tight control at this juncture would mean forcing foreign business to leave."

"Okay, even if there really were losses in 1995, what about before 1994, when they made money? They did nothing about the problem at that time either."

The deputy mayor replied, "The Environmental Protection Department is a functional government department and it is their business. They can bring the violators to court. We will not interfere. We can be accused of interfering if we start preventing you from prosecuting a case in the court."

I raised the issue of medical checkups for women workers and the fact that the city government had "cleaned up" the medical fee from 18 to 4.5 yuan, which left enough money only for general checkups without blood tests.

The deputy mayor began to fume. "We have not said that you can only have routine checkups. We have only said you cannot collect fees arbitrarily. You do not have to make a big thing out of 4.5 yuan." As the person who was in charge of drawing up City Government Document No. 125 of 1995, this deputy mayor seemed not to know that one of the examination fees that had been cleaned up was the fee for blood tests.

It is understandable that every level of Putian's government has given much hard thought to protecting the valuable investment of foreign business. But why are certain leaders always so concerned that the bosses will run away for less than 4 fen per pair of shoes, while at the same time, they are not concerned about the threat to the health of tens of thousands of women workers and the damage to the lives and environment of 2.67 million local residents caused by the failure to install purification equipment?

In actual fact, looking at Putian's situation, the enterprises that are concerned about the rights of women workers all have good business records. For example, Xiefeng Shoe Company protects its staff and workforce very well and has a thriving business. The company has not fled because it had to spend money protecting its staff and workforce. On the contrary, last year it injected another $14 million in Putian. But Qingshun Shoe Company, which frequently abused and bullied women workers to the point that the whole factory went on strike, collapsed and fled the country to avoid repaying debt.

Those leaders flying the flag high for "protecting foreign business interests" should remember that the less than one hundred shoe-factory bosses are not the only ones making a contribution to the development of Putian's economy. How much blood and sweat of women workers are included in the net output of 6 billion yuan produced by foreign enterprises? Every year, 100 million pairs of shoes are made by the hands of a few thousand women workers. If it were not for their silent sacrifice, it would not be possible for the leaders to take pride in the economic indicators. They need your concern and protection as well.

Comments

The article caused quite a stir among several bureaucracies in Beijing, one of which was the ACFTU. The ACFTU immediately sent an investigation team to Putian and instructed the local trade unions to press the foreign investors to do something about the problem. Half a year later, when I visited Putian, only three out of more than one hundred Taiwanese factories had installed air-purification devices, even though the equipment was not that expensive. The local trade union and environmental protection agency were too weak to enforce any changes. The reporter's sharp questions directed to the city's leaders clearly show that the problem was there to stay. So long as the footwear industry can replenish its labor supply every two or three years, there is little incentive for factory management to rectify the problem. The only positive change I observed during my visit was the local residents' heightened awareness of the dangers of the toxic adhesives. Unlike in Guangdong province, local Putian people worked on the production lines. They were loath to let their womenfolk work at tasks that involved direct contact with adhesives. But their caution was not extended to alerting the migrant workers of the danger. The other positive outcome, if one can describe it as such, is that the local trade union, after persistent persuasion, was able to get the Taiwanese investors to grant their workers at least two days off a month and two evenings a week without working overtime. These improvements, however, still violate China's Labor Law, which states that there should be at least one rest day each week.

CASE 12

When the cause of an occupational disease is not readily visible to the naked eye, or when the symptoms are delayed, managers in China can more easily avoid taking corrective measures, as with the exposure to toxic adhesives in the Putian case. But in the following case, more surprisingly, despite limbs being repeatedly maimed by machines, management seemed completely blasé. Within a period of three years in this Taiwanese-owned and managed cutlery factory in Fujian province, there were 142 industrial accidents among 400 workers. The injury rate of workers stood at 23 percent and among these, thirty-five people lost part of their limbs and two received head injuries. By any international occupational safety and health standards, these are incredible figures. Yet according to the article, there are Asian-invested enterprises in China with even worse records.

A PRICE THAT SHOULD NOT BE PAID*

An Investigative Report on an Occupational Safety and Health Story in a Taiwanese-Funded Enterprise

> *Editorial note:* The number of workers injured and subsequently handicapped in a cutlery factory owned by Xiamen Jiamei Company is atrocious and shocking. Chaotic management, intensive labor, obsolete facilities, and the absence of safety instructions and supervision are all causes responsible for the appalling conditions. However, the inferior quality (*suzhidi*) of the workers and their lack of awareness in using the legal system to protect their own rights is also pathetic, disconcerting, and worrisome. Fortunately, this case has already attracted the

---

*Translation from the Chinese text: Fei Xu, "Buying fuchu de daijia: yijia taishang duzi qiye gongshang shigu de diaocha baogao," *Zhongguo gongren* (Chinese Workers), No. 4 (1993), pp. 22–25. Translated by Anita Chan.

attention of the authorities. It is hoped that the problem will soon be resolved.

Reportedly, the industrial relations in some private and foreign-funded enterprises are very tense and the occurrence of industrial accidents is frequent and serious. We hope that the enterprises will learn the lesson and strictly abide by the "People's Republic of China Regulations for Foreign-Funded Enterprises." We also hope that the trade unions and employees in these three-capital enterprises[9] continue to heighten their legal awareness to use the laws to protect the workers' rights.

A Frightening List of Names of the Injured and Handicapped

At the end of October 1992, some workers of the Taiwanese fully funded Xiamen Jiamei Cutlery Factory visited the city trade union, the procurator's office, and the media. They were all workers who had sustained industrial injuries.

On October 27, an investigative team made up of staff from Xiamen city trade union, the labor bureau, the procurator's office, and other government departments arrived at the factory.

Based on a list of names provided by factory management, there was a total of thirty-six injured workers. The company admitted that this was not a complete list. As for the exact number of workers who had been injured and subsequently handicapped, the factory trade union chairman, Liu Yinshan, said, "Each time a worker was injured the details were sent to the city insurance company to be filed. The factory does not have the records."

Company Director Zeng Zhengdao explained, "The company began operation in July 1989. It is a labor-intensive industry. I was deeply affected by the occurrence of so many accidents. We have tried to make some improvements. Furthermore, each time an accident occurred, the company conducted an investigation and imposed monetary penalties on team leaders and those responsible; this included the factory manager." Mr. Zeng also said that in addition to the compensation paid by the insurance compay, the factory also paid 50 percent above that amount. Finally, the trade union chipped in almost 100 yuan.

Mr. Zeng pointed out that workplace accidents are not unrelated to the inferior quality of the workers. Many workers have gotten into the factory through all kinds of connections. Their educational level is low. Thus, very often the same kinds of accidents happen again and again because the workers do not learn from their mistakes. Educating them is useless. According to his investigation, 80 percent of the accidents "should not have happened."

The investigative team inquired as to whether the workers were given any training before they commenced work. The trade union chair explained that new workers have all been given training. Normally new workers are shown the regulations and then each one is assigned to an experienced worker to learn from for about half a month. During this period they are not given production quotas.

Then the company brought out three sets of photocopied materials printed on company letterhead. The first set, dated August 7, 1992, was entitled "Production Safety Regulations" and contained eleven articles; the second, drawn up on September 17, 1992, was "Details on How to Handle Industrial Injuries"; and the third, dated July 10, 1992, was "Regulations Before Becoming a Regular Worker." The contents of the last document consisted of the following: introduction to the company, disciplinary education, industrial safety education, and physical education. I made a quick calculation of the last document: the main body of the document consisted of only 250 words, excluding punctuation.

According to the records of the insurance company, Jiamei Company has had 142 industrial injuries since the factory began operation. Among these were twenty-six people with fingers severed at various lengths, crushed, or broken by instruments such as presses, electric saws, electric knives, and anvils; nine people with arms that are either broken, numb, or disfigured, or no longer function normally after their arms and sleeves got rolled into shavers or wheels; one person with a face paralyzed because of brain damage; one person's eye was damaged because of fragments flying out of shavers; and another has a broken leg. In addition, 104 others have sustained various degrees of injuries. The injury rate based on the total number of workers employed is 22.6 percent, an incredibly high number.

On November 15, 1992, the Industrial Safety Committee of Xiamen city issued a document entitled "Investigative Report on the Industrial Accidents of Xiamen Jiamei Cutlery Industrial Company."

The city's deputy mayor, Ye Tianze, commented, "The labor bureau and public safety and fire departments should immediately devise a system to improve the rules and regulations of this factory."

Only then did this appalling case begin to attract the attention of the authorities concerned.

The Workers' "One-sided Story"

On October 27, 1992, when I went to Jiamei Company to cover the story, the moment I got down to the shop floor some workers who had been injured and had heard of my visit immediately crowded around me. They eagerly took off their gloves, showed me their maimed hands, and proceeded to tell me the details of how the accidents had happened. Some of them, although they were grown men, were not embarrassed to show their tears.

One worker from Guizhou, who was only twenty years old, came to the factory on March 21, 1992. After seven days he was placed in the polishing workshop. After three days his left hand was caught in a machine. Now the soft tissues of his left arm are damaged.

Twenty-four-year-old Qin Gui is from Jiangxi. He was assigned to work in the cutting workshop. On September 19, 1991, he had asked someone to stop the machine so that he could make some adjustments. By accident, the other person pushed the "On" button, and this resulted in two sections of his left hand's middle and ring fingers being chopped off. Qin is one of the few workers who possesses an urban-residence permit. After the injury, he tried to go back home to be recruited to work in a mine. But the local labor department told him that missing two fingers was considered to be a serious injury, and that he was not qualified to work in the mine.

Thirty-three-year-old Zeng Zhentan is a local peasant. He joined Jiamei's timber factory in 1990. On October 16 of that year, his right thumb (two sections) and second finger (one section) were cut off by an electric saw. After he recovered, he went back to work in the timber workshop. On October 18, 1991, his already maimed right thumb was sawed a second time.

On November 11, 1992, one of the deputy chairmen of Xiamen City Trade Union and a staff member from its liaison office came to Jiamei to hold a meeting with the injured workers. Thirty or so workers attended the meetings. They all eagerly reported the details of the accidents and expressed dissatisfaction with the low industrial compensation they had gotten. The session went on until midday with no sign that it would come to a close. In the end, we had to ask them to state their cases in as succinct a manner as possible.

Female worker Huang Caifeng could not stop weeping as she raised her maimed right hand. She came to the factory in February 1990. That same year, on November 17, the machine she was operating went out of control, severely injuring her right hand: she lost one section of the index finger, one and one-half sections of the middle finger, two sections of the ring finger, and three sections of the little finger. The entire right hand no longer stretches out. Basically, it no longer functions. She is only twenty-three years old. Her family is in the countryside and she is not yet married. Her future is bleak.

Not long after the meeting began, a group of injured workers who no longer worked at the factory arrived on the scene. They had heard about the meeting and had made long journeys to Xiamen so that they could tell us their stories. Yi, a female worker from Guizhou province, began working at the factory in March 1991. The accident happened one June evening when she became entangled in the large amount of discarded material scattered near the work station. The machine was inadvertently turned on and she lost one section of her right index finger, one and one-half sections of her middle finger, and one section of her ring finger. After she recovered, the factory sent her to work in the sorting workshop, but because her fingers were still numb, she could not perform her duties. So the company gave her 2,825 yuan (this amount included wages due to her during the injured period, two relief subsidies totaling 100 yuan, food expenses during her recovery period, and medical fees) and told her to go home. Then she was told that "When the compensation fee from the insurance company comes through, it will be sent to you."

After the cases of these injured workers were publicized, there was a strong reaction from Jiamei's high-level management. The company's general manager, Mr. Hong, said that to report such industrial accidents in the newspaper was to damage the feelings of Taiwanese compatriots. He said that since July 1992, Jiamei Company had implemented a series of new measures. The number of injuries had declined by a large margin—"almost down to zero." The several mainland Chinese who occupy high-level management positions in the factory also came forth to express their support. They said that one should look at the shortcomings of Taiwanese enterprises from a more detached and comprehensive angle, and that the stories related by the injured workers were "one-sided." Many industrial accidents occurred because the workers did not follow work procedures set down by regulation. They also said that the bosses were actually very concerned. Many times they had personally sent the injured workers to the hospital by car.

Causes of the Accidents

According to a report compiled by the Xiamen City Industrial Safety Committee, the accidents were caused by chaotic management and lax safety precautions. Workers were only given simple safety and technical instructions. Facilities were primitive and dangerous, and labor intensity extremely high. There were no health and safety precautions taken against noise, dust, and toxic chemicals. Machines were crammed on the shop floor and did not have safeguards. The production quotas, paid at a piece rate, were far too high. Workers were required to fulfill quotas of almost two thousand pieces an hour using machines that should only be used to produce at a rate of 1,000 pieces an hour. This very intensive workload can easily lead to mental exhaustion, which in turn increases the chances of workers committing errors and thus contributing to accidents.

A female worker, Jiang Zengfeng from Anhui province, began working at Jiamei in March 1991. On June 18 of that year, she was injured by an electric saw. All five of her left fingers were injured. Her index finger no longer functions, and her middle and index fingers have both lost two sections. A letter she sent to me stated:

> The reason these accidents happen is that the boss buys some obsolete machines from Taiwan and the mainland. These machines have poor safeguards. In addition, some cadres keep on raising the production quota. The workload is too high. There is too much overtime. All these have caused the workers to work under stressful conditions, which, therefore, leads to a large number of accidents. Furthermore, new workers do not receive any specific training. All the training they get is to follow veteran workers around for a few hours and then they are placed at work stations. This, too, contributes to accidents.

According to the report, "Jiang Zengfeng's analysis may be biased, but some of the facts are true."

Injured worker Zhao Chaoli said that some machines were wobbly and looked extremely unstable. The workers reported this to the company, but nothing was done. So the workers tried to solve the problem themselves by tying the machine up with leather belts, and then continued working.

Another injured worker, Liu Huai from Jiangxi, started working on June 13, 1992. On June 15, he was placed at a work station. When he noticed that an "out of order" sign was hanging on the machine, the team leader told him the machine had been repaired, so there should be no problem. Well, an accident happened. His right arm was crushed and burned up to his shoulder. A large piece of skin was torn off. When I visited him in December in the hospital, he had not yet recovered. He said that when the accident happened, the new workers next to him did not even know how to turn off the machine. He was saved by a veteran worker who rushed in from outside.

Liu's accident provides good evidence that not all new workers have been given half a month of training by veteran workers. It shows that when many of the new workers start working, they have little idea of how the machines operate.

Lessons Learned from Paying a Price?

In many three-capital enterprises situated along the coast in the special economic zones, there has been a noticeable rise in industrial accidents. This should be cause for alarm.

The central government's Industrial Safety Committee carried out an investigation of Jiamei's factory, and discovered that everywhere on the shop floor were piles of garbage, and timber was spread all over the place. The warehouse was in ramshackle condition. Cigarette butts could be seen all over the floor in no-smoking areas. The safety conditions of the entire factory were far below standard. An examination of noise levels revealed that of the fourteen noise sources, twelve exceeded the permissible limit. The dust-reduction facilities were extremely primitive. Machines had no safeguards. Workers were not provided with protective gear.

What is most worrisome is that these kinds of problems exist in various forms and degrees in many three-capital enterprises. A staff member of one of Xiamen's industrial safety departments told me frankly that, while it is true the conditions found in Jiamei were quite extreme, it is not an isolated case. Some factories are even worse!

On December 28, 1992, Xiamen city's deputy mayor, Ye Tianze, announced to a gathering of officials who had come to listen to the Jiamei investigative report, "We give foreign investors special treatment, but this special treatment does not extend to environmental protection and industrial safety."

We do have laws and regulations in such matters. But we should also admit that the laws are not necessarily flawless. Many local governments still have not passed laws that can be pragmatically implemented. For example, there are still no specific laws regarding three-capital enterprises' industrial safety protection and insurance. Although one may always consult the laws drawn up for state enterprises, in practice, government department personnel feel that there are no laws and regulations to fall back on.

Of course, laws need to be enforced. But being "ruled by men" for so long, people's legal mentality is very low. If people who have violated the laws are not aware of it, how can we expect people to defend themselves with those laws?

According to the law, foreign-funded enterprises should sign labor contracts with workers. In the contracts, conditions that must be spelled out include: dismissal, award, benefits, labor insurance, and labor protection. But during our investigation when we asked the trade union chairman, Liu Yinshan, how many of the 400 workers had signed labor contracts, Liu answered, "Not many." He was not able to give an exact number. Upon further questioning, Liu said that except for the several dozen who were assigned special tasks or were skilled workers, the rest "had not asked to sign."

According to article 70 of the "Implementation Details for the Law Regarding PRC Foreign-Funded Enterprises," "Trade unions in foreign-funded enterprises represent the interests of the staff and workers. They have the right to sign labor contracts on behalf of the workers and to monitor their implementation." That the trade-union chair had no idea how many workers had signed labor contracts was quite amazing.

More incredible is the fact that when I went to the shop floor to ask the workers why they had not signed a labor contract, some said they were not aware of it. Some even said, "We were not told to sign." One worker who had been injured said, "When I was recruited, the boss said I would be hired as a permanent worker (*gudinggong*). Even though there was no contract, he said he would not fire me."

I asked, "What if you were severely injured and the boss fired you. What would you do?"

He shook his head, "No, he would not. I was hired as a permanent worker."

To tell the truth, a "permanent worker" is no more than one who is not classified as a casual or temporary laborer. This "permanency" is not legally binding. In the event of an industrial dispute or unfair dismissal, the case cannot be resolved in accordance with legal industrial arbitration. The workers are not aware of this.

Article 36 of the "Industrial Management Regulations for Taiwan Compatriot-Invested Enterprises in Fujian Province" states:

> In the event that there are serious industrial accidents, deaths, or serious poisoning and other occupational diseases, in accordance with state regulations, management should report immediately to the government departments concerned: the local labor bureau, the health and hygiene department, and the trade union in order that an investigation may be carried out.

But Jiamei Company declared that it "was not aware of such a regulation." Had the workers not collectively brought their problems to the relevant government organs, the latter would not have known about them.

Several times during the course of the investigation, Jiamei management complained to us that the compensation paid by the insurance company was too low and this had caused workers' dissatisfaction, and that if management had not urged the insurance company, the latter would not have been willing to pay 50 percent more. In reality, according to my interview with the insurance company, the type of insurance taken out by Jiamei was "employer-responsible insurance." Under this policy, the amount of compensation is related to the premium. There is a minimum set for the premium, but not a maximum. Compensation was computed in proportion to workers' wages, overtime pay, bonuses, and other subsidies. Jiamei management told us that workers were making about 300 yuan to 400 yuan or more a month, but with the insurance company, it took out a premium of only 213 yuan of basic wage for each worker. That is why it makes sense that the compensation was so low.

The investigation shows that there are still quite a number of loopholes at the macro-management level under the economic reforms. This is a cause for deep concern. How should we deal with this problem? How should we strengthen the legal system and enforcement mechanisms? For a long time to come, we will probably have to rely on the concern of the public, in particular, the concern of the relevant government organs.

Comments

It comes as a shock that despite the horrendously high accident rate in this factory, so many workers, after being maimed, were willing to continue to work in the factory under the same hazardous conditions. A few hundred yuan doled out to the injured by an insurance company was enough to placate them and persuade them to resume work. Even more unbelievable is that some workers had been injured more than once. True, as migrants, their options to leave were limited. The alternative was unemployment back home. Still, the astonishing situation was that losing fingers and hands had become so frequent that accidents were regarded almost as normal and natural occurrences. To all the parties involved—management, the insurance company, and workers—all that needed to be done after an accident happened was to follow a certain routine: the worker would be rushed to the hospital and the paperwork would be completed, asking the insurance company to pay up. The Taiwanese manager's attitude was that, now that they rushed workers to the hospital in taxis [presumably as opposed to taking a bus or walking], and the injury rate had declined, that was good enough. The idea that there should be zero-tolerance for industrial accidents was not there. This is also the kind of foreign-funded enterprise in which the trade-union chair and managerial staff of the Chinese partner all sided with their foreign partner. As for the workers, nowhere in the article are there signs that they had asked for changes to their work conditions such as the use of safeguarded machines, better machines, or reorganizing procedures on the production lines and work stations. The main issue for the workers was one of cash compensation.

True, when the investigation team and a reporter went to cover the story, the workers were eager to display their disfigurements. They were willing to stand up and "testify." They wanted sympathy. They wanted justice. But deep down, one is left with a fear that the workers had been so much abused that they have inculcated some of the management's attitude—that their lives and body parts are indeed very cheap, sort of disposable, and can be had for a price.

The absence of pressure from the workers (or from the so-called trade-union chair who obviously was a member of the management staff) made it easier for managers to shed their responsibility by laying the blame on the workers' "inferior quality." Readers not familiar with the Chinese worldview and usage of words might find this expression strange. Could it be a mistranslation? To describe someone as possessing "inferior quality" is an oft-used

Chinese expression, imbued with elitism. It is usually used by "educated" people to describe the inferior morals and unworthiness of the "uneducated." This demeaning evaluation of the poorly educated is based on the time-honored assumption that education creates a person of a higher order. As can be seen from this case, not only did the factory director not view the workers as equal beings, even the reporter, who was sympathetic to the workers, believed that the workers were of "inferior quality."

CASE 13a

This long Kafkaesque article was published in an ACFTU magazine, written by a researcher of a union federation research institute. He was able to gain entry to the gutted site of a toy factory in Shenzhen, where a fire had caused eighty-seven deaths and more than forty serious injuries. In this article he notes obstructed passageways, barred windows, and locked fire exits, recounting in detail what he saw of the charred ruins, and reconstructing images of horrific scenes as the factory went up in flames, of the agony of being being burned alive, and of the hysteria, the pushing and shoving as women migrant workers tried to flee from the inferno.[10]

The fire was much publicized in the Hong Kong press and within China. It caused a national outcry against unsafe work conditions in the Asian-invested factories of south China. It even stirred the normally reticent ACFTU into sending an investigation team to Shenzhen. After collecting evidence, the team's report publicly condemned the local government and its various bureaucracies for neglecting to comply with fire and building regulations, holding them responsible for the fire. It accused the township government of "one-sidedly emphasizing the investment climate without taking into consideration workers' safety, and for giving in too much to Hong Kong businesses." Such strongly worded statements of one bureaucracy openly berating another in the press is unusual in China, not to mention the fact that it came from the ACFTU, a bureaucracy of little status.[11]

Toyland Inferno: A Journey Through the Ruins*

The Story of Shenzhen's "Black Friday"

For the employees of Zhili Toy Factory, September 19, 1993, was truly Black Friday. Of those scheduled to work that fateful afternoon, up to one-third

---

*Translation from the Chinese text: Yi Fu, "Feixu shang de pingdiao: Shenzhen '11.19' teda houzai shigu jishi yu fansi," *Zhongguo gongren* (Chinese Workers), No. 5 (1994), pp. 4–11, and No. 6 (1994), pp. 8–11. Translated by Jonathan Hutt.

were injured in the fire that engulfed the factory, leaving a total of eighty-seven dead and another forty-five suffering from severe burns and permanent injuries. As news of the tragedy spread, so did the sense of incredulity. Yet, beneath the grief ran an undercurrent of anger: people wanted to know how something like this could happen. This great loss of life occurred not as the result of an earthquake, terrorist attack, plane crash, or shipping disaster; it happened in an average factory. How did so many young people come to lose their lives in this tragedy? What lessons can be learned from the incident?

It was in a state of perplexity and grief that I went to the scene of the disaster to carry out this investigation and research.

Natural or Man-Made Disaster?

The Rubble

In the town of Kuichong in Shenzhen, on a street at the entrance of Xinwei industrial estate, stands a three-story structure of reinforced concrete. The scent of death hangs over its blackened exterior, a powerful physical reminder of the fire that consumed it. From a distance the site resembles little more than a large black hole. This was once Shenzhen's Zhili Toy Factory, a Hong Kong–owned concern, now no more than a charred ruin.

At the factory gates we stated our name and business. The guard, like most of the workforce here, has been recruited from the countryside. The tragic death of his coworkers has obviously taken its toll, for in a voice that had lost all its former severity and authority, he softly said, "Go on in. Just don't be too long." As the iron gates closed behind us with a clang, it was as if we had been incarcerated in another world. The cramped factory complex is enclosed by workshops and high walls, along the top of which run barricades of wire or glass shards. The smell of burned plaster spilled forth from the blackened remains of the main factory building. Besides the sound of our own footsteps there were no other signs of life. This was a scene of disorder and desolation, surrounded by a deathlike silence.

The main factory building is nestled against the northern perimeter of the factory compound. Although there were in fact four exits to the factory—one in each corner—at the time of the fire, only one was operational. In order to maximize productive floor space and to regulate the comings and goings of workers, the Hong Kong owners had ordered one of the four exits soldered shut and two others kept locked. In order to reach the one serviceable exit at the factory's southwestern corner, workers had to pass through a narrow corridor with metal railings on either side, 8 meters long and 80 centimeters wide.

We entered the factory by the southwestern door. Within the expanse of this open-plan building, breathing was difficult. What once had been the factory's equipment had been reduced to a molten mass by the fire, while the scorched raw materials heaped upon the floor resembled large piles of coke. The factory's internal wall had collapsed, and the blades of the ceiling fans had withered in the heat, drooping down like wilted flowers suspended in midair. Although fire regulations stipulate that the workshop and warehouse be housed in separate buildings, here the storage area occupied the eastern corner of the ground floor, separated from the work area by a flimsy wire partition.

Chemical fibers, foam rubber, and other flammable materials had been stored within this so-called warehouse. At its southeastern corner was the cargo lift, which according to all safety regulations, was supposed to be fitted with doors. However, not only did the lift have no doors, but it was situated in an area in which raw materials were stored. Not surprisingly, it was amid these highly combustible materials that the fire spread so quickly through the factory premises. Today, one can witness how in the kiln-like intensity of the fire the walls of the lift have acquired a brick red glaze, the metal supports contorted like two dead snakes coiled upon the wall.

Cries of the Damned

According to the report submitted by safety inspectors, the cause of the fire can be traced to a short circuit in the tangle of exposed wiring, with the melting wires generating sufficient heat to spark the initial flare-up. As the workers, most of them women, were unaccustomed to any regular fire drills, panic spread quickly through the factory. Aided by the strong northeasterly wind, the fire moved rapidly toward the southwestern corner of the factory. The rows of merchandise that were stacked in the factory's southeastern corner served as the obvious conduit for the fire, which climbed toward the first and then the second floors. The raw materials and finished products that occupied every spare corner and lined every corridor quickly became the kindling for the inferno as it continued on its path of destruction. Accompanied by cries of panic, the scramble for safety began.

Those working on the ground floor were among the first to learn of the fire and were able to reach the sole exit on that level. Though suffering from burns and other injuries sustained in the melee, they can be considered the fortunate few. Those on the first and second floors were doomed, since their only avenue of escape was to leap to safety from the windows. They risked injury or death in the fall, but there was always a slim chance of survival. However, all the windows of the factory were covered with steel bars, imprisoning their occupants, while along the northern face of the factory, the windows also had an additional layer of wire mesh. Today, one can see evidence of the pathetic attempts that were made to pry open these bars along the factory's southern face. On the northern side, one can see that the wire mesh has been ripped open, but the steel bars would not yield. Trapped behind the mesh and the bars, the young women were helpless. There was also evidence that, in the search for a possible escape route, some young women had forced open a locked bathroom on the first floor in the factory's western corner. Their hopes were in vain. The windows here were also barred, condemning them to certain death.

In the ensuing panic, what was so desperately needed was someone to take charge of the evacuation. Where were the manager and the managerial staff? They were safely in their offices on the first floor, separated from the chaos unfolding in the factory complex by a thick brick wall. While they may have suffered from smoke inhalation, their lives were not in jeopardy. More important, there were no metal bars on the windows to prevent their escape and only a meter below the window itself was the roof of an adjoining building, which provided a quick route to safety. It was said that the factory management and white-collar employees did, in fact, use this exit. But did anyone come and direct the migrant workers toward this way out? I had a careful look around and noticed that the tiles on the roof of the neighboring building were broken in only a few places, suggesting that only a few people did, in fact, know of and use this escape route. With no one in charge, this route to safety was not there for all those who needed it.

The Road to Life and the Road to Death

There was only one way out. To make use of it, the workers needed to reach the ground floor via the stairwell in the northwestern corner, and then to brave the inferno. The desire to live caused nearly three hundred workers to desperately fight their way to life by this route. If the workers, having reached the ground floor, had been able to use the northwestern exit, the outcome would have been very different. However, the exit closest to the stairwell was firmly bolted, making it necessary for the workers to plunge into the sea of fire to reach the exit at the southwestern corner. There were those who, regardless of the dangers, braved the inferno, while others hesitated, though hesitation spelled certain death. Many were badly burned in the process, but a large number of people made it to safety this way.

But tragedies also took place on this flight of stairs. As the fire grew in intensity, the smoke thickened. In the frenzy to reach the ground floor, many on the stairwell were knocked down and trampled underfoot, and within the narrow confines of the stairwell, those following behind tripped over the growing tangle of bodies. At the same time, the fire continued on its path of destruction moving toward the northwestern corner of the factory, while the toxic black smoke given off by the piles of flaming chemical fibers was carried across the ground floor and spiraled up the stairwell. The migrant workers rapidly began to lose consciousness; those pushed forward by the throng could not retreat from the encroaching fumes. Within moments they, too, lost consciousness.

When those on the outside were finally able to break open the northwestern exit with a hatchet, they were greeted by a gruesome sight. The bodies of people who had died pushing against the door—piles of them—tumbled out. Along the whole 20 meters of stairwell, they were to find a tangle of lifeless bodies, seventy-nine female workers and two male workers.

Coming to the stairwell, a site which had been examined with a fine-tooth comb by the investigative team, we saw a white notice placed next to the metal doors upon which was written "Scene of Most Fatalities." At the time of the fire, the smoke must have been very thick, for now the smoke-damaged walls of the stairway are lost beneath a layer of black so thick that tracing my finger across the wall left a deep mark. Scattered on the stairwell are the shoes of both those who had fled the fire and those who were to become its victims, every conceivable type of shoe; cloth, leather, and sports shoes in every conceivable color: red, black, and white. I counted almost two hundred of them. That is to say, almost nobody left this scene with both shoes on. One can imagine the horror of the crowd jostling for life.

A death-like silence pervades the blackened remains of the stairwell. Gazing upward, one notices the shafts of light that pour through the broken skylight as if this were the only possible source of open air. Those eighty-one young lives—how much they had aspired for open space, and yet they reached the heavens with black fumes through this scorched cavity. This was a shocking waste of lives that had yet to be lived, and here in the stairwell is the faint echo of their plea to survive. As I stood in the stairwell my heart plummeted, and gazing upward I let out a long wail, tears trickling down my cheeks.

Do Heaven and Man Have No Feelings?

This was a tragedy that could have been so easily averted. If only the cargo lift had been fitted with doors, as required by regulations, then the fire would not have spread so rapidly to the first and second floors. If only the warehouse had been located in another building, then the lives of the workers would never have been placed in such immediate danger. If only the factory had been properly wired, then the chance of a short circuit would have been greatly decreased and the fire averted altogether. If only all possible avenues of escape had been open and the windows had not been barred, then the workers would have found it easier to evacuate the factory. If only there had been someone to organize the evacuation shortly after the fire broke out, then the loss of life would have been far less. Even after the fire took hold, if only the workers had been able to use the northwestern exit nearest the stairwell, then the lives of eighty-one workers would have been spared. If only . . .

Five safety problems had been previously detected, but the problem had never been remedied. Instead, the factory management had simply gone through the motions. From the surface evidence, the fire was caused by management's failure to follow fire-prevention procedures. In substance, it is because management placed profits before people. People's lives to them were worthless. The Zhili fire was not fated; it was a man-made tragedy caused by a few heartless people. This raises an important social issue, namely, the question of worker rights.

"Protect Worker Rights"—Vice Premier Zou Jiahua

Is This Another Ye Mailing?

The Japanese film *Ye Mailing* depicts the lives of workers in the early stages of Japanese capitalist exploitation, exposing the brutalities and greed of capitalist society and the exploitation of the proletariat. Twenty-odd years later, the feelings once aroused by this film have been gradually forgotten. As I lingered over the Zhili ruins, the chill of *Ye Mailing* overpowered me.[12]

Within the metal and wire cage that is the factory, more than 250 sewing machines were once crammed into the 500-square-meter shop floor. This translates into less than two square meters for every machine and worker. Piles of raw materials and half-finished products were jammed into the same space, and even spilled over into the washrooms. This was the job environment of the workers.

I next visited the dormitory complex, which was separated from the factory by a low wall studded with broken glass and barbed wire. The workers came and went through a narrow iron gate. The dormitory itself consisted of one building, with each room approximately 20 square meters housing ten double bunks. Along the outer wall of the overcrowded dormitory, a tarpaulin was erected to accommodate an additional thirty or so double bunks. In order to enter the dormitory, one was forced to squeeze through the narrow gaps between this outdoor bedding. Every inch of space was put to use.

The scene is now desolate. Those who had been fortunate enough to escape the inferno have gathered their possessions and left. What remains are the possessions of those who perished—tossed on the beds, scattered on the ground, and lining the corridors. Letters, photographs, and once treasured possessions now lie in a heap, and others are blown down the corridors like tumbleweeds.

In general, the conditions at Zhili factory are a vast improvement over those of *Ye Mailing*'s era. Still, the moment the workers entered the factory grounds they lost their identity, cut off from the world outside by the high walls and imposing iron gates. Within these walls the employer's power was absolute, a power to which the workers were expected to submit during and after working hours. Employees could not come and go as they pleased even after work, but required written approval from a supervisor to pass through the two gates of the dormitory and the factory grounds.

A printed leave form reads:

Zhili Toy Factory Application for Leave Form

Due to illness, XXX has been granted leave for a period of X days/hours. On presentation of this document to security personnel at the main gate, the bearer is granted permission to leave the factory grounds.

Signed XXX
Date, Month, Year

Although this management method paraded under the title of "regularizing management," it was anything but. In early capitalist societies, the suppression of basic worker rights and the control of their movement was widespread. Today, such practices have almost disappeared except in socialist countries such as our own.

Song of the Migrant Workers

How do the migrant workers see their own lives? Previously, I had no real personal contact with them. What cursory information I had came from the superficial meetings I had arranged with workers. These were all of "the situation is excellent" variety. I could not say they were lies, but there was a flip side to the coin.

Amid the ruins, I came across several diaries. Though none bore the names of their owners, they were their sole legacy. Every page is a record of their emotions, overflowing with a deep melancholy. In several of these, I came across a hand-copied song of the migrant worker, which clearly expresses how these young women felt about their lives.

From Sichuan to Canton,
Thru' Ou-Yang to Shenzhen,
Home is long gone,
Mom and Dad we had to leave,
Your words forever in my heart.

They say Canton streets are made of gold,
It's been over three years,
I wish my family were near,
But my pockets are still bare.

Last night I had a dream,
Mom was with me here,
She stroked my face,
Streaming with tears.

Come New Year's Eve,
The entire family is at home,
Except for me,
Mom, I should have listened to what you said.

A day feels like a year,
It ain't so easy to be away from home,
No cash, no salt, no oil, nor grain,
To live is an agony.

From Canton to Sichuan,
Throw open the windows and look outside,
Mountain upon mountain,
Sichuan's beauty before my eyes.

This type of literature does not see the light of day in print, but among migrant workers it is extremely popular. Showing it to several migrant workers, I discovered that, especially among the workers from Sichuan, this song was well known.

"Big Sister, I Am So Tired I Cannot Stand It Anymore"

Here are several extracts taken from the correspondence of the migrant workers at Zhili Factory that I had collected:

Sis,

We're only eating two meals a day. We do a five-hour shift in the morning, six in the afternoon, and another four at night. Every one of us who came here together can't stand it either.

Your little sister
May 5, 1993

Little Sis,

I also want to pack up and go home, and never leave home again. I earn nothing. It's tough. You must go to see a doctor and stop fretting about the money. To be healthy and alive is to have everything. Make sure you aren't miserly when it comes to your medicine. You must eat both breakfast and dinner.

Your sister
October 11, 1993

The above correspondence was between two sisters from Sichuan, the elder of whom worked at Zhili. Her letter dated a month before the Zhili fire shows how much she misses home. The fire proved her right when she wrote, "To be healthy and alive is to have everything." Now she is gone; nothing is left.

Auntie Chunzhi,

The factory isn't too bad. We get three meals a day and do twelve-hour days. There's an hourly rate. On the eight-hour day shift, we get 70 fen an hour and on the night shift we get one yuan an hour for four hours. After three months, you're eligible for bonuses. When I was at the Dezheng factory, the fumes in the factory gave me a headache and I simply could not work there anymore. I've only received two months' pay for three months' work because I owed 90 yuan for the ticket to Shenzhen. That's just some 50 yuan for three months' work, a whole month for nothing. Fifty yuan ain't enough for daily odds and ends. And then, I borrowed another 60 yuan when I switched factories. I'm so ashamed, having left home and worked for six months, I can't even make enough to support myself.

Your niece,
Xinfeng
May 24 (no year)

Xinfeng,

I'd like to change factories, too, but I was afraid they wouldn't give me back my identity card, and that card is yours. I hate it here, can't stand one more day. When we were at home, we all dreamed about this wonderful place, but once we got here, we saw it for what it is. I really regret ever having come.

Auntie Chunzhi

This correspondence was between a young woman from Henan province and her aunt. Without such documentary evidence, it would be hard for many of us to believe that someone might receive only 50 yuan for three months work. Having recently moved from another factory, this young woman is quite content with three meals a day and a daily wage of 9.60 yuan. That she is happy with her lot, despite the strenuous workload and low wages, says a great deal. Yet between the lines of this letter lie misery and pain, and for the likes of Auntie Chunzhi, even this state of well-being is beyond her grasp. Her young niece would not survive the inferno.

"Boss, I Wanna Quit!"

Recruited from the provinces, the migrants working at Zhili were usually screened first by the county-level labor-management offices, which signed labor contracts with factory management. The contracts, usually of one year's duration, are printed and issued by the Shenzhen Labor Bureau. These contracts contain specific clauses stipulating the employee's rights. For example:

> When the period covered by the contract is complete, the contract becomes null and void. In such a circumstance, should Party A wish to retain the services of Party B and Party B agrees to this, the contract may then be renewed with approval from the Labor Bureau.
> Should Party B be dissatisfied with changes to either their position or their responsibilities, they may tender their resignation and will be released from their contract when both parties have completed the necessary formalities.

But in the real world, many employers either ignore contracts altogether or simply do not honor them. Instead, in order to control their workforce, employers either use a system of "security deposits," or hold onto workers' identity cards. Moreover, workers are often forced to take unpaid time off or face outright dismissal when work orders diminish. According to the standard contract:

> During the period covered by this contract, should there be no work [because of delays in the arrival of materials, for example], Party A promises to pay Party B a per diem of between 2 and 4 yuan as basic living expenses.

The factory management did everything possible to reduce such expenditures. On the other hand, when the workload was at its heaviest, there was little chance of tendering your resignation, and without an identity card, a worker was unable to leave.

At Zhili, it was not that there was ever a shortage of work, but that the work could be finished only with a vast amount of overtime. With such a heavy workload and insufferable conditions, it is hardly surprising that much of the workforce wished to resign. But this was not a wish that workers could state openly. Sifting through the debris in the dormitory complex, I came across two letters of resignation.

> To the Honorable General Manager and Factory Management
>
> Dear Sirs,
>
> I have worked here for three years. My contract expired some time ago. I have received a letter from my family asking me to return home and I hope you will approve my resignation.
>
> Resignee, Ni Li
> May 10, 1993

> To the Honorable General Manager and Factory Management
>
> Dear Sirs,
>
> I have received several letters from my family asking me to return and I find that I no longer have the heart to continue working. I hope I will receive quick approval of this request.
>
> Resignee, Chen Aihua

Both letters were scribbled with changes, suggesting that these were merely drafts. The final versions had probably been sent off to the factory administration. Dated a month and a half prior to the fire, obviously neither application had received approval and both women had continued working up until Black Friday. There was no way of obtaining a full list of the casualties, but from the information available to me, I was able to ascertain that at least one of the two seeking to resign was a victim of the tragedy.

The Return of the Prodigal Son?

There is a common saying, "After decades of bitterness, things are what they were before Liberation." This expression is very common among workers in foreign ventures and may not be far from the truth. While we should welcome foreign investment, we must also ensure that these businesses abide by our country's policies and laws. Such businesses must be prevented from undermining our socialist system and destroying the rights of our workers. Some Taiwanese businessmen return to the mainland and attempt to brainwash their employees with notions of the superiority of capitalism and Sun Yat-sen's three principles: "The communists have bungled the economy and now they have asked us to return. People had better listen to what we're saying."

With regard to management and labor practices, many foreign investors willfully exploit their workforce. There are repeated instances of verbal abuse, physical violence, and public humiliation, while the hermetically sealed workforce is virtually imprisoned and relinquishes its rights on entering the factory. Employees are commonly subjected to body searches, forced to take on extra shifts, and frequently have their wages docked. As profit is placed above both safety and the rights of the worker, it is not surprising that dangerous situations such as these continue to arise.

The events at Zhili are certainly not without precedent. Not long before the Zhili tragedy, a fire at a Hong Kong–owned clothing factory in Guangzhou claimed seventy-two lives and, while the investigations at Zhili were still under way, more than sixty people died in a fire at a Taiwanese business in Fuzhou, which left another eight people seriously injured. Quite clearly, there is little to separate the employers of today from their pre-Liberation counterparts.

Foreign observers, on the other hand, have been more critical of these business ventures, describing them as a meeting of the ruthless employer and the expendable workforce. On a trip to Shanghai, a delegation of Taiwanese union officials warned that Taiwanese businessmen were bringing with them not only investment funds, but exploitative labor practices. In order to foster investment while limiting the harmful side effects, it was crucial that people be aware of the situation from the outset.

Where Is Loyalty? Beneath the Lucre!

The sole objective of any investment is to make a profit. There is nothing wrong with this in itself. In order to achieve this goal, employers must aim to extract as much surplus value as possible, even if this means they must exploit their workforces. This is the rationale behind Marx's theory of "surplus value." The employer is the personification of capital, which calls to mind the well-known work by Freidrich Engels written 150 years ago, words that do not seem out of place even today:

> To the capitalist classes there is nothing that does not exist for the purpose of making money. Even they themselves cannot be excluded for their very existence is to make money. Beyond the quick route to wealth they know of no other happiness. Beyond the loss of wealth they know of no other sorrow.

In all fairness, the conditions at Zhili were not that bad compared to many other foreign-owned ventures, and the factory's owner cannot be singled out as being particularly ruthless. Although I have never met the owner, the impression of him held by others is that, by all accounts, he is a gentle and cultivated man and not the tyrant we might imagine him to be. I recall that in the center of the factory compound, the owner had erected a shrine to the gods of prosperity and war, on which there were written the lines "Loyalty joins heaven and earth; patriotism unites the sun and the moon." Alongside was an inscription that read, "Venus shines in the Western sky. The people rise toward the golden star of prosperity." Obviously, the owner had some respect for the notions of loyalty and patriotism, but if loyalty and the attainment of profit should be incompatible, and a choice had to be made, what then? To quote the lines from a song, "Should you ask where loyalty lies, it lies beneath the lucre." To the boss, this seems to be the only option. But are we aware of this?

There Must Be No Ye Mailing *on the Mainland!*

The profit motives of the employer are not in question here. However, profits should not be at the expense of worker rights. We do not want to see the kind of exploitation that is synonymous with the primary stage of capitalism moved to the mainland. The mainland is not *Ye Mailing*. China seeks foreign investment, but not investors who exploit and control workers. We do welcome mutually beneficial development. If the question of the position and rights of workers in these foreign ventures is not resolved within the letter of the law, then horrific events such as those that transpired at Zhili will continue. Beyond the practical considerations that arose from the disaster, there is an issue with a more far-reaching social impact, namely, conflicts between employer and employee.

Reacting to the disaster, Vice Premier Zou Jiahua pointed out, "This entire situation could have been avoided if foreign companies had not placed profit above the lives of their workers. The number of similar companies is not small and safety conditions are anything but good." He also stated, "In Shenzhen, and in particular regarding foreign companies there, we should increase union activity to guarantee worker rights." Not only do these comments highlight how the origins of the Zhili disaster can be found in the labor–capital relationship, but they also illustrate the fundamental role of the Chinese government in this relationship, namely, as the protector of worker rights.

Yet how do foreign investors manage to do exactly as they please? These are issues worthy of examination and attention.

How Much Responsibility Should the Government Take?

Li Youwei, "Every Level of Government Must Take Responsibility"

On the day of the disaster, the mayor of Shenzhen, Li Youwei, was in Beijing. Hearing news of the fire, he returned to Shenzhen and rushed immediately to the scene of the tragedy, where, acting on the instructions of the central authorities, he assumed direct control of the operations.

To the residents of Shenzhen, the second half of 1993 had been a period of continuous disaster. First, there were the torrential rains that inundated large parts of the city. Then, on August 5, there was the explosion of a petrol tanker. Finally, on November 19, the Zhili disaster claimed the greatest fire death toll in more than thirty years. Shenzhen citizens find it difficult to speak of the incident without great emotion, "Shouldn't the leadership take responsibility for such a huge disaster?"

The concern expressed by the citizens of Shenzhen was not without foundation. Because of the present system, many bureaucrats are able to abdicate responsibility even when a disaster like this happens. Officials are so adept at passing the buck that we never see them tendering their resignations, or in any way accepting responsibility. As we shall see, the case here is somewhat different.

At the meeting hastily convened to attempt to address the disaster at Zhili, Mayor Li stated:

Because we are the ones who want to have such businesses, and we are the ones who solicit foreign investment and issue the necessary permits, every level of government must take responsibility for the events of Zhili. We are all government employees. We must not overemphasize the employer's role in this affair. First and foremost, we ourselves are responsible.

The matter must be handled with the utmost seriousness. I am willing to accept whatever the central authorities decide to do with regard to this incident.

In all fairness, Mayor Li had only recently taken up this post. It was impossible for him, as the person ultimately responsible, to take care of all details. To blame it all on him is really to make him bear the mistakes of others. On the other hand, with every office there are responsibilities, and even if someone has been mayor for only twenty-four hours, he must still take responsibility for everything that happens within that period. Personally, I feel the mayor's desire for some disciplinary action is praiseworthy because such courage and moral fiber are not usually seen in high-ranking officials. Moreover, Mayor Li raises an important point: when an incident occurs, all government officials at all levels are responsible.

Amid the Ruins Fluttered the Banner of a Safety Production Award

Situated in the western corner of the first floor, the factory offices were untouched by the fire, but scattered across the floor are all manner of reports, documents, personnel files, and migrant workers' identity cards. I crouched down on the floor to go through these secret documents that were once inaccessible to outsiders. Suddenly, a noise from above caught my attention. Looking up, I saw several banners fluttering in the wind. Next to them were several other banners with citations. I noticed one in particular:

> Awarded to this progressive work unit for work in fire safety management procedures.
> Government of Bao'an County,
> Kuichong Town, December 1991.

What an irony: a fire safety banner blowing over the fire-scorched ruins.

That the factory was a potential fire hazard was apparent even in the planning stage. The combined factory and storage area, the open lift, and the bars across the windows all blatantly violated fire-safety regulations. The illegal wiring and the obstruction of fire exits following construction further increased the dangers. Nevertheless, this was assessed as a progressive work unit in fire-safety management procedures. The local town government was clearly aware of the severe fire risk at Zhili factory, and while pretending to address such matters, went out of its way to appease the Hong Kong owner. If the events at Zhili had not been so serious, the local authorities may have been able to hide behind some bureaucratic smoke screen. However, after the fire, as more information came to light, it was discovered that the responsibility for the tragic events at Zhili went much beyond this.

Government for the Masses or Government for the Bosses?

In the first half of 1993, the Shenzhen City Fire Safety Bureau dispatched a team of inspectors to Kuichong township. As a result of their preliminary inspections, a majority of the eighty-five factories and fourteen other enterprises were declared fire hazards. Of these, forty-five had combined factory, warehouse, dormitory, and refectory facilities in a single building. In the Zhili factory itself, the team found thirteen problem areas that required attention. Some factories had up to twenty problems. To implement these changes would not only require capital outlay, but would also affect production. Although they received official notification of the necessary modifications, employers did not rush to implement the recommendations, at best giving them only the most perfunctory attention. Despite this, the town government did not ensure that the modifications were made; instead, it worked on behalf of the interests of the Hong Kong owners, using all manner of underhanded practices to help them acquire the necessary fire-safety certificates. On May 28, the town mayor, Zeng Weidong, wrote to the Shenzhen City Bureau of Fire Safety requesting that fifty factories be granted the fire-safety certificates. The letter reads as follows:

To the Shenzhen Bureau of Fire Inspection Teams,

Our town has completed our inspection of the safety modifications, and at present, most meet the requirements. We express our deep gratitude for the Inspection Team's suggestions in its investigative report, which is so supportive of Kuichong's economic development. After discussion in the town government, we agree to issue fire-safety certificates to the fifty factories. Should the permits not be issued, this could well affect our program of economic development and we fear that Hong Kong businessmen may take the matter up with the (Shenzhen) municipal government. We hope that we can resolve this issue together with the other parties involved. We look forward to receiving your approval.

Respectfully yours,
Zeng Weidong, May 28.

This letter is brief but it says a great deal. First is the question of meeting safety requirements. The letter implied that while the modifications had not all been made at the time the letter was written, they would have been completed by the next inspection. The second point is a warning that Hong Kong investors may take the matter up with a higher authority in an attempt to sway their decision. This would appear to be in response to the pressure brought to bear on the local authorities by the foreign investors for a speedy resolution to this affair. Finally, the expression of thanks for the contributions made toward Kuichong's economic development may also include covert business deals between the town government and members of the fire-safety inspection team.

On the day this letter was written, a meeting was held in a small conference room at the town government office. At this meeting, the town mayor proposed that the 5- to 10-yuan daily meal subsidies paid to Bureau of Fire Safety inspectors amounting to 1,000–1,500 yuan be increased to a total of 5,000 yuan per person or 15,000 yuan for the three-member team. The inspectors thereupon approved the permits for the fifty factories in Kuichong. This was simply a cash-permit transaction. In effect, the town mayor paid a total of 15,000 yuan for twenty-two permits (the other twenty-eight would be issued by the bureau) for factories that had not met the safety standards.

Thus, a business transaction at the expense of workers' safety was concluded in the name of economic development. At Zhili, only six of the thirteen points that required attention were dealt with, and then only in a haphazard fashion. Nonetheless, that was considered as having met safety standards. On the mayor's list of fifty factories, Zhili was number seventeen.

Why should this town work so hard for the Hong Kong investors? According to the county government's own explanation, it was all for the economic development of Kuichong. Individual officials and even the county government (they said) gained almost nothing from these ventures. Also, they claimed that factories like Zhili pay little in rent or taxes, and much of that goes to the village authorities, anyway. The town authorities receive nothing, yet must cover all manner of crippling expenses, such as public security and administration, and the cost of providing public utilities.

What a clean image! But the reality is very different. The county government and Zhili alone have a murky relationship. The county economic development company charged with overseeing economic development and the Hong Kong owner concocted a phony contract in which it was stated that a monthly rental of H.K.$2,500 was to be paid for the use of the 500-square-meter premises. In a supplementary agreement, H.K.$24,000 is the rental price of the larger 2,400-square-meter complex. The difference between the two contracts is as much as ten times. That is, in five and one-half years, between its opening in May 1988 and the fire, undisclosed rent totaled over H.K.$1.4 million. This came to light after the Zhili fire.

It is clear that government employees saw the legal system and the safety of workers as little more than a plaything. When government employees represent the interests of foreign business, then we are justified in asking exactly for whom these officials are working. With conflicts between employer and employee back on the agenda, the government must now come up with a strategy to deal with the situation. Though the matter is complex, there is little question about their priorities. That this is a government for the people and not for the employer is what distinguishes China from capitalist nations. Consequently, the government must, first and foremost, protect the rights of the employee. Any government that uses the notion of economic development as a pretext for sacrificing worker rights is both corrupt and criminal.

Corruption and Accidents Go Hand in Hand

In January 1993, a team of safety inspectors from the Shenzhen Bureau of Public Safety conducted a semiannual blanket inspection of more than eighteen towns in the Bao'an and Longgang districts. A three-person team comprised of a Wu, a Li, and a Lu came to Kuichong. Faced with so important a task, one might have expected them to be fastidious in the way they executed their duties, but sadly, they seemed more concerned with turning this into a money-making exercise. Knowing that few employers had made any effort to implement the necessary changes, the team of inspectors used this information to pry open the wallets of the foreign investors. On May 24, at a meeting with the local authorities at which five factory owners were present, the team informed them that factories in Buji village had been subject to fines, and more than twenty factories had been closed in order to complete repairs. So as to seem less severe, the team stated they were prepared to issue certificates to factories that made three or more of the necessary modifications. When they had addressed these matters, the owners could come to the hotel at which they were staying, where they would issue the certificates. The employers clearly understood the hint. The representative of Zhili's owner delivered a package containing H.K.$3,000 and left with the necessary certificate. From my investigation, I have discovered that an additional twenty-nine certificates were issued. The question is: How many other bribes were paid?

The inspection team sought to extort money from both the factory owners and the local authorities as well. On examination of the accounts, it could be traced that the team had received 6,000 yuan from the local government for living expenses, and another 15,000 yuan in exchange for twenty-two blank safety permits. Furthermore, issuing the eight permits as trump cards, they asked for more money. In total, they received bribes amounting to 30,000 yuan. A public organization that should be the guardian of public safety was, in fact, run by profiteers who helped to shelter businesses that broke the law. They are the accomplices to manufacturing disasters. Only when corruption is eliminated can disaster be averted, for the two go hand in hand.

Shenzhen's Stony Silence

As news of the tragedy spread, there was a public outcry. The whole country was shocked. Veteran reporters converged on Shenzhen in order to cover the story, hoping they could whip up public opinion. In the course of these investigations, reporters ran into unexpected obstacles. On the day of the fire, as reporters congregated at the site, the local government sprang into action. Officials refused to answer any inquiries and banned any government employee or reporter from speaking to the survivors. The township propaganda office refused to grant reporters any interviews, stating that all further announcements would be press releases issued by the municipal news bureau. The scene of the disaster was then closed off to all reporters.

If the authorities had been preparing for legal action, their attempts to prevent details from leaking out would be quite understandable. Yet this does not explain why the rest of the Shenzhen media were silent. At one time, this would have been considered front-page news or exclusive reporting, but now there was little more than a few brief "press releases." It was as if everyone involved had come down with a case of laryngitis.

I addressed my concerns to a few of these veteran reporters: If they failed to investigate fully and make their findings known, weren't they failing in their responsibilities to their readers and society in general? Surely, such indifference would jeopardize the very relationship between the press and both the people and the Party?

All of them shrugged and shook their heads. "Sorry, mate, but how can we dare to disobey orders from on high?"

Chinese Laborer, Workers' Daily, Guangming Daily, Chinese Women, and *Chinese Youth*, along with several other major publications, all devoted an entire page to the fire, while the *People's Daily* published a supplement containing reports of the fire and various editorials. The incident was reported across the nation, and in some smaller publications there were a number of insightful remarks, such as those published in *Yangcheng Evening News*, for example, "There isn't a convenient scapegoat to pin this one on."

I asked the Shenzhen authorities why they had controlled the local media. Their response: To prevent any negative impact on the investment climate and to maintain social stability. I cannot accept such an explanation.

The majority of investors in Shenzhen are from Hong Kong, where there was detailed coverage of the tragedy. These reports, with their accounts of personal tragedies and their strong condemnation of the illegal factories, prompted a public outcry both in Hong Kong and elsewhere. The Chinese government could not possibly prevent the matter from being discussed in Hong Kong. Moreover, how can social stability be maintained by attempting to stifle public opinion? The only information available to the people of Shenzhen came from rapidly spreading rumors or from abroad. Surely, a situation such as this only fosters distrust and suspicion.

Ferreting Out Corruption: Tracing Who is Responsible

As the smoke surrounding the events of November 19 began to clear, the real reasons for the events at Zhili became known. The tragedy cannot be blamed on a simple electrical fault or bad management. Rather, it involved a complex web of social, economic, and political factors: unlawful and exploitative employers, irresponsible bureaucrats, and self-seeking opportunists, all of whom acted with complete disregard for human life.

Although the employers are held accountable, what about the bureaucrats and opportunists? Should they not also be liable for their role in this affair? We have already mentioned the role of the various safety-inspection teams, but what about their immediate superiors? Are they not also responsible? In their investigations the team of inspectors from the municipal Bureau of Fire Safety violated regulations, and having secured approval of the safety permits from their divisional head, they used the information they had gathered for the purposes of extortion. Should the municipal authorities not also be liable for the part they played in this tragedy?

I recall an item from a news broadcast on Shenzhen Television shortly after the fire, "The central government investigative unit on corruption has completed its work in Shenzhen and expressed satisfaction with the work done to date." Were the people of Shenzhen overjoyed by this news? Many people stated quite clearly that the guilty parties had better not show their faces anywhere near the factory.

Upholding the Sanctity of Labor

How Much Are Migrant Workers Worth?

Following the fire, the still badly traumatized survivors were unable to return to the factory dormitory and were housed at the Kuichong Recreation

Center. For "security" reasons they were kept behind locked gates and under tight security. The survivors were told that under no circumstances were they to talk to anyone about events at the factory. If something untoward happened to them, they themselves would have to be responsible for it.

Fortunately, I had the opportunity to meet one of the survivors, a young woman from Henan province. She told me, "I was the lucky one. Two of the girls who went with me to Shenzhen died and another was badly burned." As she talked of the tragedy she stuttered, looking all around her, as if she were guilty of divulging some state secret. Sensing her terror, I hurriedly changed the topic. After she had already been through so much, I did not want to cause her any further distress. I still cannot understand why the victims should be made to feel as if they had committed a crime.

If the living were treated like this, then what about the dead? The matter of compensation for the victims' families was resolved quickly, and those put in charge of the matter felt it went more smoothly than expected. The victims had come from all over China—Sichuan, Henan, Hubei, and Hunan—from the impoverished backwaters to a city of immense wealth. Yet their destination brought them not wealth, but only tragedy and death. A fifty-year-old peasant from Sichuan who came to collect the body of his daughter only had this to say: " I never should have let her come."

Compensation payouts varied according to geographical and family conditions, ranging between 20,000 and 40,000 yuan. While this is a large sum of money for someone from a peripheral, old, backward, and remote area, to the employer it is merely a drop in the ocean, what they might spend on a single banquet. The value placed on human life can be seen by comparing these figures with the market value of another commodity, namely, pets. On the open market, prices range from 50,000 yuan for a Pekingese to over 240,000 yuan for a Mexican Chihuahua. Perhaps this is not the most scientific comparison, as one cannot really attach a price tag to human life in this manner. Yet, in our present socialist system, doesn't it appear that the life of the average worker is cheaper than either a family pet or a banquet?

It is not so much compensation figures that I am quibbling about, but the social status and fundamental value of the workers themselves. Since you employers use standard international business practices to seek investment opportunities in China, when an accident happens, should you not also follow international procedures with regard to compensation? In a market economy, a small to mid-sized business will surely go bankrupt if only a few employees die, not to speak of such a serious accident. Yet the eighty-seven lives of Zhili are not worth an ordinary two-story house.

The Rising Sun: The Special Economic Zones

The Special Economic Zones (SEZs) have surpassed all previous models of rapid economic development, and Shenzhen's developing economy is a prime example of this economic miracle. Within the past ten years, industrial and agricultural output has been increasing at almost 40 percent annually. What was once a sleepy backwater has been transformed overnight into a cosmopolitan commercial city. One of the major reasons for this success has been the CCP economic reform policies and the development of new technologies and business practices. Yet, without the blood, sweat, and tears of hundreds and thousands of migrants' physical labor, this would never have been possible.

Of the total population of 2.6 million people, more than 1.8 million are migrant laborers not native to Shenzhen. They constitute over 98 percent of employees in the compensation-trade[13] and three-capital enterprises, 92 percent of the construction industry, and 86 percent of the commercial and service industries. Consequently, when we speak of "Shenzhen people," we really should be referring to these "hired laborers." Not only do they make up 70 percent of Shenzhen's population, they are also the principal creators of the region's prosperity. With an average age of twenty-five years, the Shenzhen workforce is, in the words of the talented worker-turned-writer, Anzi, "a rising sun on the move, a youthful tribe on the move." It is they who are sustaining this brilliant, special economic zone.

But what about their working conditions and the standard of living here in the Shenzhen SEZ? When I addressed this question to Party Secretary Li Haoceng, he expressed concern:

> Today everyone talks about how everything here is just fine and great. But does anyone know how this was achieved? We must not forget the million-plus migrant workers who made this possible. And look at them now, where they live, what they eat. For those of us in our four-room apartments, it is hard to realize how tough it is.

Dreams of Gold

This million-strong workforce surges into Shenzhen carrying with them many dreams: some of wealth, some of status. But how many can rise to join the ranks of the bosses? They are really no more than daydreams.

In my possession, I have a collection of about fifty monthly pay slips that I gathered from the Zhili site. Of these, Sun Shuni got the highest pay that month, earning 627.90 yuan. Zhang Yanyu got the lowest—only 139.60 yuan.

From this, 35 yuan was deducted for meals, 3.50 yuan for accommodation, one yuan for a service fee, 19 yuan in fines, 10 yuan for the deposit, and 40 yuan for miscellaneous items. This left a net wage of 33.10 yuan. Another worker, Zhang Tinglan, received a net wage of 35.20 yuan. Except for two people who did not work for a whole month, for all fifty people [whose pay slips were in the collection] the average monthly wage was approximately 260 yuan for working thirty or thirty-one days. That means for working about twelve hours a day, their income was less than 9 yuan [U.S.$1.10].

In comparison with wages throughout Shenzhen, those at Zhili were average or better. According to a survey carried out in October 1993 by the Shenzhen authorities, over 40 percent of wages were lower than the minimum wage set by Shenzhen city. On average, overtime was three to four hours each day for a seven-day workweek. The greatest amount of overtime in one month was 150 hours. Yet the hourly overtime wage for some can be only 50 fen (half a yuan), or even nothing. On the other hand, defaulting on payment of wages is a common phenomenon, with employers intentionally withholding wages for as long as three or four months. The payroll is used as operational funds, or just sits in banks collecting interest. In the course of this investigation, it was discovered that in Nanshan District alone, wages in arrears amount to more than 500 million yuan.

The majority of workers soon discover that the streets of Shenzhen are not paved with gold. According to official statistics, over 900 million yuan was sent out of Shenzhen over the Chinese New Year, of which over 400 million yuan was remitted by migrant workers. While this may seem like a large amount, dividing it by the large number of 1,800,000 migrant workers, the migrants only remitted an average of 200 yuan per person.

Sacrificing Youth

Married women or slightly older women have difficulty finding work, as many factories have a policy of not hiring anyone over the age of twenty. In most factories, all the workers are women of about twenty years of age. They are full of energy, have quick reflexes, and have no family responsibilities. The bosses make their money from this youthfulness. As for the laborers, they are gambling their youth for a better tomorrow—the long exhausting working hours and heavy workloads are draining their physical strength and energy. The young women age prematurely.

I visited a joint-venture factory where workers were primarily engaged in manufacturing and assembling components for electrical equipment with the aid of a magnifying glass. A health and safety expert who accompanied me asked the workers whether they took measures to rest their eyes during or after work. "Never," they replied. When we asked the factory management, we received little more than an evasive response. In the opinion of this expert, unless workers in this industry take the appropriate measures, they risk severe and permanent damage to their vision within two months. Looking through the magnifying glass for only a few minutes was enough to give me eye strain, and yet the young girls did so for ten hours a day. One can only presume that since the local government selected this factory as a model factory for us to visit, the conditions must be considered better than most.

In Shenzhen, I also attended a migrant-laborer forum. There, I learned from the participants that none planned to stay for long. Some had a wait-and-see attitude, while others said they would stay between two and three years. It was only later that I realized this was not because they did not wish to stay, but simply because they had become so exhausted, they could no longer manage to continue working. Once the bosses have squeezed every drop of sweat out of them, they are allowed to go.

A Bowl of Scattered Beads

How do we put the Shenzhen migrant labor force of 1.8 million people into comparative perspective? In 1919, the entire industrial workforce in China totaled 2.8 million, and based on this, the Communist Party built its class foundation. This is to say that today's Shenzhen workforce alone constitutes 70 percent of the manufacturing workforce of previous years. As Karl Marx pointed out, "Numerically the workers have attained their critical mass. But it is only when they have become organized and are guided by knowledge that this numerical strength can be transformed into a decisive factor in determining whether victory will be theirs or not."

In Shenzhen's foreign ventures, workers are unorganized. Their effectiveness in advancing their personal interests and in playing a social role is greatly disproportionate to their numerical strength. According to statistics, unions are established in only 20 percent of the three-capital and compensation-trade enterprises, with union membership covering only roughly 10 percent of the workforce. In fact, many workers have no idea about what unions do. When they encounter difficulties in the workplace, the idea of seeking help from the union does not occur to them, they cannot find one, or having succeeded in contacting one, the union cannot solve their problems. As capital–labor conflict escalates, in a majority of cases, the employer has many resources at his disposal to handle the situation, while the workers are left to fight their own battles.

What about in foreign-funded enterprises where unions have been established? While there are some that attempt to protect the rights of the worker, many others are unions in name only. Some of them are even "bosses' unions." I visited one industrial park where there were some 400 foreign-funded factories. Of these, sixty of them had unions, yet almost all of the trade-union chair positions were occupied either by factory directors or factory managers. At one union meeting, the trade-union chairman, who also happened to be the general manager, frankly acknowledged that "unions have a dual responsibility to protect both the interests of the workers, and also the interests of the boss."

I could not contain myself and asked, "What if the interests of the employer and the employees are in conflict? Whose interests should the union protect?"

The chairman was at a loss for words. Everyone there was embarrassed. According to the local township trade-union chairman, none of these trade-union chairpersons who are also (PRC-side) managers dares to confront the boss on the workers' behalf during an industrial dispute. This phenomenon seriously jeopardizes the interests of the worker. This was exactly the situation at Zhili, where the trade-union was not set up according to legal procedures, and there was no factory committee. Yes, the factory had a manager who doubled as a "trade-union chairman." But what good does this "chairman" do for the workers?

In sharp contrast, the workers have no organizations, yet their employers have their array of associations: the Hong Kong Entrepreneur Friendship Association, Investors Society, Employers Social Club, and the like. In Shenzhen, the employers' associations are organized at the "village" level. But these villages are not real villages, but former villages that have now been turned into industrial estates. These estates vary in size, from a small one housing a few hundred enterprises to a large one with up to a thousand. In one typical estate, there are over 500 enterprises, 80 percent of which are foreign owned. Here, the local employers' association is known as the Hong Kong Entrepreneur Friendship Association. While these go by many different names, there is little difference between them. They do not have much formal structure. They are really avenues for bosses to meet, socialize, play golf, exchange views, and discuss business. For example, at the time when the Zhili factory was being inspected for fire safety, employers in Kuichong were gathered at their club to discuss how to handle the inspection and obtain the necessary certificates.

Faced with such a powerful adversary, the workers in foreign ventures have little leverage for a variety of reasons. First, local governments overlook the value and necessity of unions. Second, there is the strength of the employers' associations, which have both obstructed and controlled the unions.

Finally, on joining the workforce, migrant workers have to surrender their identity cards and their rights as free citizens.

There are reports that the Shenzhen Municipal Trade Union has begun work to establish a greater presence in foreign ventures, and to clean up and revamp "bosses' unions" and those unions that exist only in name.[14]

Protecting the Laborers—An Urgent Task for SEZ Development

Following the establishment of the market economy, a new social group, a stratum of laborers (*laogong*), has emerged, especially in the SEZs. In a broad sense, laborers are defined as those who are employed by others. Their major source of income derives from directly producing by either physical or mental activities, in contrast to those who run or manage enterprises. They are the "white-collar" or "blue-collar" workers. In a narrow sense, "laborer" usually refers to a "blue-collar" employee.

Both in the Chinese labor movement and in the international labor movement, the word "laborer" is not a pejorative term. It is a widely accepted concept. Eighty years ago, during the May Fourth Movement, the pioneer of the democratic revolution, Cai Yuanpei, used the term "the sanctity of labor." Since then, both the Communist Party and labor organi- zations have frequently used this term to mobilize this massive labor class. Under the present transition to the market economy, which has caused a change in labor relations, the labor stratum that seemed to have disappeared for a while has reemerged. Theoretically, the labor stratum constitutes the main portion of the working class. That is why laborers are masters of the state. But in real life, laborers' rights and their social status are to a large extent not respected or protected. This situation is particularly serious in the foreign-funded enterprises. The Zhili fire disaster is one extreme example.

According to incomplete statistical records, between 1992 and 1993 there were over 7,000 complaints of workers' rights violations. Of these, there were more than 1,000 cases of industrial disputes and more than one hundred strikes involving several tens of thousands of workers. Among them was one factory where the conditions were not as bad as Zhili's. But when three strikes broke out and were threatening to escalate, the municipal government reacted swiftly and gave the matter serious attention. On May 28, 1993, the Standing Committee of the Shenzhen People's Congress passed the "Regulations on Labor Conditions in the Shenzhen Special Economic Zone" to try to regulate labor relations. The reality is that labor protection in the SEZ continues to be a serious problem to the extent of adversely affecting the zone's economic and social development.

The tragic events at Zhili should be a catalyst that motivates the government, the employers, and the unions to fulfill their responsibilities and to work together to protect the rights of workers.

First, in their deliberations and rulings on management–worker relations, government representatives must maintain a fair and impartial attitude. Protection of workers' rights is not only a fundamental responsibility of a government, it should be an inherent element in a market economy and a national characteristic of socialist nations. All levels of government must execute their duties fairly, stamp out corruption, and not blindly pursue economic development at the expense of labor.

Second, in their pursuit of profit, employers must both respect and safeguard the rights of their employees. This is not only a legal obligation; it is a prerequisite for both business stability and sustained development. Internationally, there is a growing trend toward a kind of management–labor relationship that is built upon mutual respect and cooperation. Such business practices require people who are moral and have a respect for law, and understand that imposing harm on others can ultimately only harm themselves.

Finally, all unions must address the issue of how best to represent the interests of workers and defend their rights. Especially in the SEZ, unions must make every effort to maintain a fair and level playing field for the workers. Protecting workers, mediating, and stabilizing labor relationships are primarily trade-union functions that help the economy develop. Organizing workers, turning them into a powerful social force, and educating workers so that they become aware of their rights and develop effective means to protect themselves; being of service to the workers; speaking out on their behalf; and taking action when necessary are all responsibilities of the trade union. This is the crucial role that the trade union can play in creating a progressive and stable society and developing a socialist market economy. It is also the trade union's *raison d'être*. The various levels of the Shenzhen city trade union have contributed greatly to this task, but there is much still that needs to be done.

The Shenzhen Zhili fire disaster epitomizes the many loopholes in the current state of labor protection. This fire should have shocked us into realizing that labor protection is not only the urgent task for ensuring economic development in the special economic zones; it is also an immense social, political, and economic problem that awaits resolution in this stage of transition to the market economy.

We believe that no matter what, socialist China should be "the laborers' world" (Li Daqiu's words). "The sanctity of labor" should not be merely a slogan of socialist China, it should also be realized in practice.

CASE 13b

A year after the Zhili fire, six factory and government officials were prosecuted and found guilty.[15] The Hong Kong owner was sentenced to two years in jail, but within a few months he was able to go back to Hong Kong on parole.[16] The wounded survivors received around U.S.$5,500 each from the township government.[17] But the money, as can be seen from this letter written four years later by one of the Zhili survivors describing her life back at home in Sichuan province, could barely compensate for her losses.

This letter was addressed to a staff member of a Hong Kong labor nongovernmental organization (NGO) that has kept in touch with some of the victims, and has been relentlessly staging an international campaign to secure additional compensation for the victims by publicizing the plight of the survivors. The NGO is aware that once publicity and public sympathy subside, those responsible—the Hong Kong investor, the local Chinese government, and individual officials—will seek to get away with paying as little compensation as possible.

The NGO's campaign has also raised the issue of the responsibility of the multinational corporation for which all of the Zhili factory's production was destined. In the era of globalization, NGOs, trade unions, consumer groups, and human rights groups in the developed countries argue that such multinational corporations are responsible for the well-being of the workers who manufacture their products. They should be obliged to monitor the work conditions of their suppliers to ensure that the products are not made by exploited labor. The Zhili Toy Factory fire became the focus of a "Fair Games" campaign that in 1997 finally succeeded in getting the Italian company Artsana S.p.a./Chicco to promise to pay a total of U.S.$180,000 in compensation to the fire victims. This amounts on average to just over $1,000 for each deceased and injured worker, a pittance even by Chinese standards. But it seemed that at least some justice had been achieved.

The Zhili story did not end on this note, however. Artsana S.p.a./Chicco, having enjoyed international publicity for its "responsible behavior," did not deliver on its promise. In 1999, the Hong Kong NGO discovered that the victims still had not received any of the promised money. It had entrusted the funds to the Hong Kong philanthropy Caritas to distribute the money, but with full knowledge of Caritas, the company diverted the money to other charities in China.[18] At present, the NGOs have therefore renewed their international campaign against the Italian toy company.[19] The ongoing Zhili saga underlines the low priority that is paid to the victims of OSH tragedies, not only by corporations that would prefer not to address the issue, but also by charitable organizations.

Four Years Later—A Letter from One of the Survivors

Dear Mr. Shek,

How are you? I received your letter of July 11 on July 30. I was so excited to get your letter that my emotions could not subside for quite some time. Really, several years have passed and you can still remember me. I am just too moved. I sincerely thank you for your concern.

After the fire in Shenzhen in 1993, I stayed in the hospital for half a year. The sufferings of those days took away my courage to live. I was in pain the whole day long, and the psychological burden was unbearable. Day in and day out I was covered in tears. Luckily, there are friends like you to help, support, and encourage us. Only then could I see a glimmer of light. Although the burns could not completely heal after half a year, the government forced us to leave the hospital.[20] What wrong had we done? We can only blame our bad fate. Heaven is so unfair.

The rough journey home reopened all my wounds. Yet the local doctors and hospitals would not take me in. Their verdict was that I was a hopeless case. My family was distraught. In the end, we got a practitioner of Chinese medicine who tried to revive me as if I was a dead cat. I thought I would die. By a stroke of luck, combining Western and Chinese medicine, my life was gradually snatched from the hands of the god of the dead. It took a full two years. But it was even more painful than before. It was like being stuck at the bottom of a well; the whole day long I could only lie in bed unable even to turn my body. I saw no sunlight. Days went by like years. After another half a year, with persistence, I was able to sit in a wheelchair. Then, gradually, I could stumble around with crutches. I tried repeatedly until I could move around with crutches for quite a distance. But I seldom go outside. I dare not go back into society. Of course, I do not walk in the streets at all, scared of people staring, pointing, and talking about me. So all I can do is stay at home and do nothing. Thinking about it, I was naïve. I had thought that once the wounds on my arms and legs were healed, I could go outside. Only now do I realize that arms and legs cannot grow again. I have to learn to accept people's stares. I am still rehabilitating at the county town. But I believe that with your encouragement, I will learn to adapt to society and to life. Thanks for your blessing.

Mister, perhaps you are very busy. What kind of work do you do? Can you tell me? 1997 is the year Hong Kong returns to the motherland. It is also a year of travels. I am sending you a very special stamp that I have saved and cherished. It has the picture of the Great Wall on it. I also hope that you can find time to come to the mainland for a visit. Come here to have a look. On behalf of my family and our village elders, I welcome you to be our guest.

You are such a good person, I wish you good fortune all your life, and that you have the magic touch in whatever you do.

You can phone this telephone number and ask for me: . . .

August 1, 1997
Yours,
Handwritten by Chen Yuying,
someone who knows so little.

Notes

1. *Workers' Daily*, March 31, 1999, p. 8.
2. This is a reference to the enormous statue of Mazu, goddess of the sea, that has recently been erected on Meizhou Island on the coast of Fujian province. The Fujianese are proud that Meizhou is said to be the birthplace of the goddess.
3. Of these three hydrocarbons, benzene is the most toxic and has been banned in many developed countries. Adhesives manufactured in China up to the 1990s still contained a high percentage of benzene. Adhesives manufactured in Taiwan tend to be toluene-based with much less benzene. See Meei-shia Chen and Anita Chan, "China's 'Market Economics in Command': Footwear Workers' Health in Jeopardy," *International Journal of Health Services*, Vol. 29, No. 4, 1999, pp. 793–811.
4. I was in Putian in August 1996, and in one village, where a factory making Nike shoes was located, several villagers I talked to expressed concern about the health of the women working in the factories and the effect on the lychee trees.
5. Ironically, the Mazu statue was built with Taiwanese money that accompanied the Taiwanese investment that poured into the region.
6. The term referring to people's "high" or "low" quality is often used in Chinese to mean people who are educated or less educated. But implicit in the term is the belief that people who have more education are morally superior to those who have less education.
7. Deputy Factory Manager Zheng is probably a manager from the PRC side of the joint venture. As can be seen, although ranked "deputy manager," he has little power in the factory.
8. Within the parentheses is the reporter's rebuttal of the deputy mayor's explanations.
9. The "three capitals" (*sanzi qiye*) refer to fully funded enterprises, cooperation enterprises, and joint ventures.
10. The author related his feelings to me in Beijing in 1996.
11. *Workers' Daily*, December 26, 1993.
12. *Ye Mailing* is a Japanese film that was shown in China in the mid-1980s, about the mistreatment of Japanese workers during the era of Japanese modernization. It was popular with the Chinese audience who could identify with the harsh lives of the workers.
13. Compensation trade is an arrangement whereby the Chinese side adds value to a product and gets back compensation in kind from a foreign business.
14. Subsequent field work undertaken by Anita Chan in the Shenzhen area in 1995, 1996, and 1997 indicated the situation had barely changed.

15. *Workers' Daily*, December 14, 1994.

16. *Ming bao*, September 5, 1997.

17. *Tiantian ribao* (Everyday News), Hong Kong, March 31, 1994.

18. The diversion of the funds was confirmed in a letter from Chicco's law firm to the Hong Kong NGO.

19. See "Toy Campaign: 6th Anniversary of the Zhili Fire, Dossier No. 6, Special Issue," compiled by Asia Monitor Resource Center and the Coalition for the Charter on the Safe Production of Toys, Hong Kong, November 1999. Also see *South China Morning Post*, November 20, 1999, p. 5.

20. On the pressure the local county government applied on the survivors of the fire still in the hospital, see Hong Kong's *Tiantian ribao* (Everyday News), March 31, 1997.

The fortified gates and guard tower of a foreign-owned footwear factory in China.

Migrant workers waiting at a railway station.

Workers are often held virtual prisoners, as in these dormitories covered by iron bars.

Workers making Keds shoes in a factory in Jiangsu province that is owned and managed by South Koreans.

Workers filing out of the Keds shoe factory after a day's work.

Workers from the Yue Yuan company, with metal rice bowls in hand, make their way to the factory gate to punch their time cards for the evening shift. This company in Dongguan, southern China, employs about forty thousand people to make brand-name sneakers, including Nike, Adidas and Reebok.

Migrant workers making shoes in an enterprise owned by a farmer in a village near Shanghai. The filth, exposed wiring, uncovered glue, bare hands and lack of exhaust fans are all clearly evident.

A textile workshop owned by a farmer in Guangdong province's Xiqiao township, a major center for textile production. Workers are not protected against the deafening noise from the old machines.

Migrant workers making bricks at a village outside a country town in Jilin province.

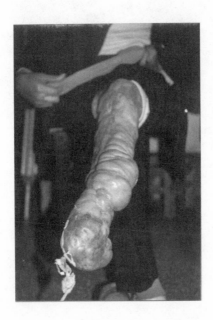

The stump of a Zhili fire victim still awaiting compensation *(see chapter 14, case 13).*

Lawyer Zhou Litai *(fourth from the right)* and some of the workers he shelters while helping them fight for accident compensation *(see chapter 4 on occupational health and safety)*. All of these workers are missing at least one hand.

Chapter 5

Violations of the Right to Work

Serious violations of labor rights and incidents of corporal punishment in state enterprises are not frequently reported by the Chinese press. The problem of being deprived of work in the state sector has become widespread and has received steady media attention. Unemployment is not the only problem. In the cities of China's interior and northeast provinces, reemployment is not only very difficult, but also requires a large sum of cash. When the industrial reforms began, the new labor market was supposed to work on meritocratic principles. One could expect to compete for jobs on the basis of qualifications. But by the mid-1990s, as described in case 14, a different kind of "job market" had emerged. It has become a normal practice to pay a lot of money to buy a good job, or even a job that promises just a steady income. Such jobs are still available in healthy state enterprises, although they have become rare. Other possibilities are to buy a job in one of the new subsidiaries established by state enterprises and large collective enterprises, or in one of the new shareholding companies that some of the state and collective enterprises have been transformed into.[1] If the enterprise appears financially sound, the risk of putting up a year's wages is generally perceived to be worthwhile. Case 15 is a good example of the difficulties confronting workers of a state enterprise that was in the process of transforming ownership.

CASE 14

The department store in this case was established by a local bureaucracy, the city's financial department. While getting rid of some of its old staff, it simultaneously recruited new employees—on the condition they provide capital and fees amounting to about two years' salary. In China a plethora of confusing terminologies has emerged for "raising capital," in which the real intent is extorting money from ordinary people who just want a regular job.

How Should We Evaluate This Kind of "Investment Capital"
Through the Recruitment of Workers? A Report on How
Yanzhou Department Store Hires Employees*

Not too long ago, this paper received a call to our news hotline asking our
reporters to come and investigate the main Yanzhou Department Store in
Shandong province which, during the recruitment of staff in September of last
year, asked every newly recruited staff member to pay 15,000 yuan as an "investment capital fee" (*jizi kuan*) and a further 2,000 yuan in "training fees."

*The Receipts Given to New Staff Members Proved That Each Person Had
Indeed Paid His or Her 15,000 Yuan Capital Fee and 2,000 Yuan Training
Fee, of Which 1,400 Yuan Was Designated as a Security Deposit.*

After receiving this phone call, a reporter rushed to the department store to
look into the case.

This problem started last year around the middle of September, when the
Yanzhou Department Store, under the aegis of the Yanzhou Municipal Gov-
ernment Finance Committee, used 5.7 million yuan to buy the Hua Yuan
Market, located in the southwest corner of Yanzhou's railway station. It was
decided that after renovation the name would be changed to Commercial
Tower. This project was rushed to be completed before the Lunar New Year.

In order to find employees for the Commercial Tower, the Yanzhou Department Store applied to the municipal labor bureau in the latter half of September for permission to hire state workers under a contract system. After obtaining
permission, between September 26 and October 13, the Yanzhou Department
Store administered comprehensive literacy and medical tests to all of those
who registered, and a list of those who passed was made public. At the general
meeting of those who were chosen, the staff of the political-work department
stated that the enterprise was short of capital, so new employees had to pay
15,000 yuan of capital fee, 1,400 yuan of security bond, and 600 yuan as a
training fee within five days. The principal of the capital fee would be returned
in five years, plus 15 percent interest per year. After these amounts were paid
in full, workers had to report to the Yanzhou City Business School for training.
The Yanzhou Department Store recruited a total of 126 new employees, who
then underwent job training and military training, and started work at their
posts on January 28, the opening day of the Commercial Tower.

What needs to be stated here is that the 600 yuan training fee collected

---

* Translation from the Chinese text: Wang Wei, "Zheiyang de zhaogong jizi gai ruhe
kan?—Yanzhou baihuogongsi zhaogong qingkuang caifang lu," *Zhongguo laodong bao*
(China Labor News), May 4, 1996. Translated by Paul Levine.

from new recruits by the Yanzhou Department Store was in accordance with the Shandong Provincial Regulation for Management and Charges for Employment Training.

Why Is There a Need For a Capital Fee? For Its Part, the Enterprise Stated That This Was Necessary to Solve Its Shortage of Capital. In Order to Pay These Capital Fees, the Families of the New Recruits Had to Shoulder a Heavy Burden.

The second day after our reporter arrived in Yanzhou, the general manager of the Yanzhou Department Store, Zhang Haihe, was interviewed to discuss the collection of capital and the reasons behind it. He had been working overtime nonstop for a number of days and was obviously exhausted. He explained: "Our company bought the Hua Yuan Market for administrative and political reasons. The key point is that my company has limited capital. We have no capital to spare other than the 500,000 yuan of deposits that were paid during the signing of the contracts. In order to find capital, I went to many banks in Jinan, Jining, and Yanzhou City. But because they are in their fourth quarter, the banks would not loan any money, so I returned empty-handed. As a result, after the company's board of directors met and reviewed the situation, they decided to borrow money from all of our employees. The employees in current employment each paid 5,000 yuan, and the new recruits paid 15,000 yuan. These will be returned with principal plus interest by the end of five years at the rate of 15 percent per annum. This capital loan plus the municipal government's financing enabled us to pay in full the amount needed to buy the property rights to the Hua Yuan Market. Of course, lower-level staff could not tell the difference between the concepts of finance capital and investment capital, so it was all written up as "investment capital fees." As for the security deposit, it was collected according to the company's usual practice, and as all of the existing employees had paid this, why shouldn't we collect this from the new recruits?

On the same day that Zhang Haihe was interviewed, our reporter also separately interviewed the parents of some of the new recruits.

The father of one new recruit, a retired worker from a state-run enterprise, said that the recruitment of his daughter cost him half of his life savings, and he had also borrowed 10,000 yuan from her uncle in the village. He said that it was understandable to collect money from new recruits, since the enterprise was short of capital, but the amount should not be too large.

Another father is an employee of a state-run enterprise. He said: "I only receive a monthly salary of 320 yuan. My wife is jobless and we have to bring up three children. How can I save anything? I had to borrow money from six other families to cover the 14,000 yuan for my daughter. I borrowed the last 3,000 yuan from my work unit. "After my daughter's recruitment, I told my second son, 'you go into the army as a cadet next year.' I heard you don't need money to get a job after being a soldier. I don't know what the world is coming to when you need that much money to get a job!"

Is This Investment Capital (jizi) or Is It Finance Capital (rongzi)? The Government Departments Concerned Have Different Opinions.

The head of the Finance Committee for Yanzhou city, Bai Fengling, thinks that "the capital collected during the recruitment process was finance capital, not investment capital. This is because finance capital involves paying back both the principal and the interest, but investment capital is nonreturnable. Another point is that we don't merely use the ability to pay money as the condition for recruiting workers. Borrowing funds from the staff to help a company get over a rough patch when it is in trouble is a way to realize the spirit of 'the worker being the master.' It also accords with the municipal government's general guideline to try to use the uncommitted capital in society. As for collecting a employee security deposit from employees, all of our enterprises are doing it, so what's wrong?"

The head of the labor bureau, Kong Fanrui, was of the opinion that "this kind of activity should be classified as raising investment capital from recruits, since one of the conditions for their participation in the training course is their ability to pay the 15,000 yuan capital fee and the 1,400 yuan security deposit." He said that the labor bureau had reported this problem to the municipal government many times. On December 5 last year, in the published summary to the major reexamination of the implementation of the Labor Law, the labor bureau reported to the National People's Congress and the municipal government that "there was a strong reaction from employees about enterprises asking for capital at the time of recruitment. Out of all the municipal and township enterprises in Yanzhou county that were examined, twenty-one collected differing amounts of money in this manner."

The deputy Party secretary of the Yanzhou City Party Committee, who is also the city's deputy mayor responsible for labor matters, thinks that this phenomenon of raising capital at the time of recruitment is a problem of the economic-development process. Due to the shrinking of state credit and enterprises lacking in capital, at present a minority of enterprises collect "investment capital fees," while most use finance capital, and some issue shares.

To change labor relations from management by administrative fiats to management by law, it is very important to differentiate between creative internal management and the strict observance of the law.

So how should we look at this recruitment of capital carried out by the Yanzhou Department Store? After our reporter returned to Beijing, experts in this field were interviewed for their opinions on this matter.

The division chief of the department under the Ministry of Labor responsible for labor relations and monitoring labor disputes, Fan Zhanjiang, systematically analyzed the way the Yanzhou Department Store recruits employees and raises capital:

> I feel that in reality this is a capital-borrowing activity undertaken within the enterprise. Why do I say this? First, the scope of this capital raising is targeted at the entire staff within the enterprise. Second, this capital has interest, and the principal will be returned at a specific date and is not noncompensatory. Third, the list of recruits was drawn up based on the results of a physical checkup and an entrance examination. However, when carrying out this activity of raising capital within the enterprise, the Yanzhou Department Store was not very rigorous in some areas. Borrowing capital should take place under voluntary principles and should not be mixed in with the process of recruitment.

Fan Zhanjiang also said that in the process of collecting a security deposit from new recruits, the Yanzhou Department Store committed a procedural error. According to the letter dated July 3 of last year from the general office of the Ministry of Labor and the general office of the State Economic and Trade Commission, which was in response to a "request for instructions about whether or not to stop the practice in an employing unit of requiring employees to pay security-type monies or buy shares," it is specified that when a work unit, based on its specific management needs, is permitted to collect security deposits from its staff and workers on a voluntary basis after labor relations have been established, the collection is not a violation of the Labor Law. However, the employing unit cannot use the threat of terminating labor relations as a means to force its staff to pay this deposit. This is a process that should be carried out on a voluntary basis only after labor relations are set up. This is mainly to guarantee that the employing unit and the laborer enter the process of establishing labor relations on a basis of equality.

The opinion of Zhou Wanling, head of the legal consulting division of the Legal Affairs Department in the All-China Federation of Trade Unions, is that to be employed is a realization of the citizen's right to work. This is clearly defined in the state constitution and in the Labor Law. When an enterprise recruits workers after being granted permission by the Labor Department, the enterprise can draw up specific requirements, such as the level of education and the height of employees, but it definitely cannot attach conditions relating to raising capital. This method used by the Yanzhou Department Store also exists in other places as well. In reality, these units are demanding capital as a condition for recruitment, and the result is that they are disenfranchising the labor rights of those who cannot pay these fees. Relevant departments should pay a high degree of attention to this problem.

The collection of an internal security deposit by enterprises is also against the law. Our country's existing statutes stipulate labor responsibility, which includes completing production tasks abiding by enterprise regulations, and so on, but definitely not paying security deposits. The law is strict and new content cannot be added at will. Although there are those in Yanzhou who say that borrowing capital by an enterprise is a way of realizing workers' consciousness as masters, Zhou thinks that this view is erroneous. True, under a market economy, the benefits of the staff and workers and the enterprise are often linked, but "internal capital borrowing" and the establishment of labor relations should not be taken as interconnected. The borrowing of capital is within the realm of civil relations, while labor recruitment falls within the realm of labor relations. If the two are mixed, then this practice should be assessed and judged in accordance with the Labor Law.

I asked other experts for their opinions on this matter, but they felt that it was relatively complicated and hard to get a handle on, so they were unwilling to express their opinions. This reflects the fact that the period of switching from administrative management to the current management of labor relations has been relatively short. Many entrepreneurs—and even experts—find it hard to differentiate the boundaries between being creative and enterprising in management practices and observing the law. This is a major question that should invite a high degree of attention.

Comments

There are several interesting points to note about this new department store. Although no longer an old-style state enterprise, it is a subsidiary of a local state "bureaucracy," and still has a number of state-enterprise trappings. It still has close ties with its supervisory bureaucracy and officials, and when recruiting employees, it needed approval from the local labor bureau. The enterprise still has a political-work department (zhenggong ke), which no longer carries out the role it had in Maoist times (e.g., propagating Communist Party documents and imposing ideological control), but nonetheless is an intra-enterprise institution with authority and power. It was this department, not the personnel department, that announced to the successful job applicants that they needed to pay 17,000 yuan each to obtain a job. Notably, it used the rhetoric of collective good although it was no longer a state enterprise.

On the other hand, the new department store adopted quite a few of the practices of non-state enterprises. For example, it made new recruits go through a program of military-style training, similar to that run by Taiwanese-funded enterprises in China.[2] It collected a security fee, similar to the "deposit" deducted from the wages of migrant workers in non-state enterprises (see Chapter 2). The training fee and security fee, which amounted to about four months' salary, would certainly have deterred new recruits from leaving even if they found working conditions intolerable. But the main purpose of collecting these fees was to underwrite the new venture's lack of capital. In this respect, these "deposits" were not the same as the deposits demanded of migrants. The employees in this case were local people with residential rights. And the amount that was required was many times greater than the sum demanded from migrant workers. Migrants could not afford to pay that much, but urban families, desperate to find work, scraped together the money to buy a job. The more widespread this phenomenon has become, the more people seem to accept it as the norm. This is reflected in the remark made by the father of one of the new recruits that, "it is understandable to collect money from new recruits since the enterprise was short of capital." Notably, "training fees" in this locality have become so common that they have been accepted and legalized by the local authorities in contravention of national regulations.

It is interesting to compare the different positions the various officials took over the legality of raising capital from recruits. Their interpretations of the law varied depending on the bureaucracy they worked for. The city financial committee had a stake in the department store, therefore, the chair argued that what they were collecting was really finance capital, which is legal, not investment capital, which is illegal. The city labor bureau chief, as an overseer of industrial relations, on the other hand, classed this activity as "raising investment capital from recruits." In fact, the labor bureau had told higher level authorities earlier that this practice was a problem. The Party secretary of the city admitted that the practice was improper, but argues its inevitability, because accumulating capital is necessary for economic development. As a Party secretary, he could not be too blatantly pro-management, but being an official with a vested interest in development, he cleverly chose a middle road that fit his position and interests. At the national level, the official from the Ministry of Labor took a similarly neutral-sounding stance. Although his interpretation favored management more than labor, he was extremely adept at using legalistic language. The pro-labor stance of the legal consultant of the ACFTU, on the other hand, was unequivocal. He condemned this kind of practice as a violation of labor rights in a sociopolitical climate where the expression "labor rights" needs to be used with caution. One important development highlighted by this report is that China's political system has changed from being monolithic to being fragmented by bureaucratic interests.

It could be asked why the department store wanted to buy a shopping mall when it did not have the capital. Instead, it preferred to violate state regula-tions by forcing its employees to lend the company money. One legal and fair way to go about this would have been to distribute shares to the employees by turning the company into a kind of shareholding cooperative. This would have meant the employees would have partly owned the company; making them pay, but not giving them shares, deprived them of the right of ownership.

CASE 15

This article describes how the foreign partners of a joint venture that had formerly been a state enterprise laid off all the company's workers. Rules and regulations exist to protect workers in such circumstances, especially older workers. Workers are supposed to have some say in the transition pro-cess—the staff and workers representative committee is supposed to be con-sulted, and the trade-union chair has a right to representation on the newly created board of directors. The problem is that very seldom do workers and trade-union representatives fight for these rights. Very often, management's power meets with no resistance.

This case is unusual in that the state enterprise did not have a workplace trade union. One emerged out of the workers' strike, although the details are not provided in the article. The chair put up a battle under the most adverse circum-stances—when the foreign investor was determined to lay off all of the 1,100 employees. Individual trade-union officials who have the courage to take a stand are fighting a losing battle in an environment that is so adverse to labor.

NOT A SINGLE ONE OF THE 1,100 EMPLOYEES OF SHENYANG CITY'S HARMONY COMPANY ESCAPED THE MISFORTUNE OF A MASS LAY-OFF—WITHOUT DISCUSSIONS WITH THE BOARD OF DIRECTORS AND STAFF AND WORKERS REPRESENTATIVE COMMITTEE*

The Scale of These Layoffs Is Rare. The Axe Also Fell on the Head of the Union. This Incident Has Aroused Concern in Many Quarters and People Are Waiting to See the Outcome.

On April 26, a notice of two-hundred-plus words posted on the side of the Shenyang Harmony Department Store announced the store's decision to can-cel labor contracts and lay off more than one thousand one hundred employ-

---

* Translation from the Chinese Text: Hou Yongdong, "Shenyang 'xiehe' da caiyuan, yi qian yi bai ming yuangong wuyi xingmian—meijing dongshihui he zhigong daibiaohui taolun," *Liaoning zhigong bao* (Liaoning Staff Paper), June 3, 1996. Translated by Paul Levine.

ees, including the store's trade-union chair. According to our understanding, this is the largest number of layoffs at one time at one enterprise since the founding of the PRC.

From interviews, our reporter understood that the store is owned by a commercial joint venture made up of the former Shenyang Northern Trade Tower and a solely owned, foreign-invested enterprise, Harmony Department Store Company Ltd. All of the one thousand one hundred employees were originally employees of the Northern Trade Tower. The store's trade-union chair and its committee members were carefully evaluated before being elected by the staff and workers representative committee and the trade-union committee on May 18, 1995. This was later approved by upper-level departments. The whole process was in complete accordance with the Trade Union Law.

According to our understanding, this large-scale layoff was the sole decision of the foreign partner of the store, and was not discussed by the board members and the staff and workers representative committee.

According to Ms. Jiang Baohua, the chair of the store's trade union, on April 23, a representative from the foreign partner sent a staff member from the personnel office to inform her that the store was going to lay off female employees over forty years of age and male employees over fifty years of age—a total of more than one hundred fifty people. Jiang Baohua immediately expressed the opinion that this was not in accordance with the present national "Double-ten" policy (employees who have worked more than ten years and who still have ten or more years to go before the legal retirement age have the right to sign long-term contracts and contracts for unspecified lengths of time).

The foreign representative said to Jiang Baohua, "You only need to attend the decision-making meeting and you don't have to speak." Seeing this, Jiang refused to attend this meeting. Three days later, the decision to lay off all of the one thousand one hundred employees became official.

According to the foreign representative, the term "lay off" (*cai yuan*) is not the right word for the situation; rather it should be termed a "termination" of labor contracts. His reasoning is that the signed labor contract between staff members and the store began on the January 1, 1994, and ended on December 31, 1995, a total of two years. When the contract term is up, not renewing the contract with staff and workers is a legal action. However, according to related laws and policy regulations of the PRC, the enterprise should notify staff members one month before the expiration of a labor contract as to whether or not the enterprise intends to renew the contract with them. In this case, the store was in continuous operation for four months after the completion of the contracts, and paid another three-months' salary to employees before management announced what they called a "nonrenewal of contract" decision. Relevant departments of the Shenyang Municipal Labor Bureau clearly state that this type of situation and the contents of that notice do not constitute a termination of contract, but rather, that this is a situation in which employees are laid off, even though the notice emphasized that this decision was made for the survival and development of the enterprise. It was a reorganization effort to solve current problems. But to lay off so many people in one stroke is seen as unacceptable by the staff and workers and all sectors of society.

The foreign representative stated that the store's joint-management agreement clearly spells out the right of the foreign representatives to terminate labor contracts and to lay off staff members; therefore, this decision should be considered as normal. But at the same time, the agreement also states that any major decisions require discussion by the board of directors, and laying off more than a thousand people at one time is definitely not a minor matter.

During the interview, the head of the trade union, Ms. Jiang, filled in some of the background to the dispute. When the store was initially set up, the foreign partner promised staff members a minimum wage of 500 yuan, but before the Lunar New Year last year, the foreign party independently decided to lower the minimum wage to 200 yuan, and to set the remaining 300 yuan as a floating wage. This decision caused the employees to go on strike, and the store to close for three days. The trade union was created after pressing demands from the employees, and with the mediation of higher-level bureaucracies. She said that even though the trade union had been formed, it was only an ornament and it had no say in policy decisions, not to speak of democratic monitoring or control. The foreign party requested that the trade union organize union activities outside of the eight-hour workday. But the nature of the enterprise determines that the possibility to do this is minimal.

All along, the foreign side never contributed a single cent toward union operating costs,[3] and the union does not even have its own bank account. At the end of last year, the union tried to organize a cultural night to raise funds, also planning to hold a question-and-answer game show related to the Labor Law and the Trade Union Law, but it was canceled because the union could not get the foreign partner's approval.

Our reporters talked to a few female employees in front of the store who were still arriving at work, but had been barred from entering the shop. According to the workers, when the store was first opened, more than ten employees fainted due to the chemical fumes given off by the construction materials piled inside the shop, but management did nothing about it. Since the store opened for business, employees were not even able to enjoy their entitlements such as a supplementary stipend for inflation and extra money to cover working during seasonal hot and cold spells. Working extra shifts and hours had become normal but overtime pay, as stipulated by the law, did not exist. What made the employees all the more furious was that telephone fees incurred by the various departments in the shop were deducted from staff and workers' salaries at an average of approximately 20 yuan per month per person. The union tried repeatedly to approach the foreign party about these problems, but with no success.

During the last couple of days, when some employees continued to come to work but were denied entry, they waited outside on the steps and insisted on going to Jiang Baohua to sign in. The demand was very simple: "We want to work, and we should not lose our jobs without just cause or reason." Jiang Baohua also said, "Nobody can fire me from my position as chair of the trade union except the staff and workers representative committee."

At present, all of the relevant government departments in the city are actively trying to mediate a resolution to the problems. All levels of society are watching closely to see when the Northern Trade Tower will again open for business, when the 1,100 employees can return to their posts, and when the head of the trade union will be able to resume her duties.

Comments

In a follow-up newspaper report twenty days after this was published, the stalemate had still not been resolved.[4] That the protest could drag on for so long reflected the workers' ability to use the trade-union structure to fight for their legal rights. But in an environment so hostile to labor, even the most resolute protest is likely to fail. This case does illustrate, though, that democratically elected trade-union officials can take their jobs seriously. That is why, no matter how weak the trade unions and their officials, managers of all stripes are not willing to tolerate their presence—just in case the trade unionist turns out to be a fighter. Notably, the number of unions at state enterprises declined from 194,760 in 1996 to 154,593 in 1997; and state-sector union membership fell from 58 million in 1996 to 51 million in 1997.[5]

Notes

1. For details on why these subsidiaries are generally profitable see Ding Xueliang, "The Illicit Asset Stripping of Chinese State Firms," *The China Journal*, No. 43, January 2000, pp. 1–28.

2. Anita Chan, "Boot Camp at the Shoe Factory: Where Taiwanese Bosses Drill Chinese Workers to Make Sneakers for American Joggers," *Washington Post*, November 3, 1996, p. C1.

3. According to the Trade Union Law, workplace unions are entitled to receive 2 percent of the enterprise's payroll.

4. *Laodong daobao* (Labor Bulletin), June 22, 1996.

5. *Zhongguo gonghui tongji nianjian* (The Chinese Trade Union Yearbook, 1997), Beijing: State Statistical Bureau, 1998, pp. 99 and 106; and *The Chinese Trade Union Yearbook, 1998*, pp. 108 and 119.

Chapter 6

Violations of the Right to Organize and of Collective Action

We have observed that when workers can no longer tolerate the situation in their factories they tend to informally seek outside help—from the media, the government, the local labor bureau, or the trade union. There is a state-regulated structure and procedure that workers can resort to. This avenue to resolve conflict with management has become more and more common. The Chinese Industrial Relations Regulation, passed in 1993, required workplace industrial-mediation committees to be set up to resolve as many conflicts as possible before resorting to arbitration beyond the workplace level. The mediation committee is to be composed of representatives from the staff and workers representative committee, the enterprise, and the workplace trade union; with a union representative presiding over the committee. If unresolved, the conflict can go to an industrial-arbitration committee made up of representatives from the locality's labor department, trade union, and a government bureaucracy in charge of economic affairs. After 1993, cases of industrial conflicts increased by more than 50 percent a year; the rise is much more rapid for collective disputes than individual disputes.[1] By 1999, a total of 270,000 mediation committees and more than three thousand arbitration committees of various levels had been set up in China.[2] In the first half of the year, the arbitration committees dealt with 55,244 cases, involving 230,000 people. This was a 58 percent and 71 percent increase, respectively, from the first half of 1998.[3] At the time of writing, the results of these cases were not available. But in previous years, workers have tended to win. For example, in 1995, 52 percent of employers lost their cases compared with 20 percent of workers. In 1996, employers won in only 20 percent of cases.[4] That is to say, workers stand a good chance of winning if they appeal through the proper channels.

Case 16 shows an example of how employees of a branch of the Bank of China tried to utilize this legal structure and collectively sought arbitration outside the workplace.

Case 17 is an example of a collective action that was considered by the authorities as having gone beyond the law—a few young intellectuals attempting to organize migrant workers as part of their political agenda to bring democracy in China.

CASE 16

This case discusses an attempt at genuine collective bargaining, initiated from the grassroots in a state enterprise, that was ultimately crushed by management and local authorities. The incident occurred in a branch of the Bank of China in a remote county town in Guangdong province. The story is a firsthand account from the perspective of a reporter of the Southern Daily, *Guangdong's Party newspaper. The account of the struggle between the reporter and the local authorities is symbolic of the struggle between good and evil in today's China.*

The kind of venue in which this incident happened partly determined the outcome of this labor dispute. In remote outback areas, those in power are omnipotent and blasé about the law. The reporter had a premonition of the hostility that would await him before he left Guangzhou to cover the story. So he took a friend along, a reporter from the China Youth News, *a popular newspaper known for its candid investigative reports. Like two policemen on the beat, always in pairs in a rough neighborhood, the two ventured forth. No harm came to them. But to challenge powers that be with probing pro-labor questions, they needed courage and mutual support. They had to know when to flaunt the power of the media and the right to freedom of the press, and when to use the higher status and authority endowed to them by virtue of being from the seat of provincial power, the provincial Party committee. These all had to be signaled to their opponents with finesse at appropriate moments.*

In the course of the reporters' investigation, the alignment of power within the hierarchical structure became obvious. The bureaucracies and officials who were sympathetic to the workers, or at least willing to mouth the norms set down by the Labor Law, were the county labor bureau and its industrial-relations arbitration committee, the county-level trade union and its legal department, and the county court. Siding with management were the county government, the county Party committee, the county-level financial sector trade union, the local police, and the national headquarters of the Bank of China. But in the end, the former had to succumb to the power of the latter. The arbitration committee rescinded its original ruling that was in the employees' favor. The protagonist of the industrial dispute, a bank teller, lost her job. The reporter's newspaper continued to lend support to the workers.

It openly ridiculed and challenged the Bank of China by carrying the scandalous story on the very page the bank had its advertisement. In the end, media publicity proved helpless when it came up against those in power.

POWER AND THE LAW: WHO MISTREATS WHOM?*

As a reporter for Guangdong's *Southern Weekend*, I get a special kick out of going to the letters department to read incoming mail. For any reporter who cares about society, readers' letters are undoubtedly a source of information. One day last August, I was spending the morning browsing in the letters department when a letter from a cadre in the Nanxiong county branch of the Bank of China caught my attention. The letter revealed that on May 8 last year, eight off-duty tellers from the branch presented a petition to the manager signed by all the branch's tellers. It asked the manager to address the long-standing issue of employees' rest days and night shifts.

Until two years ago, the tellers had enjoyed one day's rest every week, as stipulated by state regulations. But in 1993, the bank branch laid down new rules requiring them to work every day, 365 days a year, without a full day's break. In addition, every night there had to be someone on night shift, and whoever that was had to continue working the following day. Either one man or two women could do the night shift, and the chief teller was exempted. The tellers would rotate through the morning, afternoon, and night shifts in a cycle throughout the year.

When conventional channels failed to win the attention of the tellers' superiors, the public-spirited Liu Guangwen led an initiative to present a petition to their superiors expressing the shared concerns of the tellers. The petition began with "esteemed leaders," and then immediately affirmed that "under the correct leadership of the bank's management, and with the united effort of all the staff, business has flourished and the economic gains have been heartening. This is the spirit that has inspired the front-counter tellers." Then the petition used the mildest language to point out that the tellers had not had any days off for a long time and their night shifts were too frequent. Finally, it expressed the hope that management would consider giving the staff "four days off a month" and also "arrive at a reasonable solution of the problem of night shifts."

In response to the petition's two requests, the manager, Liu Dan, immediately agreed to giving tellers two days off a month; she said that the issue of night shifts required the collective consideration of management. For a time, the tellers' hopes were raised. But they became uneasy when it was clear that

---

* Translation from the Chinese text: Zhu Defu, "Quanli he falu: daodi shei buxiangxin shei," *Shanghai wentan* (Shanghai Literary Forum), December 1996, pp. 23–27. Translated by Christopher Buckley.

management was not honoring its promises. On May 18, eleven off-duty tellers went again to the manager's office and asked Liu Dan what was happening. This time, Liu's tone had unexpectedly hardened. She berated the staff: "Go and write a self-criticism. And write down exactly how this illegal assembly of yours happened."

That afternoon, the bank management notified the entire staff of a meeting that night. The assistant manager, Zeng Qingliang, announced: "This action of yours was concerted, premeditated, and planned. It was an illegal action with political overtones. The ringleader has been removed from her duties to think things over. Everyone who took part in this action must write a self-criticism, and must take the initiative to cooperate with the internal inquiry."

On June 12, the Nanxiong branch of the Bank of China concluded that the incident was:

> provoked by a handful of people using the pretext of a widespread desire of bank tellers to increase their rest time after the implementation of the five-day work system. Hiding behind falsehoods and disobeying their section leaders, they used liaising, assemblies, and petition delegations to directly intimidate management. Their unreasonable demands gravely damaged the reputation of the Bank of China.

Based on this verdict, Liu Guangwen was to be punished by dismissal. She was given three months to find a new employer, and during that time would only receive the basic wage. After that, there would be no reconsideration: all her wages and welfare payments would be stopped and she would be forced to resign. Of the two other staff members who were active in this incident, one was punished by having it recorded in her records, and the other by administrative warning. Both also had three months of bonuses deducted from their wages. The several Communist Party members who took part received internal Party disciplining.

Over the next fortnight, all of the bank tellers lived in dread. More or less every teller who signed the petition was individually spoken to by the bank management. They were ordered to "confess" any extremist statements Liu Guangwen had made, and then to sign their "confessions." It was at this time that, at the request of the bank management, the internal-security police of Nanxiong County Public Security Bureau also began investigating whether the incident was political in nature. Later, it was decided that categorizing the incident as political was too tenuous, and so no such allegations were made.

But sustained by her faith in the law, Li Guangwen began the arduous task of appeals and petitions. In her appeals to the authorities, she defended herself thus:

> Firstly, enterprise employees have a right under national law to make reasonable requests in writing to their superiors. Clause 41 of the constitution stipulates that: "Citizens of the PRC have the right to offer criticisms and suggestions to state organs and personnel." Clause 49 of the Enterprise Law stipulates that: "Employees have the right to participate in the democratic management of enterprises. They have the right to make complaints and suggestions about production and work." Secondly, clause 36 of the Labor Law demands that the work hours of workers do not exceed forty hours a week. The work hours of the front-counter tellers of the Nanxiong branch of the Bank of China have exceeded the limit set by the Labor Law by 23.2 hours, and they exceed the limits set by Order 174 of the State Council by 27.2 hours. Clause 3 of the Labor Law stipulates that workers have a right to rest and vacations; clause 38 stipulates that employers should ensure that workers have no less than one day's rest a week. But the tellers of the Nanxiong branch have not enjoyed this right for almost two years.

In response to accusations of the "misdeeds" committed by the staff, Liu Guangwen had more to say in her defense. First, the petition to the bank management conveyed in written form the heartfelt concerns of all the tellers, and stated that "expressing their opinions is the right of every citizen." Describing this as a "disgraceful incident" was clearly not in keeping with the law. Second, management said that Liu Guangwen "hid behind falsehoods and surreptitiously stirred up uninformed workers to assemble and petition." Actually, prior to these events, the staff had repeatedly approached the section management with their problems and bent over backward for them. And what law is there to say that employees cannot directly approach their superiors with their problems? Since the issue of employees' rest days had been around for many years, what was so "misleading" about it? Third, the petitioners were accused of "intending to stir up trouble in massed assemblies and strikes," and "scheming to pick a day to assemble in front of the bank before the vaults were opened with the clear intention of striking." This was a vestige of the Cultural Revolution: the tendency to shoot first and ask questions later.

In mid-May, in keeping with the spirit of the Labor Law, Liu Guangwen presented a written appeal to Nanxiong County Labor Bureau's Labor Arbitration Committee. It requested that the committee conduct a truthful investigation of the whole affair and render a just verdict. At the same time, Liu Guangwen also sent this appeal documentation to the *Southern Daily*, without writing a separate letter of appeal to the newspaper. Her intention was that she was sending the newspaper a formal copy of the document that was sent to the Labor Arbitration Committee.

Having read the letter, I talked it over with the head of the letters-to-the-editor department, Li Changhui. Li encouraged me to look into the affair. When I contacted Liu Guangwen at a phone number given in the letter, she recounted in detail the course of events and her own reactions, and I felt that her ordeal was sure to rouse people's compassion. As the reporter for one of the Party's newspapers, it was my duty to give her a fair hearing.

When I was discussing this with other leaders, however, they believed that despite the fact that the story was newsworthy, it was also extremely sensitive and they warned me to be careful. It was then that I had some misgivings, and I put off researching the story for a long while. In these months, Liu Guangwen bombarded me with phone calls, keeping me up to date on developments and her own hardships. Finally, my conscience as a reporter was stirred and in late October 1995, I decided to make a trip to Nanxiong. My good friend and Guangdong reporter for the *China Youth News*, Lin Wei, gave me support and solidarity during this trip. Not for the first time, we set out together as a team.

By train from Guangzhou to Shaoguan, and from there to Nanxiong by bus, is a journey of several hundred kilometers. It took us a whole day, setting out in the morning at a bit past seven and arriving in Nanxiong at a bit past seven in the evening. Nanxiong is in the far north of the undeveloped mountain region of northern Guangdong, bordering on Jiangxi. The economic mainstay of the county is tobacco. Economic backwardness and distance from the central powers invariably encourages dominance by power holders. Like the bandit kings of old, their power has been unfettered.

It is the practice of the *Southern Daily* not to seek out the local press secretary or even the reporter stationed in an area when doing a critical report, so as to avoid putting them in an awkward spot or affecting their careers. But out of politeness, when I arrived in Nanxiong, I contacted the local press secretary, Zeng Tao. I explained in some detail the objectives of my visit in order to get his views about the incident. Initially, Zeng Tao was very friendly. The following day he arranged an interview with the heads of the bank. We had heard Zeng was very busy, and we knew all too well that it would not be appropriate to get him involved in an interview of this sort. We suggested that he go on with his other work and not bother about us. But Zeng Tao insisted on sending someone else from his office, Little Zhang, who it was rumored was undergoing training to take over as press secretary.

Having heard and considered Liu Guangwen's appeal on July 17, the Labor Arbitration Committee of Nanxiong county determined that the actions of enterprise employees who express opinions to their superiors and make reasonable requests are protected by law. If what she said was wrong, it concluded, it was only the way in which it was said that made it difficult for her superiors to accept. The committee members unanimously determined that the Nanxiong bank's punishment of Liu Guangwen was excessive and not in keeping with the seven conditions justifying the dismissal of state enterprise employees. On August 14, the panel convened a mediation session between the parties.

The bank refused mediation and presented the following reply. First, the work hours of the tellers had never exceeded those laid out in the Labor Law, because the night shifts were done at the request of police authorities and did not count as work hours. Second, employees' democratic management of an enterprise can only be exercised through the staff and workers representative congress, otherwise it is unlawful. Third, the appellant had entered the bank manager's office during her work hours and had severely disrupted the administrator's normal work duty. Fourth, the bank's own investigation after the event proved that the appellant had repeatedly made "statements with malicious intent" throughout the activities.

The key to deciding whether the Nanxiong branch's handling of the affair was correct depended on two issues: whether the night shifts of the staff counted as work hours (and hence whether the request of the staff was reasonable), and whether staff could directly raise complaints and suggestions with their superiors in written form (and hence whether the behavior of the staff was lawful).

On October 26, we went to the office of the bank manager, Liu Dan. To our astonishment, Liu Dan, who had made such a brutal decision, turned out to be a refined and demure woman, about thirty years old. We had heard that several hundred thousand yuan had been spent on redecorating the bank manager's office, and the imposing grandeur could lead you to think it was not a bank in a poor mountain district. We cut straight to the question of whether night shifts counted as work hours. Liu replied vehemently: "How could the night shifts count as work hours? It wasn't us who told the staff to turn up. It was the police who demanded that we do it. On night shift, you don't have to use a computer. You can chat, sleep, watch TV. It's not the same as going to work."

The reporter then asked: "So, are night shifts optional for employees? Can you not take up the job?"

"You must be joking!" Liu Dan blurted out without careful thought, "How on earth could they come and go as they please? If anything goes wrong, it's their responsibility." According to the relevant judicial interpretations, rest time refers to the time when workers can arrange their time as they see fit without the need to engage in production and work. As a young female bank manager, Liu Dan had her difficulties: "Their demands aren't totally unreasonable. But if we went along with them, it would be tough. That's the truth." When asked what she thought of the arbitration committee's recommendation of mediation, Liu Dan replied dismissively, "The fact that the labor authorities didn't take Liu Guangwen's scheme to go on strike seriously is only because the strike didn't occur. But if we didn't prevent her, she might have caused a real storm."

Mr. Zeng, a deputy manager, sitting by her side, added: "These days the labor bureau doesn't have any standards to stick to. They're bone idle and spend the day thinking of ways to make trouble using the Labor Law."

Under the persistent questioning of reporters, Liu Dan possibly came to recognize she had treated Liu Guangwen too heavy-handedly, but she would not admit her mistake. Her excuse was: "How can a work unit apologize to an individual? If we admitted our mistakes, what authority would the leaders be left with?" When seeing us out the door, she delicately pleaded with us not to write a report: "Otherwise our bank will be seen as weak-kneed. Keeping things under control takes priority over everything else."

To prove the correctness of her actions, Liu Dan pressed us to interview the county's financial sector trade-union chair. Only after we arrived at the county People's Bank did we discover that the union chair was a nonsense position filled by a deputy manager from the bank. The chair (representing the interests of labor) and the bank manager (representing the interests of capital) had been fused into one. This was truly a trade-union organization with Chinese characteristics. Whether the trade union could effectively represent the interests of workers was highly doubtful. Zhang Yunpeng, the bank manager-cum-trade-union chair, took the same view of the matter as the Bank of China. His disgust with Liu Guangwen carried heavy emotional overtones: "From my perspective as a deputy bank manager, this type of employee simply can't be allowed to exist. That would be disastrous. I'm not sure whether that's the law or not, but if you work in a bank your monthly wages are more than those of a county head. And then you still demand rest days. That's just absolutely unconscionable." Deputy Manager Zhang placed himself in the position of a leading manager without showing any signs of embarrassment; these were not a union chair's words of support for Liu Guangwen. This type of trade-union chairperson was simply an insult to the term "trade union." When I pointed out that the way the matter would finally be handled depended on the County Arbitration Committee, Zhang struck back: "Even if the verdict was overturned that won't make a difference. Nowadays it's not hard to get rid of someone. When it comes time to reduce staff numbers we can reduce you, or we can get the personnel department to transfer you to a failing enterprise." He was saying in so many words that whoever dared to offend management would have to bear the consequences. Interestingly though, Deputy Manager Zhang's son is one of the bank's tellers who signed the petition. "I told him not to take part, but he just had to go and do it. What a son of a bitch." Zhang's face was filled with hatred toward his unfilial son.

When they were interviewed, the deputy chairperson of the Nanxiong County Trade Unions Federation, Huang Shixia, and the head of the federation's Legal Department, Zhu Xingfa, both believed that Liu Guangwen and others were legally entitled to collectively make written complaints and requests to their superiors. The petition expressed the shared desires and requests of all the bank tellers and there was nothing questionable in it. The Bank of China's treatment of Liu Guangwen was excessive. Huang and Zhu's attitude to the burning question of whether night shifts counted as work hours was unequivocal: "Of course night shifts count as work hours." Zhu Xingfa said with deep feeling: "This should never have been a big deal. But Little Liu was too impatient. She changed the request into a petition only to highlight the importance of the issue and catch the attention of management. But all that did was provoke them. The word 'petition' is too thorny, and it easily leads people to associate it with something more serious."

The trade-union deputy chair, Huang Shixia, said the bank was plainly distorting the law in accusing Liu Guangwen of engaging in illegal activities simply because her request did not go through the staff and workers representative congress. Here, Huang raised another doubt: "As far as I know, the bank branch hasn't convened an employees' congress for two or three years. How are employees supposed to raise their requests?"

The head of the arbitration section of the Nanxiong County Labor Bureau, Zhang Xuyu, observed that the Bank of China's treatment of the appellant was clearly inappropriate. This was shown in two main ways. The first was in politicizing the issue and using political terms at the drop of a hat. As soon as the bank saw the word "petition" they became neurotic. Second, the bank was too heavy-handed and did not follow the relevant state laws and regulations. Zhang explained that after receiving Liu Guangwen's appeal on July 17, the full arbitration committee met on October 18. The members unanimously agreed that this "petition" incident expressed the personal interests and reasonable requests of the employees, and it was in keeping with the Labor Law. Although some people said things not beneficial to unity and went about it inappropriately by choosing the format of petitioning, the Bank of China inflated the issue into something far too grave. Liu Guangwen's actions did not constitute one of the seven types of behavior that are reasonable grounds for dismissing state enterprise workers. Liu, the deputy director of the labor bureau, also made it clear that: "The night shift has objectives and tasks, so of course it should count as working time. It was wrong of the Bank of China to punish staff for harboring intention to strike."

To protect the legitimate interests of a laborer, the arbitration panel issued the following judgment on August 18: "The appellee's treatment of the appellant was excessive. The case should be classed as a serious misdemeanor to be dealt with by administrative penalty. We recommend that six months of work-target allowances be deducted from her wages." Zhang Xuyu showed us the original of the arbitration judgment and said that copies would also be issued to both parties the next day. He also invited the two of us to attend the arbitration session. I felt that the judgment smelled of horse trading. Nevertheless, given the realities confronting the labor bureau, that it could even make this decision was already an accomplishment. The bureau had no choice but to leave the Bank of China management with a way to save face. Law with Chinese characteristics is frequently affected by this kind of unsavory relationship.

When chatting with the leaders of the labor bureau, I frankly offered my own views of the Liu Guangwen affair. Generally, it was contestable that the bank was in the wrong. Little Zhang from the press office, who had been accompanying me all this time without saying a word, darkened as he heard my views, and then he slipped away. To where I did not know. When it was time to finish for the day and I still had not seen him, I returned to the hotel for dinner, and in the dining hall of the hotel I saw Little Zhang and Press Secretary Zeng Tao sitting in a corner. Zeng's face was gloomy and embittered. After I sat down, Zeng remained resentfully silent. When he did speak it was to accuse me of bringing him trouble:

> When you came to Nanxiong, we were never under any obligation to put you up. Now that we're putting you up, you go and raise a storm. After you've finished, you can just dust yourself off and leave. It's us in the press office who'll take the blame from the leadership. If things don't go smoothly and the leaders get their tempers up, maybe we'll be transferred to work in a township.

Having heard him out, I couldn't hold my temper either. I said:

> As soon as we arrived in Nanxiong, we came and gave you the whole rundown on what we were up to. We didn't hide anything, we explained very clearly that this trip was just an investigation. How we'll write the report is something we can discuss after the interviews are done. What did I do to get your temper up like this, Zeng Tao?

After returning to our guest house, we went to the service counter to make a long-distance call back to Guangzhou. The clerk said the phone was broken. We were puzzled because it was working perfectly well that morning—how could it be broken now? After we went to our room, Lin Wei went down again to ask to make a call. Another clerk told him that the telephone line was cut. I felt there was something fishy going on, and when Liu Guangwen came to see me, I got her to go down and make a call. The telephone worked without a hitch. Now I got the message: people were restricting our freedom of communication.

The next day, when interviewing the deputy secretary of the county Party committee, I decided to get to the bottom of things. Zeng Tao was still with me as we ate breakfast. We both maintained a wary silence. Deputy Party Secretary Qu, who already knew what we were up to, began on Liu Guangwen as soon as he started speaking: "If you've got a complaint, you can raise it with your superiors in private. How come you have to use a petition to do it? It just shows that these people have no organizational discipline. If we don't come down hard, what would happen to discipline? Would the leaders have any face left?" When we directly asked him what he thought of the affair, Qu said without hesitation:

> Legally speaking, I don't know whether they're wrong or right by raising complaints in this way. All I know is that they really shouldn't go about it in this manner. Down at the grassroots, you can't always talk about the law. There are lots of real problems to deal with. For example, wages in the Bank of China are so high that people are desperate to get a job there. If you get such good conditions and you still make a fuss about this or that, what sort of person are you? If workers in every enterprise carried on like this, how could you keep a lid on things?

Having listened to his ramblings, which were bereft of the slightest knowledge of the law, I said I also had something I wanted to raise with him. I told him about the telephone. I also pointed out that as a correspondent for the official newspaper of the Guangdong province Party committee, the relevant state regulations gave me priority access to communications, but in Nanxiong my freedom of communication had been restricted. This was an extremely serious mistake. Qu instantly denied any knowledge of it; Zeng Tao turned deathly pale and flustered, protesting that he did not know anything about it, either. Observing Zeng Tao's shifty features, we both felt that we had his number.

After hastily getting rid of us reporters, Deputy Party Secretary Qu sent us to talk to the deputy mayor in charge of labor affairs, Li. The first thing that startled us was the sight of Li swaggering out of a posh limousine. At the time, the central government was cracking down on cadres using cars above their rank, and the central work team was still supervising the campaign in Guangzhou. Deputy Mayor Li stuck to the same story as Deputy Party Secretary Qu: "Liu the bank manager told me about this. I've heard that Liu Guangwen was always up to no good. If you've got a complaint, there's still no need to engage in illegal organizational activities." When it was mentioned that the labor bureau intended to arbitrate on the case, Li said quite bluntly: "I heard yesterday afternoon about how the labor bureau planned to arbitrate the case and last night I called Li, the head of the labor bureau. I asked him not to rush into announcing it—wait until County Party Secretary Guo returns and we'll take it from there." When I pointed out that this was bureaucratic interference, Deputy Mayor Li loftily replied: "The arbitration committee works and handles cases independently. It doesn't have to answer to me. But you need to be careful about everything. The concern of the leadership is not administrative interference."

It was at this point that I had a vague premonition: the ruling of the arbitration committee would be buried. And that afternoon, when we went to the labor bureau to hear the announcement of the arbitration decision, not one of the comrades on the arbitration committee who was scheduled to attend was present. An old woman announced in words which were clearly prepared that the previously scheduled announcement of the arbitration decision would have to be postponed. The reason was that section head, Zhang Xuyu, had gone down to the countryside to attend to a major industrial accident.

I understood the real reason. That afternoon, before the offices closed, I stormed back into the labor bureau and caught Li, the head of the labor bureau, in his office. At first, he was evasive. He would not admit that he had been overruled by the county leadership. When I repeated to him what I had heard Deputy Mayor Li instructing him over the telephone that morning, he finally owned up. But he repeated: "The county wouldn't interfere. The arbitration committee is not a toy. Taking into account the opinions of the relevant county leaders is simply showing them respect." He fulsomely promised: "Take it easy. After a few days, we'll make our announcement. The outcome won't change at all."

From this day onward, I refused all of Zeng Tao's attentions. I went out to eat wherever I wanted, and when I left Nanxiong I didn't ask him for any discount on the guest house bill—I paid what was asked. We wanted to let people know that we would not abandon our integrity as people and reporters to pander to them or to beg for petty favors. We would do as much as we could afford to do; if we did not have any money, we would go hungry and sleep on the streets. We would never yield to these contemptible forces.

I also went to interview the Guangdong Province Labor Bureau about this affair. A leader in the labor relations section made it quite clear: there was nothing illegal in Liu Guangwen's actions; the reaction of the Nanxiong branch of the Bank of China was wrong and should be corrected; and the arbitration committee of the county labor bureau should handle its cases independently and should not be subject to bureaucratic interference from any source.

On December 8, 1995, the *China Youth News* "Freezing Point" special column featured a report by Lin Wei and me: "Defending Lawful Rights or Assembling to Stir Up Trouble—An Investigation of an Employee's Petition." It exposed the background to the Liu Guangwen affair, and its publication provoked intense reaction. Within days, the editorial office received hundreds of letters and telephone calls supporting Liu Guangwen. The *China Youth News* sent out other reporters to interview some legal specialists of the All-China Trade Union Federation and the head office of the Bank of China. On January 19, 1996, the *China Youth News* published a front-page article, "Labor Law Under Interrogation—Interviews with Experts Aroused by an Investigative Report." It explored the Liu Guangwen affair in depth. These two reports created a storm in Nanxiong. It became a main topic of conversation throughout the county. But certain people in Nanxiong did not face up to the criticisms made by this Party newspaper or mend their ways; rather, they were outraged and doubled their efforts to exact revenge on Liu Guangwen.

Subsequently, on December 22, the *Southern Weekend* featured my half-page report that further exposed the facts behind the Liu Guangwen affair. Ironically, the bottom half of the same page carried an advertisement for the Bank of China, "Choose the Bank of China, Realize Your Dreams." It was said that people in the Bank of China's head office blew their tops after seeing this. But the result of this outrage was not that they investigated or intervened in illegal actions of the bank's subsidiary offices. Rather, they addressed their accusations to the media that exposed the facts. Apparently, the chief of the Bank of China sought out the *China Youth News* and threatened to take it to court. But no writs were issued. The head office of the bank remained mysteriously silent about the content of the report. But they did stop placing ads in the *China Youth News*.

The *Jilin Daily* reprinted my article in full on January 8, 1996. Other newspapers have also reprinted portions of it. This reflects the widespread nature of this kind of incident, and why it aroused that much public media attention. The Liu Guangwen incident is not that unusual in this country.

What is most dismaying is that the intervention of the mass media not only failed to encourage a satisfactory resolution to the affair, it brought even more pressure to bear on the fair-minded Nanxiong County Labor Bureau.

When I was investigating in Nanxiong, the attitude of the labor bureau was open and uncompromising. But after our investigation, it caused certain leaders in the county Party committee to interfere in the handling of this affair. The reports of the *Southern Daily* and the *China Youth News* not only failed to raise certain Nanxiong county leaders' knowledge of and respect for the Labor Law, it deepened their shared hatred for the foe and increased the pressure they placed on the labor bureau. Beset from all sides, the Nanxiong County Labor Bureau could only bow to appease them in order to protect itself. It overturned the relatively just decision it had previously issued. On January 4, 1996, the Bank of China used the argument of inapplicable law to restore the Nanxiong branch's punishment of Liu Guangwen that had been rescinded.

But not even this already compromised and craven judgment of the Nanxiong County Labor Bureau was enough to satiate the Nanxiong branch. Under the orchestration of certain leaders in Nanxiong's Party committee, the vengefulness of the Nanxiong bank branch knew no bounds. On January 18, 1996, it applied to the county court to uphold its own punishment of Liu Guangwen and quash the labor bureau's judgment. The county court accepted the case on February 6, and it held its first open hearing on March 11. Since then, nothing has happened. But my own intuition is that Liu Guangwen has little chance of winning, for reasons that need not be stated.

As I and the *China Youth News* reporter, Lin Wei, see it, Liu Guangwen is a fighter defending respect for the labor laws. She may yet end up a martyr. Her deep faith in the Labor Law is stirring proof that the legal consciousness of ordinary Chinese is on the rise. Calls for upholding the law are beginning to be converted into real actions taken in the name of the law. The outcome of these actions may be tragic, but they hint at a future full of promise.

There are two anecdotes about this affair worth recalling. First, after the report was published, a friend joked that the title of the story should not have been "The Law Doesn't Believe in Power or Face"; it should have been "Power and Face Don't Believe in the Law." I did not know whether to laugh or cry at his joke, which revealed so much about China's national conditions. In any case, the facts demonstrated the harsh truth of his joke.

Second, before this year's Spring Festival, a gang of people from the Nanxiong County Party Committee came to Guangzhou to enjoy a feast in honor of all sorts of powerful gods—in the name of paying New Year's respects. At the dinner banquet for the big names in the Guangzhou news media, the Nanxiong deputy Party secretary cast an eye around before offhandedly telling a comrade from the *Southern Daily*: "How come Zhu Defu from your paper didn't come tonight? If he had come, I would have given him a good tongue-lashing.

Our comrade sternly replied: "Zhu Defu didn't go after you, so you should all be satisfied. If you still want to give him a tongue-lashing, you're really looking for trouble."

For a long time, I have not heard any news of Liu Guangwen; I am not sure what has happened to her. I feel much regret for my own inability to deliver justice to her. I also feel guilty that our barging in made things even more complicated, and placed Liu Guangwen in an even tighter bind. It may be that Liu Guangwen's efforts will not alter her own fate, but they must bring good to those who succeed her, because ultimately, her efforts show those who think they have nothing to fear because they have power that a legal consciousness is beginning to penetrate society and will not go unchallenged.

Afterword

I wrote this essay in one sitting and then called Liu Guangwen. I asked how the court case was progressing. Liu laughed bitterly that it was half a year since the case was convened (August 6). The law stipulates that ordinary civil cases must be completed within half a year, and can be extended for another half year with the agreement of the chief judge of the court. Liu has repeatedly gone to the court to inquire after the progress of the case, and it seems that the court has no intention of completing it on time. A concerned legal official privately counseled Liu Guangwen to forget it—no small fry was going to beat a big fish like that. Now Liu is worried that the court will let the case drag on until she despairs. And it does seem that this fear will be realized. Since the event blew up, Liu Guangwen has been unemployed for a year and three months. The Labor Law that has been out for over a year has done nothing to protect her. This sobering fact should remind us that bringing a law to fruition is difficult. But faithfully following a law in order to govern is an even more arduous undertaking.

CASE 17a

Li Wenming and Guo Baosheng, the two protagonists of this case, are members of the intelligentsia, outsiders who became advocates for the workers. But their support for workers was not merely to solve workers' bread-and-butter problems, or their daily abuses, or even to fight for independent trade unions. It was part of their idealistic struggle to establish political democracy in China.

Four documents[5] are used to illustrate the nature of this case. First is the provincial indictment charging Li and Guo with counterrevolutionary crimes (case 17a). Although it is an official document, it contains interesting details of Li's and Guo's "subversive activities." These include circulating writings by Wei Jingsheng, China's famous political dissident at the time; holding discussions on topics that were unequivocally political; networking with labor advocacy groups in Hong Kong; and attempting to establish an illegal organization for migrant workers.

The second document (case 17b) is an excerpt from Li Wenming's eloquent and emotional defense. He focused almost entirely on his right to freedom of expression and argued against accusations that his activities could in any way be construed as subversion. He did not try to defend himself by arguing that his actions were altruistic in aiming to help the migrant workers, and completely sidestepped the accusation of setting up an illegal organization.

An unexpected spin on the case is found in the third document, an excerpt of the defense statement made by Li's brother, Li Dongming, in which he directly addresses the accusation that Li Wenming and others set up illegal organizations (case 17c). According to Li Dongming, Li's activities initially had the enthusiastic personal support of the head of Shenzhen's city government and the head of the city trade union. Disseminating knowledge of the Labor Law among migrant workers in Shenzhen was an official Shenzhen government program, which Li was in charge of. It had the personal stamp of approval from Shenzhen's Party secretary. It was only after Li began building contacts with democracy-movement activists that he ran into trouble. The indictment understandably failed to include this important background information.

The fourth translation is a rousing short essay published in the Migrant Workers Forum, *the news bulletin published by Li Wenming and his friends calling on the workers to unite (case 17d). The essay is an appeal to social justice, juxtaposed in the bulletin with articles like "What Is a Trade Union?" which explain the ABC's of trade unionism.*

Li and Guo were detained and incarcerated in 1994, but another two years passed before they were officially charged with counterrevolutionary activities. During that period, international labor-rights and human-rights organizations mounted a call for their release. On the day they were to be officially tried, some twenty reporters from the Hong Kong news media turned up at the court in Shenzhen to observe the trial, only to be told that the trial had been postponed.[6]

Half a year later, Li and Guo were declared guilty and were each given sentences of three and one-half years, retroactive from the day they were detained. Effectively, they had another six months to serve. For such a serious charge, the sentence was lighter than expected.[7] In another six months, Li and Guo were released on schedule.[8] International pressure and the fact that their labor activities originally had the authorities' stamp of approval might have had some effect.

STANDING UP FOR WORKERS' RIGHTS—AN ACT OF SUBVERSION?
THE TRIAL OF TWO SHENZHEN LABORERS*

*Shenzhen Municipal People's Procuratorate of Guangdong
Province Prosecution Indictment
Shen-Jian-Qi-Zi* (1996) No. 203

Since March 1993, defendant Li Wenming has been secretly liaising with Zhang
Jianjing and Wang Zhongqiu of Beijing, Song Xianke of Hunan, and other
such persons of reactionary ideology. In his discussions and correspondence
with them, defendant Li Wenming frequently revealed his anti-Communist
Party, anti-socialist, counterrevolutionary ambition. While holding a contract
to run *Shenzhen Youth* magazine's public-relations department of Bao'an county,
he used Apartment No. 704, Block 23, Binjiang New Village, Shenzhen mu-
nicipality, as his base, in the name of publicizing the "Regulations on Hiring of
Labor in the Shenzhen Special Economic Zone," and organizing an essay com-
petition on the topic of the "Migrant Workers Tide" *(dagong chao)*. Flaunting
the banner of upholding workers' lawful rights and interests, he illegally set up
organizations such as the "Federation of Migrant Workers," the "Association
of Migrant Workers," and other such organizations. He co-opted some mis-
guided and ill-informed workers to join these illegal organizations, and by
such means as publishing a [magazine called] *Migrant Workers Forum* (Dagong
guangchang), writing reactionary articles, and convening meetings and making speeches, he carried out counterrevolutionary propaganda and incitement
and conspired to subvert the government.

On the evening of March 11, 1994, defendants Li Wenming and Guo
Baosheng assembled Kuang Lezhuang, Fang Yiping, He Fei, Zeng Jiecheng,
Lan Chunquan, Wu Chun, and Liu Hutang (all dealt with separately) and
others to Apartment No. 704 in Binjiang, and presided over a forum on "Strategies for the Democracy Movement." Defendant Guo made a speech based
on his essay, "Strategy for the Struggle for Democracy in the Mainland." He
stated: "The main obstacle facing the democratic movement at present is the
despotic system of the Communist Party. In fact, the democratic movement
itself is nothing less than a decisive life-and-death struggle between the democracy activists and the despotism of the Communist Party." He appealed
for "all the democratic factions to unite in order to strengthen their resources
and influence."

---

* Reprinted (with slight copyediting) with the kind permission of the *China Labor
Bulletin*, Issues 32 and 33 (December 1996), pp. 8–9.

Later on during the meeting, defendant Li Wenming expressed his agreement with the views of defendant Guo Baosheng, and added: "If we carry out the democratic movement, we need to improve our economic situation. We have now registered a company in Beijing (namely, the Beijing Yi Ma Company, registered by defendant Li Wenming) and should strive to set up branch companies in Shanghai, Wuhan, Chengdu, and other big cities. These bases can then become liaison points for the democratic movement across the country."

On the evening of March 18 that year, defendant Li Wenming assembled Kuang Lezhuang, Fang Yiping, He Fei, Zheng Wuyan, Lan Chunquan, and others at Apartment No. 704 in Binjiang, and presided over a meeting at which speeches were made on the topic of migrant workers living in China's cities who have no local residence permit, no work permit, and no citizen's identity card. At the meeting, defendant Li Wenming presented an analysis of China's four social strata: peasants, workers, the middle class, and the intelligentsia. He raised the counterrevolutionary proposition that in order for the democratic movement to erupt in the cities, it should make use of the workers, unite the workers, be active among the workers, and follow the successful path of the East European experience, thereby bringing to an end the totalitarian rule of the Communist Party.

Toward the end of March 1994, defendant Guo Baosheng went back to Beijing, where he typed up his manuscript "A Strategy for the Struggle for Democracy in the Mainland" and made three photocopies. Upon his return to Shenzhen, he gave one copy each to defendants Li Wenming and Kuang Lezhuang. At the same time, he gave copies of reactionary articles written by Wei Jingsheng that he had brought back with him to defendant Li Wenming, and also to Kuang Lezhuang, Fang Yiping, He Fei, Lan Chunquan, Zheng Wuyan, Wan Xiaoying, to a journalist named Lin from the Hong Kong newspaper *Shen Bao*, to a Hong Kong social worker named Du, and others, for them to disseminate, thereby creating an extremely bad influence. These articles included "My Defense Speech in Court," "Three Transformations and Eight Prospects: A Preliminary Evaluation of the Political Situation in Post-Deng China," "Social Organizations and Publications at Universities Since 'June 4th,'" "The Best Instruction Given to Us by Mao Zedong," "The Wolf and the Lamb," "A Joint Discussion of the Hong Kong Question with Friends from Hong Kong," "The Fifth Modernization: Democracy and Other Things," "More on the Fifth Modernization: Democracy and Other Things," and "Sequel to More on the Fifth Modernization: Democracy and Other Things."

On May 12, 1994, defendant Li Wenming was detained under investigation, and on May 13, defendant Guo Baosheng traveled to Guangzhou and went into hiding. In a Guangzhou guest house he wrote the reactionary article "South China's Labor Movement—the Chinese Democratic Movement," which he then photocopied and mailed to places beyond the country's borders in an attempt to expand his influence.

The accuracy of the above facts is attested to by witnesses and witness testimony, by the notes and photographs taken during on-site examinations, by forensic-scientific expert evaluations, and by the documentary and material evidence that was seized. The facts are clear and the evidence is accurate and sufficient, and confessions by the two defendants have been placed on file.

It is the view of this procuratorate that defendants Li Wenming and Guo Baosheng, in disregard of the nation's laws, openly conspired to overthrow the People's Government, and that their actions violated Article 92 of the Criminal Law of the PRC, constituting in each case the crime of conspiracy to subvert the government.

> For the attention of:
> Shenzhen Municipal Intermediate People's Court
> Acting Procurator Liu Hanjun, July 15, 1996
> [Official Seal of the Shenzhen Municipal People's Procuratorate of Guangdong Province]

CASE 17b

"Let History Be the Judge"—Li Wenming's Statement to the Court*

The nature of the judgment at today's proceedings is threefold: ideological, historical, and also a judgment of conscience.

Throughout my life, the core of all my considered ideas has been the desire for historical progress: a strong country, a prosperous nation, a happy people, the construction of genuine democracy and the rule of law, the building of a healthy system of social criticism and appraisal, a complete change in the corrupt and autocratic working methods of cadres in some sections of the Communist Party, and the expansion of the reform process in a manner which benefits all working people. All of these can produce a prosperous and contented country.

Broadly speaking, the main point about my case concerns the question of propagating political opinions. I firmly believe that there is not one article in the Chinese law that could confirm I have committed the crime of counterrevolution or of conspiring to subvert the government. Indeed, even using

---

* Reprinted with permission from *China Labor Bulletin*, Issue 35 (March 1997), pp. 9–10.

the evidence set out in the official indictment, it is still impossible to come to this conclusion. The case itself and the arguments on which the indictment is grounded are mutually contradictory. There are six points that can negate the charges of counterrevolution:

1. we had no program to oppose the government;
2. we had no leaders;
3. we had no real strength;
4. we had no plans for action;
5. we undertook no operations or activities; and
6. there were no serious consequences.

In my personal understanding of history, the word to "conspire" does not exist. I believe that we should openly, and in the full light of day, proceed to strive for progress for mankind. I believe that a civilized and dignified system of government should have the capacity to accommodate these ideas. A government that tolerates dissent is one that respects its own policies; and a government that acknowledges conscience is one that acknowledges history.

CASE 17c

LI DONGMING'S STATEMENT IN COURT IN DEFENSE OF HIS BROTHER, LI WENMING*

Finally, I would like to turn to the indictment itself, which cites as evidence my brother's behavior after he traveled south to Shenzhen in 1992. In my view, his behavior does not constitute the crime(s) outlined in Article 92 of China's Criminal Code:

1. Li initially came to Shenzhen in order to use his vacation period to help both me and Tang Shengwen find a job. The reason he stayed was the result of the insistence of Huang Shouzhu, the general manager of the Sichuan Famous Products Marketing and Promotion Center, who took a liking to Li and persuaded him to stay in Shenzhen and learn as much as he could.
2. Li Wenming then found work as a reporter for the Bao'an county office of the newspaper, *Shenzhen Youth*.
3. Another important point is related to the contracts issued by the press agency's public relations department. Due to a shortage of available funds, the owner (manager), Mr. Chen, divided the agency up into several separate departments and ordered that all the original

---

* Reprinted with the kind permission of the *China Labor Bulletin*, Issues 32 and 33 (December 1996), pp. 10–11.

journalists sign individual contracts. Li Wenming signed up for the public-relations department that had its office at Apartment 704, Block 23, Binjiang New Village. Far from being a counterrevolutionary stronghold, this was simply the address of the public-relations office.

4. The Migrant Workers Tide project was the brainchild of Li Wenming and Kuang Lezhuang, and initially received the personal support of the local government leader, Zhou Xiwu. Moreover, the logo for the Migrant Workers Tide project was written in the personal calligraphy of Shenzhen official trade-union leader Lu Zhaowu. The whole project was extremely successful and made a positive contribution to the cultural activities available to workers in the city of Shenzhen. It had no connection whatsoever with the Federation of Migrant Workers and was not a front for setting up an illegal workers organization.

5. The aims of the Federation of Migrant Workers were to protect the legal rights of workers and to enrich the cultural life of workers outside work hours. Its objectives were therefore praiseworthy from the outset and, moreover, the federation did apply to the civil-government department and the official trade-union office for registration. In keeping with official procedures for all such federations which require the approval of both the local government administration and the official trade union, the federation, during its preparatory stages, publicly issued a statement outlining conditions of membership and completed all the relevant forms. Thus, the Federation of Migrant Workers cannot be called an "organization" as such, and certainly not a counterrevolutionary organization. The city government and official trade union are now taking the interests of workers very seriously, and legislation to protect their interests is gradually being introduced. This was exactly the intention of Li Wenming and Guo Baosheng.

CASE 17d

"IT ALL DEPENDS ON US"*

Friends, brothers, and sisters who labor for bosses, when you walk through thoroughfares and narrow lanes, you see luxurious hotels and karaoke clubs lining the streets. But friends, how many times have you been inside?

Why is it that we who labor for bosses can't enjoy what we are entitled to enjoy? We've got a tiny bit of wages and we have to count pennies. We have

---

* Original text taken from *Dagong guangchang* (Migrant Workers Forum), date unknown, probably 1994. Translated by Anita Chan.

to think of our elderly parents at home and our brothers and sisters who need to go to school. We want to go to night school to further our education but our bosses strip us of our rights. Overtime, overtime, and more overtime. Why are these bosses so ruthless? Because all they know is to make money at the expense of our rights. They think that so long as they buy our time, they can treat us in whichever way they like. Besides, my friends, have you really gotten the money that is wrung from your time and your sweat? None. It is all docked!

Friends, brothers, and sisters, who is concerned about our sufferings? If only someone would come to show some sympathy, saying "Oh, it is really tough," we would be satisfied. But why is it that we can't even get something this simple? When you get off work, you have to stand in a long queue to get some warm water to take a bath. You don't even have the strength to wash your clothes. You are simply too exhausted. You drag your tired body to bed, but in no time, the hour to start work again is already here. It is not easy to get out of bed, you want to sleep a bit more! But the time machine is heartless. Such long hours of heavy labor have turned us into machines, yet even machines get oiled, but not us. Your eyes are puffy and red from lack of sleep. Suddenly, you are wide awake because a needle has poked through your finger.

On March 1, 1994, the Shenzhen City Labor Bureau released a new regulation on labor employment that eliminated the distinction between casual labor and formal full-time labor. Henceforth, all workers will be called employees (*yuangong*). The eight-hour workday and five-and-a-half day week applies to all workers. Yet there remain innumerable cases of violations of this regulation.

We are the resource and wealth of society. Without us, these so-called bosses would not exist. Why are we scared of the bosses? You think the bosses are not scared of us? That's not true. It is not that the bosses are not scared of us, it is that we are scared of ourselves. One, two, ten, or twenty of us can be fired by the boss because there are so many other people hovering outside the factory gate wanting to take your place. But what if there are one hundred, one thousand, two thousand of us? You think the bosses really don't care? You think they can still ignore our existence? Of course not. We have technical skills; we are skilled workers. To replace us with unskilled workers would be like breaking their own rice bowls. We do mean something to them.

Higher wages, shorter work hours, better living conditions, better work conditions—all these are not going to drop from the sky. We have to struggle for them ourselves.

Friends! Unite! Struggle for our democracy!

Struggle for our freedom!

Struggle for our rights! This is our only way out!

Notes

1. *Sichuan gongren bao* (Sichuan Workers' News), August 29, 1997.
2. *'Zhonghua renmin gongheguo qiye laodongzhengyi chuli tiaoli' jianghua* (Talks on "Industrial Conflict Regulations of Enterprises of the People's Republic"), Beijing: China's Resources Publishing House, 1993, pp. 35 and 65.
3. Qiao Jian, "Xinjiuye jizhixia de Zhongguo zhigong laodong guanxi" (Chinese Staff and Workers Industrial Relations Under a New Employment System), in Rui Xin, Lu Xueyi, Shan Tianlun, eds., *2000 nian Zhongguo shehui xingshi fenxi yu yuce* (Analysis and Forecast of China's Social Situation, 2000), Beijing: Social Sciences Documentation Publishing House, 2000, p. 361.
4. *Workers' Daily*, August 16, 1997.
5. The documents have been shortened to save space.
6. *South China Morning Post*, November 11, 1996.
7. "Shenzhen Court Sentences Chinese Labor Activists," news bulletin issued by Human Rights Watch/Asia via e-mail, June 3, 1997, hrw-news@igc.org.
8. *Dongfang Daily*, November 13, 1997.

Chapter 7

Indentured Labor Abroad

China has entered the global economy, and Chinese workers have entered the global labor market by offering their services overseas. According to one estimate, by 1996 some 300,000 Chinese workers labored overseas through arrangements made by Chinese ministries.[1] The three cases in this chapter show that a form of indentured labor is now flourishing under the management of these government ministries. Reports of gross abuses of overseas workers have been filtering back to China and finding their way abroad. Workers who protest their treatment abroad run the risk of being placed on trial by Chinese officials when they return to China. The threat of litigation and imprisonment has become a new instrument of domination.

The first case in this chapter (case 18) involves a group of Chinese seafarers on a Greek boat. The second and third cases are about workers sent to the Commonwealth of the Northern Marianas, a U.S. territory in the Western Pacific, and to Yap in Micronesia.[2] The two Chinese bureaucracies authorized to export labor are the Chinese Ministry of Foreign Trade and Economic Cooperation (MOFTEC) and the Ministry of Labor. They monopolize the labor-export business through licensing lower-level agencies to set up labor-recruitment companies. These usually carry the name of "an international economic technical cooperation company" (*guoji jingji jishu hezuo gongsi*) of a province, city, or county.[3] Other ministries and bureaucracies cooperate in helping to recruit workers of specific skills for certain kinds of industries or jobs.[4] For example, the bureaucracies in charge of the textile industry will help in the recruitment of textile workers to labor overseas. The factories in the host countries may be owned and managed by foreigners, but they may also be owned and managed by Chinese bureaucracies, by bureaucrats under the guise of collectives, or by private business people of Chinese nationality (see case 19b, statement by Sui Jianwei).[5] Even city-level police or judicial organs sometimes set up employment centers to recruit labor.[6]

Exporting labor in this way has become a modern form of indentured servitude. Workers are bonded the moment they sign a contract with the Chinese agents. Prior to departure they have to pay an enormous "deposit," often scraped together from borrowed money. The jobs often promise high returns, but in fact, employees are normally cajoled into signing contracts that are blatantly to their disadvantage. Given misinformation and sometimes told deliberate lies, workers trust that these labor-service companies, which are tied to local bureaucracies, are reliable. The stakes are high in this business of exported labor. The lure of large sums of hard currency tempts both the workers and the recruiting and labor-export companies. One consequence is that, compared with other Asian workers, the cost of obtaining an overseas job is much higher for Chinese workers, on average $2,000 to $6,000, at least five times more than the deposits paid by Filipino exported workers.[7] The workers leave for the overseas job heavily in debt, in the belief that they can easily repay the money with a short stint of work abroad. The Chinese workers are not aware that once in debt their employers can exploit them to the fullest, and the bigger the debt, the worse their circumstances will be. China profits handsomely by exporting workers. In 1994, China made U.S.$8 billion from exporting 200,000 laborers.[8] In 1998, MOFTEC signed overseas contracts in engineering, labor services, design and consultancy worth $11.7 billion.[9]

In many respects, this bondage is similar to the "deposits" paid by Chinese migrant workers inside China. But there are differences. First, the exported workers are more vulnerable because the deposit is much larger, reaching as much as ten thousand yuan or more. Second, once in a foreign country or at work on a boat, isolation and language problems aggravate their sense of disorientation and insecurity. With no means to address their grievances, and in constant fear of being sent back to China before the contract expires and before earning enough to pay back the deposit, workers are deterred by the prospect of a life in debt and do not protest. Exported workers sometimes succumb to physical, sexual, and mental mistreatment, to being cheated out of a large chunk of their promised wages, and to working even longer hours than those imposed on migrant workers inside China. They are "trapped in hell," as they themselves describe it.

There is a further difference between China's exported workers and domestic migrant workers. Workers abroad have a chance of being delivered from their plight by foreign pro-labor organizations or foreign government departments. In case 18, the seafarers were helped by the International Transport Workers Federation (ITF), the international trade union for maritime workers, and in case 19, the Chinese workers in the Marianas were helped by the Marianas and U.S. labor departments. These agencies were able to retrieve for the workers the wages that were illegally kept by the employers and by the recruitment and labor-export agents. They were also able to secure promises from management to stop abusing workers. It appeared that justice had been done.

But, as shall be seen in all three cases, a nightmare awaited the workers upon their return to China. Chinese officials and others who made money out of the business were not going to let meddling foreigners deny them these profits, and a lot of future money. They reasserted control. The deposit system had been set up to ensure that exported workers could not run away or rebel, and would meekly serve out their full term of labor. Powerless to resist host-country authorities, Chinese officials assert their power over the workers once they are no longer under foreign protection. Back in China with their hard-earned back pay, officials threatened workers with confiscating their money, suing them in civil courts, or charging them with political crimes that could send them to prison. This was the scenario in all three cases collected here.

CASE 18

This is the nightmarish story of eleven physically abused seafarers who worked on a British boat that was flying a flag of convenience.[10] This is the only case in this book that involves abusive employers of Western nationality. The seafarers successfully sought help from the International Transport Workers Federation (ITF) while the boat was anchored at an Italian port. They were later relentlessly prosecuted by their Tianjin labor-recruitment agency, a company set up by a city-level bureaucracy. The eleven were arrested and all of their possessions were confiscated, including a total of U.S.$95,000 of backpay. The three seafarers who were regarded as the ring leaders were detained for over two years before being tried for the serious crime of "leaking state secrets"—the plaintiff charged that in telling the ITF the amount of their wages, they had revealed confidential information. Although the charges were dismissed and the sailors were finally released, their names were never cleared and their confiscated backpay was never returned to them.[11]

Exporting Chinese seafarers to work on foreign boats has become a lucrative and rapidly expanding business. By 1997, about ten thousand Chinese worked on non-Chinese boats, still way behind the Filipinos, the largest national group at around four hundred thousand. But China has been aggressively competing in this global business. One way to achieve this is to sell the labor of Chinese seafarers at the lowest possible price in the international labor market and to ignore any subsequent abuses. The ITF predicts that China will soon to be a major supplier of labor to the seafaring industry.[12] The subhuman working conditions that exist on boats are not new. What has changed is that three-quarters of the seafarers in the world today are Asians,[13] and among their governments, the Burmese and Chinese are the most tolerant of mistreatment. It is no coincidence that both of these countries are "socialist," to the extent that the state or its recruitment agents hold economic and political power over their laborers. When business and government become one, the state's power is nearly absolute. According to the ITF, Chinese recruitment and labor export agents take some 80 percent of the wages paid to the seafarers by the shipping companies. What is more, they allow employers to mistreat the seafarers at will.[14] The nature of the seafaring profession is such that seafarers have opportunities to come into contact with ITF inspectors who board boats to monitor work conditions. The Chinese recruitment and labor-export agents preempt the potential threat of this contact by making seafarers sign contracts that make any such contact with foreign trade-union organizations a violation of their contracts and a potential criminal offense. According to the ILO's Convention, such practices violate the right to freedom of association. I have on file a contract signed by workers before their departure to Hong Kong with their Tianjin recruitment agent, the same agent that recruited these seafarers. Article 4 of the contract states:

"Export personnel going to Hong Kong are strictly forbidden to contact any organization (including the Hong Kong Immigration Department) and associations. If found in violation of this regulation they shall be immediately fired and have to shoulder all economic responsibilities (including back pay given to the exported personnel due to pressure, wages, penalties borne by the employer, and expenses accrued from sending replacement personnel) and all the violator's foreign exchange will be confiscated. In addition, the violator will have to bear all legal responsibility."

As can be seen in this case of the seafarers, the Tianjin International Economic and Technical Cooperation Company did exactly as stated in this article.

GIVE BACK MY DIGNITY: AN INVESTIGATIVE REPORT ON THE CASE OF M/V ARCADIA—CHINESE SEAFARERS "LEAKING STATE SECRETS"*

The ocean is such a vivid reflection on the capriciousness of life itself—tranquilizing when it's calm and peaceful, and terrifying when it's stormy.

The eleven Chinese seafarers in this story were accustomed to the harsh conditions at sea. But when they themselves were subjected to brutal treatment, they could no longer remain calm and composed.

---

* Translation from the Chinese text: Jiang Shengyang and Li Siuling, "Huan wo zhuanyan—'Akaido' hao zhonggong haiyuan 'xiemian' xunzhong," *Gongren ribao* (Workers' Daily), March 24, 1995. Translation provided by International Transport Workers Federation.

"The whole thing was a nightmare." Even after four years, when Mr. Hua Chungui, the second mate, recounted the experiences to the reporter, he was still shaken.

A Living Hell on the Ocean

Four years ago, when the eleven Chinese seafarers, including Hua Chungui, the second mate, Zhang Aizhao, the third mate, and Gao Xiaohui, the second engineer, were boarding the *Arcadia*, they did not foresee that they were entering a living hell on the ocean.

For years, many foreign vessel owners chose to employ the services of Chinese seafarers because of their commendable personal and professional qualities. Ever since the open-door policy, some Chinese companies have been collaborating with overseas shipping companies to export labor by sending Chinese seafarers to work on foreign vessels.

After the Tianjin International Economic and Technological Cooperation Company (hereinafter referred to as the Tianjin International Company) signed an agreement with representatives from Golden Light Shipping Ltd. in Greece between March 1991 and February 1992, one of Tianjin International Company's subsidiaries in the Development Zone sent eleven Chinese seafarers, including Mr. Hua Chungui, to work on the *Arcadia*, a cargo vessel.

Arcadia is an "expedient vessel" flying a flag of convenience—it is owned by a British company but registered in Panama. Apart from the captain, the chief mate, the chief engineer, and the first engineer, who were all white Europeans, the crew was made up entirely of Chinese seafarers.

It is incredible that while the West has been chanting about human rights and individual liberty on every possible occasion, the Chinese seafarers employed by a Western vessel owner are bullied, abused, and generally treated like slaves in this modern age.

The foreigners on board the *Arcadia* despised the Chinese seafarers for no apparent reason. Their sense of racial superiority was omnipresent. They verbally and physically abused the Chinese seafarers at will, calling them "pigs" in Greek. They threatened the seafarers with the sack at the slightest sign of disobedience.

According to Hua Chungui, during the thirteen months on board the *Arcadia*, almost every member of the Chinese crew was verbally abused, and hardly a day went by without some of them being beaten. In August 1991, Wang Jianmin had barely arrived on board with his luggage when the captain ordered him to start working. Wang intended to explain that he had just come on board. He didn't finish his sentence when the captain gave him a nasty kick, causing him to feel dizzy and unable to stand up for quite a while. On another occasion, the captain ordered Wang Jianmin to lash eight large octopuses against the deck, 200 times each. Wang needed a break when he was done with the third octopus, but the captain stormed over, swearing and beating him, and would not allow Wang to rest.

On board the *Arcadia*, the most basic rights of the Chinese seafarers were completely ignored. To earn the basic wage, they had to work twelve hours (excluding meal breaks) a day, and seven days without a day off. On one occasion, the vessel went to Morocco to load wheat. The Chinese seafarers worked continuously from 6:00 A.M. to midnight, but the captain refused to let them get any rest and ordered them to continue working until 8:00 A.M. the following day, by which time they had worked nonstop for 26 hours. When some of them protested to the captain, the captain waved the contract and said in an arrogant tone, "You have no right to talk about this. We signed the contract with you Chinese."

The Chinese seafarers did the toughest, the most arduous, and the most dangerous work, but were not given the most basic forms of workplace protection. The vessel owner never issued any protective gear, and frequent workplace injuries resulted. The vessel did not carry any medical personnel or emergency first-aid facilities, nor did the vessel owner take out any medical or life insurance for the Chinese seafarers. The sick or injured were not given medical treatment in good time. Some of them were ordered to carry on working while sick—or face dismissal.

Without nonskid working boots, a seafarer named Wei Liya slipped and fell while operating on an oily deck, causing a severe dislocation of his neck. While the vessel was berthed at the port of Antwerp in Belgium, the local hospital suggested he get medical treatment immediately. When Wei asked the captain to cover the medical expenses, the captain grabbed the medical report from him and rebuked, "The Chinese sent you to work here, [if you cannot work] you might as well piss off." After the vessel arrived at Yemen, the captain announced the dismissal of Wei Liya without any severance pay, and demanded that he pay back thirty days of meal expenses. Poor Wei Liya used to be a well-built man, but he was completely broken down by the injuries, unable even to turn around to say goodbye to his compatriots.

The *Arcadia* was a living hell, and the Chinese seafarers were helpless in the vast, open sea.

Mustering Up Courage to Lodge a Complaint

Having suffered intolerable conditions, the Chinese seafarers requested help from their motherland. They sent numerous letters to the company that dispatched them, that is, the Tianjin International Company, in the hope that the company would mediate to put a stop to the inhuman behavior of the vessel's senior officers, and also to improve the living and working conditions on the *Arcadia*. However, for a whole year, the Tianjin International Company did not take any measures to safeguard the most basic rights of these seafarers. Instead, in the only letter that it sent in reply to the seafarers' complaints, the company asked them to "put up with the foreigners, don't fight back when hit, don't talk back when scolded. The foreigners have foreigners' temperaments. Do not provoke them."

The seafarers were enraged as well as disappointed: "This is preposterous. The company is asking us to bear the unbearable instead of seeking to address practical issues in a meaningful way." In the meantime, the situation went from bad to worse.

Finally, things came to a head on March 29, 1992. The captain of the *Arcadia* announced the dismissal of Li Jingjian, after he was injured, and Zhang Aizhao, the third mate. Zhang Aizhao argued with the captain, insisting on obtaining work clothes from the vessel. He had also stepped forward to help when other Chinese seafarers were verbally or physically abused by the captain. He therefore became a thorn in the captain's side.

When the news spread, everyone knew without a doubt that Zhang Aizhao had been penalized by the captain for speaking out to support suffering colleagues. Their volcano of fury erupted, "We are seafarers from the People's Republic of China, not black slaves on a pirate ship. We are exporting a service, but we don't sell our human dignity."

They unanimously agreed that they should no longer suffer quietly; it was time to take action. Zhang Aizhao proposed that they should contact the local trade union to complain about the vessel's management.

On the early morning of April 2, 1992, the eleven Chinese seafarers, including Hua, Zhang, and Gao, went to the local seafarers' union at the port of Ravenna in Italy, where the vessel was berthed, to lodge the complaints.

The Chinese seafarers were met by the union representative. During the investigation, they truthfully answered queries regarding their wages. The union representative declared that he would formally take up the matter and speak with the vessel's management, bringing their unjust treatment on the *Arcadia* to an end.

When the dock workers at the port of Ravenna heard the news, they gave their unequivocal support. They issued an ultimatum to the *Arcadia,* stating that if the vessel did not proceed to improve conditions for the Chinese seafarers, they would cut off the supply of water, fuel, and other materials to the vessel, and suspend loading and unloading.

That evening, the local union representative boarded the *Arcadia* to negotiate with the representative of the vessel's owner and with the captain.

On the afternoon of April 3, 1992, the union representative informed the Chinese seafarers that the vessel management had accepted the union's demand, had agreed to take out insurance policies for all of them, and would guarantee their human rights and the rights to get medical treatment. Workplace protective gear and personal-hygiene products would be issued immediately. The outstanding two months' wages and money for food would be immediately paid to them. In the meantime, based on wage standards set by the International Labor Organization (ILO), the difference between the standard wage and the seafarers' substandard wages, totaling U.S.$95,000, would be backdated and paid. The representative for the vessel owner also signed a letter of guarantee declaring, "The owner of *Arcadia* hereby acknowledges that we raise the seafarers' wages in line with the standards set forth in Article 109 of the ILO Charter. ... From now on, we will not take any disciplinary action against them over their work, or initiate litigation, or take any other action against any of the aforementioned seafarers."

Justice was served. To use Hua Chungui's words, "We are finally able to live and work like real human beings."

In the ten days that followed, the foreigners did not dare to verbally or physically abuse them any longer. Conditions improved. The owner's representative proposed to sign a new contract that would transfer all eleven of them to work on another vessel. The seafarers turned it down. They were determined to disembark and return to China. During their transit in London and Paris, these eleven seafarers shared one aim: head eastward, and homeward bound.

The seafarers firmly believed what they did in Italy was just and legal. At worst, they thought they would have some contractual disputes with the Tianjin International Company. They did not know an even grimmer nightmare was awaiting them.

Disaster Fell from the Sky

At Beijing International Airport, on April 19, 1992, a flight from Paris landed. From it emerged these eleven Chinese seafarers who had gone through hell. They heaved a sigh of relief: we are finally home.

Their sense of relief did not last long. They had barely walked down the steps of the plane when they were met by the stern-faced manager from the Tianjin International Company and more than a dozen officers from the procuratorate. The seafarers were pushed into a police van and whisked away from the airport.

The seafarers were stunned, saying, "What's going on?"

"You are summoned for questioning," was the reply they got from an officer of the procuratorate.

In the Tianjin City Heping District Procuratorate, and in the Tianjin International Company office, some of them were strip-searched. Their foreign currency, bank books, and personal identifications were all taken away.

It transpired later that, shortly after the vessel owner's representative signed the letter of guarantee declaring that they would "never breach the agreement," he sent a telexed ultimatum to the Tianjin International Company saying, "I am awaiting the reply from your officials in charge regarding this matter. If I do not see those people locked away, I will never again accept Chinese seafarers to work on our ships." The Tianjin International Company immediately submitted a document to the Tianjin City Heping District Procuratorate entitled "Material on Eleven Chinese Seafarers Who, Taking Advantage Brought Upon by Their Jobs Abroad, Illegally Solicited Huge Sums of American Dollars from an International Organization." The company asked the procuratorate to take legal action to enable the company to seize the $95,000 the vessel owner paid to the eleven seafarers as wages in arrears.

Between noon and 5:00 p.m. on April 20, 1992, the eleven seafarers were released in two batches. They were penniless by then and had to borrow traveling money from the Tianjin International Company in order to return home.

In the ensuing four months, no action was taken against these seafarers by the procuratorate or the Tianjin International Company. In August 1992, the procuratorate arrested Hua Chungui, Zhang Aizhao, and Gao Xiaohui, and charged them with "leaking state secrets."

The three seafarers were not government officials; they were merely ordinary workers who lived off their hard labor on the rough sea. What state secrets could they possess? How on earth could such a serious crime of "leaking state secrets" fall on them?

Let us listen to the Tianjin International Company's interpretation of events. The company held the opinion that the eleven seafarers knew very well that their complaints to the local union in Italy would lead to economic loss for the company. Nonetheless, they breached the contract in order to get extra payment for their own benefit. So the Tianjin International Company concluded that these seafarers sought to get illegitimate income by initiating complaints to the local union in Italy, during which time they disclosed the amount of their wages, which was classified information, thereby committing the alleged crime.

The prisoners were shocked to learn this, as can be seen from their response:

> To export labor is not the same as selling out Chinese workers' interests or human dignity. We reported a variety of issues and problems to the company, but the company did nothing. In the end, we asked for help from the

local trade-union organization out of desperation, and as the last resort. How could monthly wages paid to us by the Greek captain for our labor possibly be classified as state secrets of the People's Republic of China? We complained to a trade-union organization against a foreign captain—how could this action be construed as breaching the official secrecy discipline? Did we have to put up with the maltreatment by the foreign officers to be called law-abiding good citizens?

The three behind bars could not believe their fate.

Battle at Court

On August 9, 1993, after they had been detained for a year, the Tianjin City Heping District People's Court held a formal hearing on the "leaking state secrets" case.

The defense team consisted of Chen Wuyun, of the Hua Xia Law Firm in Shanghai; Wu Yigang, of the Overseas Commerce Law Firm; Guo Mengzhen, of the Zhong Zi International Law Firm in Beijing; and Yue Lian, of the Jing Wei Law Firm. Prior to the hearing, the solicitors traveled back and forth between Beijing, Tianjin, and Shanghai, diligently taking statements from those directly involved as well as witnesses in the seafarers' work units and households. They visited the government departments concerned, including the Ministry of Foreign Trade and Economic Cooperation, the Ministry of Transport, the Ministry of Labor, the Ministry of State Security, the State Bureau of Secrecy Protection, and the legal-affairs committee of the National People's Congress, and also got in touch with the union representative who handled the labor dispute on the *Arcadia*. By the time of the hearing, the huge amount of diligent and conscientious investigative work carried out by the solicitors had provided them with sufficient firsthand material. They were determined to plead not guilty on behalf of the accused, as they were confident of winning the case.

At 8:30 A.M. the court commenced. The three seafarers, detained for over a year, were led into the court in handcuffs.

After a long session during which the facts were established, the prosecution and the defense, each with their own interpretation of events, carried out a heated debate.

The central question of the case was: Was the wage of an individual Chinese seafarer a state secret?

The prosecutor first presented Document No. 30, issued by the Ministry of Labor and the State Security Bureau in 1989. It set out in chapter 2, article 8, that, "Quotations of cost of labor services in labor service export activities are . . . classified state secrets." The prosecution continued with a statement of Tianjin City State Security Bureau's interpreting of Document No. 30: "The prices for labor services (namely the seafarers' actual wages) are classified state secrets." Based on this legal standpoint, the prosecution charged the three seafarers with leaking state secrets while working abroad. Their actions had violated Criminal Act Article 186, thereby having committed the crime of "leaking state secrets."

The defense fought back fiercely. First of all, they claimed, the Tianjin City State Security Bureau was overstepping its powers in reinterpreting a document issued by the Ministry of Labor and the State Security Bureau. The interpretation was not valid, and so could not be used as evidence. The defense then presented a crucial piece of legal evidence, "An Interpretive Statement on Quotations for Labor Services in Labor-Service Export—1993 (Document No. 89)," issued by the general office of the Ministry of Labor on July 23, 1993 at the request of the Zhong Zi International Law Firm. This letter gave an authoritative interpretation of chapter 2, article 8 of Document No. 30. It said, "We have studied the issue, and would now clarify the matter regarding quotations for labor services in labor-service export as follows (the conclusion was reached in consultation with the State Security Bureau):

> Quotations for labor services in labor-service export are arrived at between the legal representative of a Chinese company and a foreign employer. It is a quotation from a commercial negotiation. Quotations for labor services and the actual wages paid to workers by the Chinese company are two different things. The actual wages disclosed by individual workers sent abroad should not be categorized as quotations for labor services.

In the light of this evidence, the allegation that the three seafarers had leaked state secrets was untenable.

The defense position was that: based on the facts established by the court, this case was essentially a labor dispute involving breach of contract and bickering over duties among the Chinese seafarers, the vessel owner, and the company that had sent them abroad. It should have been resolved through civil litigation. The Tianjin City Heping District Procuratorate has taken up the case, and has tried to use procedures for criminal offenses to resolve an economic dispute. The $95,000 seized by the procuratorate should have been passed on to the court to be handled. Claiming the status of victim, the Tianjin International Company could have simultaneously initiated civil litigation. However, the procuratorate, without any regard to its legal obligations, let the Tianjin International Company take away the money even before the prosecution process began.

The defense called for the court to acquit the defendants. It should not let our compatriots, having gone through a great deal of suffering abroad, be put in prison after returning to their motherland.

On August 18, 1993, the Tianjin City Heping District Court allowed the three seafarers to be released on bail. They left prison determined to get a just verdict.

No-Fault Appeal

Another year and several months went by. By the end of 1994, the three Chinese seafarers received the court ruling.

On December 27, 1994, the Tianjin City Heping District Court signed a criminal case verdict: the defendants Hua Chungui, Zhang Aizhao, and Gao Xiaohui had been found not guilty.

Two of them, Hua and Gao, were not satisfied with the ruling, seeing it as an incomplete verdict. They decided to appeal, making this one of the rare cases in Chinese legal history in which a defendant appealed a "not-guilty" verdict.

In his written appeal to the Tianjin Municipal Intermediate People's Court, Gao Xiaohui requested that the court establish the facts with reference to the Criminal Act and the Criminal Procedure Act, declare that the appellants were not guilty, and return to the appellants the properties that had been seized from them. The grounds for the appeal were: First, the facts described in the verdict were not correct. Although the defendants were acquitted, the court, when recounting the so-called established facts, maintained that the defendants "breached their contract with the Tianjin International Company," and that that was considered "wrong behavior." But the court did not say that "they had violated article 186 of the People's Republic of China Criminal Act." In other words, the court did not arrive at the verdict based on whether it was correct for the prosecutor to accuse the defendants of having committed a criminal act—that is, leaking state secrets. Second, the Tianjin City Heping District Procuratorate—as well as the court—did not follow the proper procedures throughout the course of the trial. The Heping District Procuratorate, for no good reason, seized the appellants' properties as well as personal documents. The properties seized from the appellants were dealt with by the procuratorate even before the court session had begun. The personal-identification documents of the appellants have not been returned. The Heping District People's Court, which first presided over the case, did not fulfill its duty to stop and/or redress the improper procedural actions taken by the procuratorate. Moreover, the court did not mention the seized properties from the appellants in the verdict, completely ignoring the legitimate rights and interests of the appellants, thereby rendering the judgment incomplete, and overstepping the fairness and seriousness of the judicial system.

On the other hand, on January 11, 1995, the procuratorate submitted a protest to the Tianjin Municipal Intermediate People's Court against the verdict of the first instance reached by the Heping District People's Court. The written protest went: "Having studied the judgment, this procuratorate takes the view that the judgment made by the Heping District People's Court blurred the demarcation line between what's guilty and what's not guilty. The court applied the law in a misleading way, leading to an inappropriate ruling on the criminal case." The protest maintained that, "The defendants Hua Chungui, Zhang Aizhao, and Gao Xiaohui disregarded rules and regulations, and disclosed their actual wages, causing economic damage to the country. Their actions violated article 186 of the People's Republic of China Criminal Act. The defendants should be found guilty for having leaked state secrets, and should be punished accordingly."

With an appeal on one side and a protest on the other, there seems to be no end to the saga of the *Arcadia*, already lasting more than nine hundred days since the seafarers' walkout. People who have faith in our socialist judicial system, which is rapidly taking shape, believe that the case will have a just verdict in the end.

Comments

Few cases of worker abuse in China have elicited protests from international labor organizations. This one did. After the three seafarers were detained without trial, the ITF, one of the most active international trade-union organizations, mounted an international campaign on their behalf. In 1995, the International Conference of Free Trade Unions (ICFTU), the international umbrella organization of trade unions of the non-socialist world, brought a formal complaint against the Chinese government to the International Labor Organization (ILO), which issued a ruling on the case in support of the seafarers.[15] That the seafarers were finally found not guilty of leaking state secrets and were released may well have been a consequence of this international pressure. But the campaign was not able to fully redress the injustice suffered. The authorities continued to retaliate against the seafarers, blacklisting them and placing an injunction on them that prohibited them from leaving their hometowns. As of 1998, the money that had been confiscated from them had not been returned, nor had their personal documents. The effectiveness of an international campaign has its limits.

One interesting aspect related to this case was the involvement of the ACFTU on behalf of the seafarers. Reading between the lines of this article *and related articles on the case, one can sense the suppressed anger and outrage of the ACFTU newspaper (*Workers' Daily*) at the behavior of the Tianjin City bureaucracies and bureaucrats. It is quite possible that the money to hire several law firms to defend their case came from the Chinese Seafarers' Union, with the support of the ACFTU. In a companion article, "Exporting Labor Should Not Sell Out Human Dignity," Zhang Shihui, chairperson of the China Seafarers' Union, wrote: "Since October 1993, when the union heard about the case, we immediately sent someone to Tianjin to investigate. Based on what we found out, we have continuously called on the relevant authorities to handle the case according to the law and to issue a ruling as soon as possible." He then asked a rhetorical question, "We cannot help but ask you labor-export companies, how can you treat your own compatriots this way? Where is your sense of justice?" As in case 14, an official of the ACFTU overstepped Chinese protocol by publicly challenging the conduct of another bureaucracy through the media. Zhang called for an overhaul of the export-labor business, arguing that to stop this kind of abuse, the Chinese Seafarers' Union should represent seafarers by signing collective contracts with recruitment and labor-export agents, and grassroots unions should be set up on boats to ensure direct communication between seafarers and the union. In the end, Zhang raises the patriotic banner: "Protecting the motherland's dignity and protecting individual legal rights are rights endowed to each seafarer by the constitution and the 'Labor Law.'"*

Nonetheless, when the ITF approached the Chinese Seafarers' Union asking it to endorse the ILO ruling on the case, it did not respond.[16] The ACFTU was willing to support the seafarers, even to the extent of offending other powerful bureaucracies, but when it was a matter of a foreign body urging it to do the same thing, the ACFTU was unwilling to openly turn against the Chinese government's policy that the trade union and the state should present a united front to the rest of the world. This incident highlights the ambivalent role and attitude of the ACFTU.

CASE 19a

International politics is no stranger to irony. The U.S. government has been the most vocal critic of China's use of prison labor, but on a U.S. territory in the western Pacific Ocean, the Commonwealth of the Northern Marianas Islands (CNMI), a form of forced indentured labor has been flourishing for a decade. On the main island of Saipan, the indigenous population was only 14,000 in 1975, but due to an influx of outsiders the population jumped to 59,000 in 1997. Forty-two percent of the population were imported contract workers and about half of this export labor came from China (approximately

*ten thousand people). Previously a sleepy Pacific outpost, Saipan has be-
come a booming industrial city. The local population has prospered by rent-
ing land to outside manufacturers who use cheap Asian labor—Filipino,
Indian, Bangladeshi, and Chinese—to make "Made in the USA" products
for sale in the United States. This way manufacturers and buyers can avoid
U.S. tariffs.[17] The Marianas government was able to gain an exemption from
U.S. Federal immigration laws to import this cheap contract labor.[18]*

SHOULD WE PAY THE ADMINISTRATION FEE?*

Investigation in the Labor Administration Fee Lawsuit Against Fu Sumei in Sanming Sanyuan District Court

> This lawsuit is not an isolated case. Neither is it an ordinary lawsuit. It
> involved the interests of more than sixty people and impaired the imple-
> mentation of our labor-export policy. Through this collective appeal, we
> can see even more clearly how necessary it is to perfect the legal system!

A Letter from Three Defendants

We were originally three women workers in the Sanming Liantai Garment
Factory Ltd. (SLGF) (a joint venture). In December 1989, we signed the "Contract for Working in Saipan with SLGF." According to the contract, we should
be paid piece rates and receive a monthly income of U.S.$360,[19] with $150 to
go to the foreign boss to cover board and transportation costs, and half of the
remainder to be turned in to SLGF. The contract also specified that 20 percent
of any income above the $360 should be turned in to SLGF. These were very
harsh terms. The U.S. Department of Labor once sent their staff to investigate
our factory. After the investigation, they requested that our boss, Chen Shouren,
pay us by the hour, not by piece, so that our incomes could be higher.

Chen Shouren immediately started maneuvering around the decision by
the Department of Labor. The chair of the board of directors of SLGF, Wang
Xingong, together with SLGF manager Zhu Guihua, rushed to Saipan. Together with Chen Shouren, they made up a contract in English and asked us
to sign. They threatened us and said, "Whoever refuses to sign the contract
shall be sent back to China immediately and be held solely responsible for
all consequences." We did not understand English and therefore had no idea
of the content of the contract. What we were told was that our pay was changed

---

*Translation from the Chinese text: Sun Yongqiang, "Zhebi guanlifei
gaibugaijiao?—dui sanming sanyuanqu fayuan shenpan Fu Sumei tuoqian laowu
guanlifei yi an de diaocha," *Fujian jingji bao* (Fujian Economic News), July 7, 1994.
Translated by Liu Dongxiao.

from a piece rate to an hourly rate, and that the administration fee was changed to 25 percent of our total wages, docked directly from our paychecks.

We clearly knew that 25 percent was too much as an administration fee and that we would have little left after paying $150 for board and transportation costs. Even with all the overtime we put in, little would be left. But we signed the contract, considering the fact that we were too far away from our motherland to rely on the Party and the government to back us up, and one comrade had already been sent back after refusing to sign the contract. We hoped to exert our young bodies to work hard and make up for the unreasonable loss. After working for twelve hours everyday for three years, we finally received our blood-and-sweat pay before we boarded the plane for home. After we came back, SLGF sued us for owing it the administration fee of 15 percent of our total salary. We did not understand the allegation. After discussing among ourselves, we found that it was illegal for SLGF to request an additional 15 percent administration fee. We therefore turned to the weapon of law and hired an attorney to answer SLGF's accusation.

On March 15, 1994, the Sanyuan District Court found that it was illegal for SLGF to engage in exporting labor because it was a joint venture and it had no right to claim labor administration fees.

Consequently, SLGF had to withdraw the lawsuit. We had thought that the case was forever closed. However, SLGF came up with another trick. It made the Sanming International Economic and Technology Cooperation Company the plaintiff, itself the third party, and us the defendant for a second time. Although we knew that the Sanming Company was involved in some labor-export activities, we never signed any contract with it. Nonetheless, on May 24, the Sanyuan District Court decided that one of the defendants, Fu Sumei, lost the case to the plaintiff. We saw no point in the decision and therefore wrote to your newspaper, asking you to investigate the case and uphold justice.

The Court Decision

On the afternoon of June 17, the reporter interviewed Chief Judge Liu at the Sanyuan District Court. Liu said: "The court has taken a cautious approach to this case. It was for the sake of being cautious that we decided that only Fu Sumei lose the case, one out of twenty defendants." (According to the Sanming Intermediate Court, the case actually involved sixty-three people.) The reporter asked: " SLGF is a joint venture. It does not have the authorization to engage in labor-export activities. Shall the contract it entered with Fu Sumei be a void contract?"

Judge Liu replied: "Both parties entered the contract voluntarily. Furthermore, the contract has already been carried out. We should treat the contract as valid."

"The verdict represents the opinion of the court," he added. Now, let us have a look at the verdict, which states:

> The "employment of labor contract" the third party entered with the defendant was based on the authorization given by the plaintiff to the third party. The plaintiff has the right to engage in labor-export activities. The contract is therefore valid. The amount of administration fee imposed by the plaintiff on the defendant does not violate the provisions of state laws and policies. The amount of administration fee agreed in the "employment of labor contract" is the representation of the true intent of the defendant. It was in accordance with articles 55 and 85 of the General Principles of the Civil Law of the PRC and therefore it is protected by the law. The plaintiff adjusted the proportion of the administration fee to 15 percent based on the fact that the management in Saipan changed the pay scale from piece rate to an hourly rate. The facts are clear that defendant Fu Sumei owed the administration fee from July 7 of 1991 to December 28 of 1993, which constituted a breach of the contract. The defendant should bear corresponding liability.

Words from the Defendant's Attorney

Fu Sumei appealed the decision to the Sanming Intermediate Court. Her attorney gave the following opinion:

1. The court's decision that the labor contract entered by the third party with the defendant was valid contradicts the provision of relevant laws. First of all, the authorization by the plaintiff was invalid. According to article 14 of the Preliminary Rules on Administering Foreign-Related Labor Cooperation, matters of pay and administration fees shall be negotiated and agreed upon between a labor-exporting enterprise and a laborer. Such matters should not have been negotiated between the third party and the defendant. Second, even though the authorization relationship could be established between the Sanming Company and SLGF, SLGF should have entered the contract in the name of the Sanming Company, not of its own. Third, as a joint venture, SLGF had no right to engage in the labor-export business, and therefore should not have entered either the "contract for working in Saipan" or the "employment of labor contract." In sum, the decision of the Sanyuan District Court was a mistake.

2. If the "employment of labor contract" is void, the article it contains regarding labor administration fees is also void.

3. The court decision stated, "It was in compliance with law that the plaintiff adjusted the administration fee to 15 percent." We maintain that the decision was wrong. Under relevant laws and regulations, administration fees shall be negotiated between a labor-export enterprise and an exported laborer. The 15 percent administration fee was unilaterally imposed by the third party without consultation with the defendant. Therefore, the fee was not the representation of the true intent of the parties concerned and violated the legal principles of equality and free will that contracts shall observe.

4. According to Section E of the CNMI's Labor Contract, as well as the Payment and Wage Distribution Agreement signed between the employer in Saipan and the defendant, the former had already docked 25 percent from the laborer's paycheck and paid it to the plaintiff.

The defendant's attorney also told the reporter that SLGF brought a similar case to the Sanyuan District Court in August 1993, suing another laborer, Jiang Xiaomin, for owing it administration fees. The court decided that SLGF won the case, which the attorney found unconvincing.

In the process of the investigation, the reporter saw the original copies of the two contracts mentioned above and did not see any indication of a principal-agent relationship between the Sanming Company and SLGF. The "employment of labor contract" bore the stamps of SLGF and its legal representative only. There was no signature by either the defendant or her family members. The time the contract was signed was left blank. In the authorization agreement produced by the plaintiff, the imprint of the stamp was very fuzzy. The then legal representative of the Sanming Company said in his testimony that he did not know the existence or the content of the authorization agreement until the lawsuit was brought up. Moreover, the authorization agreement was signed on July 5, 1988, but the stamp on the agreement bore the company's new name, which was adopted in early 1989.

The reporter also interviewed Jin Shengqiang, the director of the Law Committee of the Sanming Municipal People's Congress. Director Jin took the case very seriously. During the interview he requested that the defendant report to him the details of the case and promised that he would investigate and analyze the case thoroughly and deal with the issue in a fair manner.

Many returned laborers told the reporter the various problems they encountered. Some could not resume their household registration; some were deprived of labor insurance and welfare benefits. One woman worker asked her employer for an introduction letter that was mandatory for any marriage application. Her employer refused to issue the letter on the grounds that she owed administration fees. As a result, she could not obtain a marriage certificate. Citizens' rights provided by the constitution could not be guaranteed.

At present, the case is with the Sanming Intermediate Court for a second trial. More than sixty returned laborers involved are paying close attention to the case. The people in Sanming City are also paying close attention. More than two hundred Sanming laborers still in Saipan are paying close attention as well.

Our newspaper will continue to report on the development of the case.

CASE 19b

Reprinted here is an official statement made by Sui Jianwei, a technician working for a Chinese-owned printing factory in Saipan, in his application for asylum filed with the U.S. Immigration Department in 1999. Although his own situation in Saipan was much better than that of the factory workers, he was disgusted with the way they were treated. Risking his own safety, he helped the local department of labor in its investigation of labor abuses. At one point, he was put under house arrest by Chinese officials in Saipan, who threatened to send him back to Fujian and put him in jail for twenty years. He escaped and, under the protection of the local authorities, was able to continue working in Saipan for a few years in companies owned by other nationals. When his visa expired, he sought asylum from the U.S. government. At the time of writing, his case is still pending.

How bad were the conditions for workers in the Marianas Garment Manufacturing (MGM) factory in Saipan that had instigated Sui to muster up so much courage to help them? Here is an excerpt of the sordid living and working conditions in this Chinese official-managed factory as described by one of the workers who also filed an application for asylum. In addition to low pay, deductions in wages, and long work hours:

We were made to sign false time cards and our wages were never what was stated on the pay slip! We had two staff members helping the workers fill out their time cards. I felt like a prisoner. Every month, we had to pay U.S.$60 for food. There were eight people to a table, but only two small, six-inch plates of food. There was never enough food; we would fight amongst ourselves for the little there was. We were afraid that, as we had to work very hard, we would become ill without sufficient food. Almost every month we paid $46 for our housing. There were eight people to only one toilet, which hardly ever had any water. There was only thirty minutes a day of cold water available, which meant that we only had five minutes per day for washing and showering. In the morning, we only had one bucket of water for cleaning, which all of us had to share. Each day, we had one gallon of rainwater per worker for drinking. During the dry season we were not given the gallon of boiled rainwater for personal use. The factory brought in two ten-gallon containers for seventy to eighty people. That wasn't enough, and we went thirsty. There was no drinking water provided in our barracks. Most of us, at one time or another, would leave the barracks after work looking for water to drink and to wash ourselves and our clothes. With the lack of proper food and poor living conditions, many of us got ill but the factory would not send us to the hospital even when we were very sick. If a worker fell ill and could not work, the factory would still deduct the money for food and housing.

As can be seen, as little as possible was spent on sustaining these exported workers.[20]

Sui's statement and the above statement from a worker read like an exciting gangster-movie script using a peaceful Pacific island as a backdrop. Beneath the beauty is a story of human trafficking, forced labor, suffering, fear, extortion, violence, falsification of documents, blackmail, house arrests, and threats of long jail sentences.

Statement of Sui Jianwei*

1. My name is Sui Jianwei, and my English name is Bruce. This statement is in connection with my application for asylum in the United States. I am a native and citizen of the People's Republic of China. I entered the United States on March 21, 1998 as a 212.5(a)(2) Parolee in the Public Interest for the purpose of testifying before the U.S. Senate in a matter described below. . . . I presently live at no. # xxx Street, Seattle, Washington. This statement gives my background and my reasons for applying for asylum.

2. My request for asylum arises as a result of my activities in the Commonwealth of the Northern Marianas Islands (CNMI). This is a territory of the United States in the South Pacific with its capital in Saipan.

3. I first heard about CNMI in 1990. At that time, I was living with my wife and son in Fuzhou, China, and I was working as a supervisor in a printing shop. I was approached by a publisher in my town. The publisher arranged a job for me with the Win Fung Printing Company of CNMI, and he referred me to Zhong Fu Overseas Technology Company, the agency that referred me to the job in Saipan. I

---

*Thanks to Sui Jianwei for granting permission through the Seattle law firm representing him to reprint his statement.

paid a fee of about $600 for arranging my papers, and I also agreed to continue to pay them $80 per month for two years out of my pay. I signed a contract that said I would earn $2.15 per hour, and left for CNMI on January 31, 1991.

4. I had some problems in my job, but they were not very serious. In a year, I became a supervisor of the company, and I worked six days a week from eight in the morning until ten most evenings. In 1993, I went back to China for a visit to my wife and son. I then returned to CNMI.

5. When I was in Saipan, I made friends with other Chinese workers at the Saipan Evangelical Church in CNMI. One friend, Ms. A., worked for Marianas Garment Manufacturing (MGM), a company run by the Chinese government. My friend told me of the terrible conditions for Chinese workers at MGM. She told me that the workers often were not paid, and that the living conditions provided by the company were primitive and expensive. She also said that the company treated her and other workers very badly. I could see that the workers were being abused, and I believed that what these companies were doing was wrong. I wanted to help to change the terrible conditions of the workers.

6. In about April 1993, I was aware that the Labor Department of CNMI was bringing a case against MGM on behalf of the garment workers, and I decided to help them on this case. I encouraged Ms. A. to join me. I also encouraged and helped another MGM employee, Ms. B., to go to the Labor Department so that she could give testimony in the case. The testimony from these workers was very important in the case, and MGM knew about the encouragement and help that I had given.

7. These events happened around April 1993, when I returned from China to CNMI. In May of that year, I was ill and was hospitalized. While I was in the hospital, I was visited by Mr. Bao Zhiqiang, the head of Tianjin City Labor Ministry. He was an official of the Communist Party responsible for overseeing Chinese workers in Saipan. Mr. Bao was also involved with the Win Fung Printing Company, where I worked, and with the Grace Garment Factory, one of many Chinese factories in Saipan. When he came to see me in the hospital, he charged that I was the head of the conspiracy against MGM, and said that the Textile Ministry and the Ministry of Foreign Trade in China will lose a million dollars because of this lawsuit. He told me to get Ms. A. to withdraw from the lawsuit or I would be charged with a crime when I got back to China. He threatened that I will be put in prison for twenty years.

8. When I recovered and was released from the hospital, Mr. Bao brought me to the Win Fung workers' barracks. He told me that I was going to be sent back to China. He told the man in charge of the barracks that I was not to leave my room. My room was on the second floor, and when I stepped outside, the man who was on guard duty got angry and ordered me back. Later that night, Mr. Bao came to my room and told me that he had advised Zhong Fu Company, where I worked, that he was sending me back to China. He said I would go to jail when I arrived.

9. Once, I was able to leave my room and make a telephone call to Ms. B to ask her to get in touch with the CNMI Department of Labor on my behalf. She was able to contact the Labor Department, and an official came to arrange for my release. I believe that if the Department of Labor had not intervened, then I would have been sent back to China and put in prison.

10. I talked about my experience to Mr. John Cool, an assistant attorney general for the CNMI and an employee of the Labor Department. He wanted me to help in the case against MGM, but he told me I was in serious danger because all the owners of Chinese businesses in CNMI worked together. All the managers were members of the Communist Party. During this time, I also met Mr. Philip Kaplan, Human Rights Advocate for the Diocese of Chalan Kanoa in CNMI. I provided Mr. Kaplan with information about how Chinese workers are abused in Saipan.

11. From 1994 to March 1998, I continued to live in Saipan. I was not able to get work at any of the Chinese companies in Saipan because they all knew of my activities in exposing the terrible working conditions in the factories. They recognized me as undesirable, and all these companies are run by the Chinese Communist government. If I returned to China during this time, I would have been imprisoned for my work against these companies. From 1994 to 1998, with the help of the CNMI Labor Office, I was able to find temporary employment at several different companies, but none of them were Chinese.

12. I continued to try to expose the terrible conditions of contract workers and the violations of law that were being committed. In 1997 Mr. Kaplan asked me to talk to Mr. Tom Gray, an official from the U.S. Department of the Interior. I described to him how "Made in USA" labels were sewn into Chinese-made clothes. One time, I took him to a warehouse in the middle of the night to take photographs of clothes stacked there, waiting for the labels to be sewn into them.

About the same time that ABC Television was developing a show
on the conditions of Chinese workers at CNMI, I assisted the pro-
ducer in preparing this broadcast, which was aired on the TV show,
"20/20."

13. Because I am known as a person who has been active in exposing
the terrible working conditions in Saipan, I was asked to come to
the United States and testify before Congress. In March 1998, I came
to the United States as a Parolee in the Public Interest to testify
before the Energy and Natural Resources Committee of the U.S.
Senate. I spoke about my experiences and about the abuses that occur to workers in the CNMI. Attached is a copy of the testimony that
I gave before the Senate Committee.

14. Since I came to the United States, I have been working as a printer.
I am afraid to go back to China. My actions in exposing the abuses
that occur in the CNMI, and the assistance I have given to people
investigating the working conditions there, are viewed in China as
activities against the government. For these reasons, it is certain that
I would be in danger if I return to China. For these reasons, I am
asking the United States to grant me asylum. Thank you for consid-
ering my case.

15. I declare under penalty of perjury under the laws of the state of
Washington that the above statement is true and accurate to the best
of my knowledge.

Sui Jianwei

Comments

*In my subsequent correspondence with Sui Jianwei, he said that MGM was
fined $2 million. He further explained the official position of Bao Zhiqiang,
the person who had incarcerated him in Saipan. In addition to the various
former and current positions Bao held, as described in the statement, Bao
was also a key person in the "Chinese Companies Coordinating Group"
(Zhongzi xietiao zu) to which all Chinese officials in the CNMI belonged.
The main function of the Group was to "manage" Chinese workers to prevent them from rebelling. In addition to threatening disobedient workers,
they told the recruiting agents or their work units back in China to put pressure on the workers' families. Indeed, according to Sui, not long after he
escaped, his wife was suddenly visited by two men who simply told her at the
door: "We know your husband is abroad. Tell him to be careful!" At that
point, Sui's wife had no idea what they were talking about. Nothing short of*

a Mafia-style operation can describe what the Chinese officials in Saipan were up to.

The existence of indentured servitude labor in CNMI has been known to politicians and the government administration in the United States for several years. One possible way to stop the abuse would be to make CNMI adopt U.S. federal labor and immigrations laws. But such proposals in Congress have been blocked by the Republicans. To break this stalemate, a human rights NGO, a trade union, and the Asian Law Caucus in the United States all filed three class action lawsuits on behalf of 50,000 Saipan workers against U.S. companies, many of which were high-fashion garment retailers, charging them with unfair business practices and using sweatshop labor. In September 1999, the plaintiffs and the defendants agreed to an out-of-court settlement that included compensation for the workers, the setting up of a corporate code of conduct for Saipan factories, and a monitoring system for labor conditions by an NGO that will be paid for from a pool of money gathered from the U.S. retailers.[21] One of the terms of the settlement agreement consists of provisions strictly regulating "recruitment" fees and bans the notorious "Shadow Contracts," draconian provisions in the agreements that workers are required to sign in their home country, especially China. More U.S. manufacturers and retailers are being added to the lawsuits,[22] and at the time of writing, twenty more asylum applications from Chinese workers are pending.

My continuing research into the case reveals, though, that these settlements have had little effect. An advertisement handout dated June 8, 2000, "Information for Labor Recruitment for the Garment Industry in American Saipan," distributed in China by Sanming International Company, the very company that persecuted and sued the returned workers from Saipan in 1994 in Case 19a. In this June 2000 leaflet, exorbitant fees are openly listed: an administration fee of 25,000 yuan; a passport deposit of 600 yuan; a training fee of 500 yuan; a "guarantee" fee of 10,000 yuan (not refundable if the applicant for his/her own reason cannot leave for Saipan) and an examination fee of 100 yuan. This amounts to 36,200 yuan, about $4,500, an outlay equal to several years' wages of an ordinary state worker.[23] Unless the American NGOs can monitor the recruitment process and can monitor what happens to the workers after they have returned to China, the 1999 settlement is near useless.

In November 2000 the Human Rights Study Group of the Australian National University, made up of law school students, submitted a report to the United Nations Human Rights Committee requesting that the matter be raised with representatives of the United States. At the time of this writing, they are still awaiting a response.[24]

CASE 20

This report reveals that similar conditions exist on another island, this one in the Southern Pacific. Unlike in case 19a, the women workers on the island of Yap in Micronesia took collective action. But their protest was crushed by a Chinese official, with the collusion of the Yap authorities. The workers were flown back to Fujian province to face retaliation and litigation. They were also sued for a very large amount of money for "breaching" their contracts.

WOMEN WORKERS SHED TEARS ON THE PACIFIC ISLANDS*

Chen Jianyang, a twenty-eight-year-old peasant in Sheshui village, Cannei township, Anxi county, Fujian province, shook his head, saying that life is too harsh on him. His family earned a total of about five hundred yuan a month (about sixty dollars), a large part of which was consumed on repaying usurious loans. The loans were mainly a consequence of sending his wife, Cheng Shunzhi, to work in Yap.

Life is even harsher for Ye Baoxin, a villager in Canshan Village. She incurred debt in the same way as Chen did. She finally had to get married to earn a "bride price" to pay off the debt.

Of the sixty-eight laborers from more than ten townships in Anxi county, almost all were in debt for the same reason. It was for this same reason that they were engaged in a lawsuit against China's Xiamen International Economic and Technology Cooperation Company (CXIETCC, Zhongguo Xiamen guojijingji jishu hezuo gongsi). It was not yet clear who would win or lose the case in the end.

Their experience with Yap was too painful to recall. The only words they could find to describe that humiliating experience was that they were "sold as pigs."[25]

Painful Experiences on the Pacific island

Twenty-six-year-old Chen Shunzhi appeared nervous in the beginning of the conversation with U.S. reporters and was uncertain as to where her hands

---

* "Women Workers Shed Tears on the Pacific Islands of Micronesia," (*Nülaogong leixia taipingyang*). Micronesia is made up of a group of islands in the South Pacific, the largest of which is Yap. It is here that Kingtex garment factory, a Hong Kong–invested firm is located. Translation from the Chinese text: Lian Qingchuan, reporter for *Nanfang Weekend* (Nanfang zhoumuo), and Wang Chenggang, reporter for *Quanzhou Evening News*, *Southern Weekly*, September 18, 1998, p. 9. Translated by Liu Dongxiao.

should be. Although she had been a garment worker since the age of sixteen, this village woman seemed to know little about the world. When it came to talking about Yap, she gradually became emotional.

Last March, Chen saw a poster put out by CXIETCC recruiting workers to go to work in Mauritius. She told Huang Xiaoying, Chen Xiaohua, and other sisters in her factory about the news. All of them had worked six or seven years in the garment industry and were quite confident about their abilities. In no time, some forty workers in her factory went to apply.

They first went to the private agents authorized by CXIETCC, Lin Shuizhan and Yao Shuqing, to sign up. Soon the news changed, saying it would take longer to go through the procedures of working in Mauritius than Yap. The news also said that Yap offered better terms: "An eight-hour day with a fixed production quota and pay of $150 a month."

Tempted by the promise of $150 and the opportunity of going abroad, the workers signed up for Yap without any hesitation. Around April 10, CXIETCC and Manager Liu from Yap came to Anxi to test and recruit workers. They asked the applicants to make a certain number of pockets for men's suits within ten minutes. When more than seventy out of about one hundred applicants passed the test, Manager Liu exclaimed: "Although I have tested many groups before, the Anxi group are the best qualified. I'm sure they can do the job."

In late April, CXIETCC, through its agents Lin Shuizhan and Yao Shuqing, charged each new recruit a service fee and security deposit of 8,250 yuan (about $1,030). The two agents charged an additional 2,000 yuan ($250).

At the end of August, nineteen recruits, including Chen Shunzhi and Huang Xiaoying, received a notice to go to CXIETCC to sign a contract. At CXIETCC, a staff member told them to sign the contract immediately after perfunctorily reading the contract aloud to them. For fear of being cheated, the recruits inquired into the details of the terms of payment. CXIETCC assured them again and again of the terms: eight hours a day, one day of rest a week, base pay of $150, and a bonus for work in excess of the quota. CXIETCC also told them that they could certainly finish the quota within eight hours since the quota would be set for an eight-hour workday. "Sign right away. We are in a hurry. You have paid your money anyway. You'll see, you will not want to come back once you are there," said CXIETCC.

The recruits were eager to go abroad and were afraid of being left out. So they dared not keep asking questions. Within half an hour, all had happily signed the contract.

On August 29, the first batch of laborers boarded the plane, something many of them had never seen before, and left for the alien Pacific island.

On the day of arrival, Manager Liu surprised the happy laborers by clenching his fists and telling them: "Your fate will be in my hands in the next two years. If you don't listen to me, I will dock your pay."

Beginning on September 1, life became a nightmare. Xie Guili, a woman worker, wrote in a letter home:

> It is very hot here and rains almost every day. Rainwater is what we drink. The dorm is built with iron and wood. We are surrounded by mountains on all sides. More than forty people share one room, and there is only one bath. What's more, I'm not at all used to the food here, and want to vomit when I swallow it.

The terms of work turned out to be a complete lie. The so-called work quota took these skilled workers seventeen to eighteen hours to finish. They were required to work 1.5 hours extra without pay, the so-called *fugong* (auxiliary work). Lights were turned off after 11:30 P.M. Anyone who had not yet finished the day's quota or *fugong* would have to work in the dark.

Both Chen Shunzhi and Huang Xiaoying gnashed their teeth in hatred when mentioning their foreman's name, Cai Yangzhi. Cai had some pet phrases for them, "Yap does not believe in tears. This is not the place to talk reason. Your fate in the next two years is in our hands. . . . The Pacific is not covered with a lid. Feel free to jump into it to drown yourself!" Laborers were not even free to shed tears. Otherwise, Cai would curse them: "Well, it is not that your mother or father has just died. What the hell are you crying about?" The laborers could not argue with him, or else $5 would be deducted from their pay if they did. The laborers could not go to the restroom more than three times a day, or else they would also be docked $5.

After eighteen to nineteen hours of work, the laborers had to wait in a queue for a bath. They had to scramble for a cup of boiled water to drink (a majority were destined never to get it and had to drink rainwater). They also had to fight each other to grab some food because there was not enough for all in the short ten minutes of mealtime.

One day, Chen Shunzhi tumbled at the entrance to the stairs and fell ill. The management was blind to the tears of the sisters, and accused her of feigning illness. Chen Shunzhi was too sick to work. The management had to dock her pay. On the fourth day, she was forced to stand up and work.

After a whole month's work, the laborers finally got paid $30. And they had to sign some sort of contract in English without being told of its content. They were told it was about letting management keep their pay in custody. According to management's method of calculating the piece rates, no one could finish the work quota. As a result, no one could ever get as much as $150.

A Miserable Passage through Manila

The laborers could not send letters to their families because management would intercept and read them. They asked to telephone CXIETCC, but were not allowed. One of them heard that laborers from Tongan county (another county in Fujian province) were going home soon after their contract expired. They wrote about their situation and asked the Tongan workers to pass the information to their families. But none of their family members believed their stories!

The Foreign Economic and Trade Bureau of Anxi county was one agent authorized by CXIETCC to carry out the recruitment. In early October, the bureau heard complaints from families of the laborers and went to talk with CXIETCC, who answered: "We are a big company, so how can we possibly cheat you? The factory in Yap has worked with us for six or seven years and we know the complaints cannot be true." CXIETCC also coldly told the section chief in charge of labor affairs at the Foreign Economic and Trade Bureau of Anxi county, "Laborers from your county are finicky." On October 6, the second group of laborers waiting to be sent [inquired about the complaints and] were told: "Those complaints are not true. They made it up. . . . The first batch of laborers has already produced more than required by the production quota."

On October 19, the first group of laborers to Yap was given a one-day break after fifty-four days of nonstop work. But it was not even a full day off because they were made to do two hours of unpaid auxiliary work that day. The women (only one of the laborers was a man) felt so hopeless that they had nothing to say to each other.

They once attempted to negotiate with the management. Manager Liu replied: "Your contract is not with me but with CXIETCC. The factory simply uses your labor. You have to unconditionally obey the arrangement made with CXIETCC. You should direct your problems to CXIETCC."

What else could they say? They therefore decided to fight with their own power. On October 20 they came very early to wait for the boss on the small playground by the factory gate. But the management staff passed without even looking at them. Soon a notice came telling them go to a meeting. Manager Liu stood between two armed policemen and blurted out: "Either you unconditionally resume work, or else we ask the police to take you away."

On the previous day, they had delivered a letter to Manager Liu requesting that he lower the production quota, reduce work hours, and pay overtime rates. They had all come to earn money. No one wanted to make trouble. Pushed by desperation, all the laborers chose to be taken away by the police.

On October 21, local police forced sixty-eight laborers to board a police vehicle, drove them away, and put them under detention in an old building that was more than 10 kilometers away from the factory. The police guarded the building day and night. The management told the workers it was the immigration office.

The laborers were given two or three slices of bread for breakfast, a few spoonfuls of rice for lunch, and banana paste or lettuce with a little fish for dinner. They drank rainwater when they were thirsty. When they got hungry, they used the rainwater to boil instant noodles and seaweed that that they had brought with them. They went on a hunger strike; no one cared. They had diarrhea; no one cared. They wanted to use the phone; they were handcuffed.

On October 20, CXIETCC learned about their plight and told the Foreign Economic and Trade Bureau of Anxi county that the laborers were on strike. The general manager of CXIETCC went to the Anxi county government and requested cooperation in dealing with the laborers. Anxi county government issued an open letter:

> We hope you communicate your difficulties and requests with CXIETCC or the management [in Yap] in a restrained and mild manner, and through normal channels. Don't employ excessive actions that will bring about a negative impact and unnecessary losses to yourselves, your families, and our country. The people's government of the county is concerned about you. We wish you will fulfill the contract and that all goes well with your work.

Having been cheated so many times, the laborers refused to believe that the letter was from the county government. So, they made only one request: to go back to their motherland.

On the morning of October 30, Chen Shunzhi and twenty other laborers were suddenly told to pack their luggage. They thought they were to be moved to a different place and were so frightened that they cried. It turned out that a factory garbage truck actually took them to the airport. Each of them was given $10, two eggs, and two pieces of bread. Seeing that they were going home, they were beside themselves with joy. Cai Yangzhi sneered, "What the hell are you happy about? The police will arrest when you get back."

The plane stopped in Manila. They were supposed to change planes there. But nobody told them how. Nor were they told where they could get food. The airport security took away their passports to process their visas. So they waited—for three days and two nights. Fortunately, two Taiwanese took pity on them. They bought them some bread and told them to get some newspapers from the cleaners so that they could sleep on the floor.

Huang Xiaoying and the others, altogether forty-four people, were awakened at 4:00 A.M. on November 5. They were told to pack up and they again heard the same remark: "You will know better when you arrive."

They were given $5 for expenses on the trip. Cai Yangzhi frightened them, saying they would have to pay a head tax for leaving. "The first batch has arrived at Xiamen and has been arrested. You are now being deported."

The miserable laborers had no idea what to do at Manila airport. Luckily, Mr. Zhang Jinlang of the Taiwan Knitting Mill, came to their aid. He bought them some bread, and went to airport security to inquire about their passports. He came back to console them: "No, you are not being deported. If so, you would not have been sitting here. You would have been surrounded by police." Mr. Zhang left at one o'clock. He called the Chinese Embassy in the Philippines. Huang Defa, a third-level secretary, went to the airport and confirmed that they were not being deported. He also tried his best to arrange for their accommodation and food.

The laborers would always remember their humiliating experience at Manila airport. They said they lost face for China because they looked like beggars: pathetic, thirsty, hungry, and miserable. Some white people pointed to them saying, "China." They felt so ashamed! But what else could they have done?

Arbitration

As soon as they returned home, the laborers went to CXIETCC. They requested "a fair and responsible explanation" as well as a refund of the 8,025 yuan. (The private agents had returned the 2,000 yuan they had charged the laborers for fear of being held responsible.) CXIETCC simply ignored them. Later, CXIETCC claimed instead that each laborer should pay more than 10,000 yuan. The laborers had no choice but to apply for arbitration.

The attorney for the laborers, Huang Wenhan, said in his statement that the contract provision for "six days of work and eight hours a day during the course of employment" was an act of fraud. In stipulating that, "in times of labor disputes, party B shall be subject to the mediation and decisions of Party A," it was a "bully's contract." It should be considered void because it violates the principle of equality between the two parties. Accordingly, CXIETCC should repay the laborers a total of 437,850 yuan ($54,700) and pay them 189,000 yuan ($23,600) in compensation.

CXIETCC replied in defense that the laborers were not able to produce any evidence that they were made to work seventeen to eighteen hours a day, and therefore it did not have to repay the workers' money. On the contrary, it argued that the laborers went on strike and caused themselves to be "deported," which amounted to a breach of contract. Therefore, each laborer owed to the company 11,991 yuan ($1,500) incurred for the costs of visa fees, domestic document-processing fees, flight tickets, rent during the strike, and security and food expenses at Manila airport. The laborers should also compensate CXIETCC an alleged market loss and other losses in the amount of 1 million yuan ($125,000).

The result of the arbitration was that neither side won. The arbitration decision declared the contract valid. There was no proof for the existence of the "eight-hour production quota." Although the provision that disputes should be subject to party A was void, it did not invalidate other provisions of the contract. In conclusion, the arbitration decision refused to accept the claims of both parties.

CXIETCC, the Impossible

On September 7, the reporters interviewed Tang Min, director of the legal affairs department of CXIETCC, and the general manager, Tang Jinming. They denied the laborers' statement—item by item—as if the laborers lied throughout.

CXIETCC alleged that they had explained to the laborers major items of the contract before they were asked to sign the contract. (Tang Min did not deny that it took only half an hour to finish signing the contract.) As for how to explain away the "eight-hour production quota," Tang produced a CXIETCC document that said, "The setting of an eight-hour daily quota is based on the average speed of a group of skilled workers which in turn varies with the specific style and material used for a particular order." Tang Min further declared:

> Manager Liu made it very clear to the laborers at the time of the interview that the workday would be eleven–twelve hours long and that they should be prepared to endure hard work. . . . . Because the length of a workday has to be based on each particular order, it is not possible to write it into the contract. . . . In fact, all skilled workers were able to fulfill as well as exceed the quota every day. According to the laborers, the so-called skilled workers could not finish the quota unless they worked sixteen–seventeen hours a day.

As of the time they left Yap, each laborer had obtained, at most, a total of $35 to $40 from the factory. Tang Min further explained that the factory had closed the laborers' accounts and confiscated their savings in order to compensate for the factory's loss incurred by the strike.

When questioned about the causes of the strike, Tang Min laughed and said:

Factory management also thought they had never encountered a strike like this. They would not listen to CXIETCC's mediation and management. They would not negotiate, would not carry on a dialogue, nor put forth their demands. All they wanted was a single stubborn demand to go home.

But why had CXIETCC only communicated with the factory in Yap by telephone and fax? "Because it takes at least half a month to obtain a visa. Had the laborers given us time, we would have sent a work group to Yap to solve the problem," said Tang Jinming. According to the laborers, however, CXIETCC did not have a word with them during their entire period of detention.

According to the law of Yap, "A laborer will lose the work permit if she or he stops work. Once a work permit is cancelled, a laborer becomes an illegal resident and shall be deported."

Tang Min showed us two passports that belonged to the laborers. On them was a handwritten word, "deportation." Attorney Huang Wenhan believed the imprint was forged by CXIETCC.

When asked why the laborers did not make any demands but chose instead to go back to China, Tang Min replied: "We could not understand why, either. You'd better go ask them."

Comments

Of all the exported workers from different Asian countries, those from China are caught in a particularly difficult situation. As seen in the several cases above, the fact that the recruitment agents are Chinese government agencies, not private individuals, means that the workers are subjected to near-absolute control. Moreover, the very high charges, fees, and bonds that Chinese workers pay at the time of recruitment makes their situation abroad especially vulnerable. The labor human-rights organization that is involved in filing the class action against U.S. companies using Saipan-imported labor noted that "these exorbitant fees are one of the principal causes of workers' involuntary servitude and peonage, because they effectively force the worker to continue working for their Saipan contractors, and accept whatever overtime is offered, in the struggle to repay the enormous debt that they were forced to incur in order to get the job."[26] Again, similar to the seafarers' case, the horror stories of these Chinese workers in the Marianas did not end after they were saved by "foreigners." Once home, they faced litigation charges from recruiting agents and employers. They were stripped of their money and their original state jobs, and were plunged into heavy debt.

There are a few differences between the workers exported to the Pacific and the seafarers. In China, the former had very good jobs as skilled work-

ers in state textile and garment enterprises. They were recruited by their own ministries. It never occurred to them that their government could sell their labor in a way that reduced them to working as slaves. The employment and labor-export agents do not directly manage the seafarers on the boats, but the workers in the Marianas were directly controlled by the Chinese bureaucracies and their agents, together with the employers. On Chinese soil, foreign-invested companies are managed by the Taiwanese, Hong Kong Chinese, or Korean investors. The Chinese bureaucrats extract compliance from workers overseas by extracting money from them, threatening them, and arresting them if they do not submit.

Notes

1. Trish Saywell, "Workers' Offensive: China Joins the League of Major Labor Exporters. Sending Workers Overseas Brings in Foreign Exchange and Helps Relieve Unemployment at Home—A Little," *Far Eastern Economic Review*, Vol. 160, No. 22 (May 29, 1997), pp. 50–52.

2. I have carried out some original research on these two cases and have collected enough documentation to assert that these are not isolated incidents. Some citations will be provided in the introductions to cases 18 and 19.

3. Huang Yiping, "Economic Reform and Emigration Pressures in China," unpublished report prepared for the International Labor Organization (draft), April 1996, pp. 37–42.

4. Saywell, "Workers' Offensive."

5. Statement by Sui Jianwei describing his activities in the Marianas, as a supporting document filed with his application for asylum in the United States. Sui was a Chinese technician recruited to work in the Marianas in 1991. He began to help U.S. and local authorities investigate abuses of Chinese workers in the Marianas.

6. The city police and judiciary of Jilin city, Jilin province recruited more than 200 peasants to work in Kuwait. Among them, forty-four women who worked as domestic servants found they were practically enslaved. Some sought refuge with the Chinese embassy in Kuwait. On their return to Jilin, they got into a legal battle with their recruitment agents. *Xinkuai bao* (New Fast News), January 4, 2000.

7. Huang, "Economic Reform," p. 42.

8. *China News Digest*, October 23, 1994.

9. *China Daily*, January 31, 1999.

10. For a more hair-raising case, see *Laodong daobao* (Labor News), October 28, 1997. Several Korean-Chinese seafarers were so maltreated on a Korean-managed boat that in their desperation they murdered several of the Koreans and also a few seafarers of other nationalities.

11. As of 1998, the seafarers had not been able to get back their money. My thanks to Zhao Minghua, who followed the case during her research on seafarers, for sharing this information with me.

12. In April 1997, I carried out an interview in London with ITF's communications secretary on this particular case.

13. Robert S. Senser, "Walking the Plank," *Far Eastern Economic Review*, Vol. 155, No. 37 (September 17, 1992), p. 59.

14. Remark from the ITF's communications secretary, in my 1997 interview with him in London.

15. The ILO Chinese seafarers' ruling was based on e-mail communication between Robert Senser and ITF communications secretary, September 1996. The ILO ruling was presented to the Chinese government on January 30, 1995.

16. 1997 interview with ITF's communications secretary.

17. Robert Collier, "Stalemate in Talks on Saipan Workers: Tug-of-War Between Local Officials, Federal Government on Sweatshop Law," *San Francisco Chronicle*, January 20, 1999.

18. Phil Kaplan, "Made in the USA? The Story of the Northern Marianas Islands, Where Human Rights Abuses of Foreign Workers Flourish Under the U.S. Flag," *Washington Free Press*, July–August 1997, pp. 8–9.

19. This would have been about five times more than what they could have made in China based on an average monthly income of 600 yuan.

20. Thanks to Phil Kaplan for passing on this official document written by an MGM worker in 1994, that was appended by one of the bishops in the CNMI in his letter of appeal to the CNMI governor on behalf of the Chinese contract workers. For the description of conditions by another worker, see Robert Collier, "Saipan Workers Describe Slavery of Sweatshops: They Say American Dream Turned into Nightmare," *San Francisco Chronicle*, January 22, 1999.

21. For a series of reports and documents related to the lawsuits go to http://www.globalexchange.org/economy/corporations/saipan/monitoring.html.

22. For example, in March 2000, six more companies were being sued (Honolulu, H, March 3, 2000/ PR Newswire).

23. Thanks to the Hong Kong Christian Industrial Committee for sharing this document with me.

24. Human Rights Study Group, Law Faculty, Australian National University, "A Submission to the United Nations Human Rights Committee—Alleged Human Rights Violations in Saipan, a Territory of the United States," November 2000.

25. A Chinese expression for Chinese indentured labor in the nineteenth and twentieth centuries.

26. Global Exchange, "Status of Settlement Talks in Saipan Sweatshop Lawsuits," September 1, 1999, http://www.globalexchange.org/economy/corporations/saipan/settlement.alks.html

Chapter 8

Workers' Resistance

In a political climate that suppresses all forms of activities that smack of autonomous trade unionism, workers seek to protect their rights by either legal or illegal means. This chapter shows three ways in which workers have struggled for social justice: by collectively resorting to outbursts of violence, by protesting on the streets, and by seeking legal solutions. The legal path, as will be seen, seems to be increasingly accepted by the authorities. It is encouraging that China's new legal structure, which has gradually evolved over the past two decades, is beginning to help workers,[1] notwithstanding the widespread assaults on workers' rights that we have documented in this volume. Increasingly, the authorities have come to realize that a legal system can serve as a useful mediating mechanism to resolve labor disputes and preempt social disturbances. The authorities seem particularly amenable to allowing disputes over industrial accidents to come to court.

CASE 21

To a certain extent, this case is quite similar to case 10, in which migrant construction workers exploded in uncontrollable anger and rose up in a riot against local police and local authorities. In case 21, however, the workers are not migrants; they are former state workers. The riot was on a small scale, and instead of the local authorities, it was the Taiwanese bosses who were injured in the mayhem.

The upheaval was organized by none other than the chair of the workplace union. He had the temerity to organize the workers because he had the backing of the Chinese factory director, who also happened to be a person of some local importance as a delegate to the county-level people's congress. Indeed, the incident even had the tacit approval of the local city government. The report suggests that the animosity between the two partners of the joint

*venture ran deep. It was not clear why the Chinese managers and the Tai-
wanese managers were at loggerheads, but the workers took advantage of
this division to vent their anger.*

*The case involves a number of people, and it is not always easy to follow
who belongs to which side of the joint venture. The following is a list of the
protagonists:*

On the Chinese side:
- Director Wu Caigeng
- Deputy General Manager Tang Mingqi
- Head of Labor and Wage Department Wu Haiying
- Trade Union Chair Chen Zhaoyuan
- Finance Manager Da Zuxing
- Production Manager Zhang Kouhua

On the Taiwanese side:
- Deputy Director Zhou Guiliang
- His wife, Wang Meifang
- General Manager Fang Zhongjun
- Deputy General Manager Zhu Zhenlong

This report received full-page coverage in Taiwan's main newspaper, the
Central Daily. *As might be expected, it is totally biased toward the Taiwanese
managers.*

SEVERAL DOZEN WORKERS BESIEGED AND TAIWANESE BUSINESSMEN INJURED; THE VICTIMS' PAINFUL ACCOUNT

**Workers Beat Up and Injure Zhou Guiliang, Fang Zhongjun,
and Two Others of the Far East Concrete Factory***

One year after the Qiandao Lake Boat Incident,[2] on March 6, the Far East Concrete Factory [Yuandong shuini chang], a joint venture operated by Taiwan businessman Zhou Guiliang and the Jurong county Concrete Factory in Zhenjiang
city of Jiangsu province, yet another violent incident took place. Workers beat up
and threatened the management of the Taiwanese partners when they demanded
an increase in their "floating wages." They even said they would "drive the Taiwanese businessmen out with a broomstick." The violence raised serious concern among members of the Taiwanese business community about their own and
their spouses' personal safety and the fate of their businesses on the mainland.

*Zhuang Ronghong, "Jiangsu 'Yuandong shuini chang' taishang Zhou Guiliang,
Fang Zhongjun deng siren zao gongren oushang. Shushi gongren chengbao weiou.
Shouhai taishang tongshu shimo. Yuji youcun," Zhongyang ribao (Central Daily)
(Taipei), March 30, 1995. Translated by Anita Chan.

In the incident, the deputy head of the board of directors, Zhou Guiliang, and his wife, Wang Meifang, General Manager Fang Zhongjun, and Deputy General Manager Zhu Zhenlong were all beaten, injured, and forced to sign a "treaty." That evening, Zhou, Wang, and Zhu gave up protecting the factory and moved out of the factory compound to stay temporarily at the Zhenjiang Hotel. General Manager Fang flew back to Taipei to seek help.

Subsequently, the victims filed letters of complaint to the Jurong county, Zhenjiang city, and Jiangsu province governments, to the PRC Taiwanese Affairs Office, and the Overseas Chinese Association. But as of today, they had not received any reasonable response.

In addition, Wang Meifang, who also holds U.S. citizenship, filed a complaint with the U.S. consulate in Nanjing. It was reported that the consulate had expressed its concern to the Chinese authorities, but nothing else has happened since. The three who retreated to stay in the hotel are actually captives. All they can do each day is to act as the Chinese party's rubber stamp. They have completely lost their rights to manage the factory.

The Far East Concrete Factory has 1,000 staff members and workers. At the time of the incident about half of them, led by the trade-union chair and some important cadres, participated in besieging and beating up the Taiwanese businessmen.

* * *

"Don't beat my wife. She is pregnant. No, you can't beat her! Don't beat her anymore!" Just then, a metal spittoon flew across the room, hit Zhou on the head, and cut short his plea.

That morning, Zhou had sensed a strange atmosphere already brewing in the factory. Very early, Zhou Guiliang finished drawing up the wage-scale table and handed it to Finance Manager Da Zuxing. Zhou also instructed Da to get ready to go into Zhenjiang city to remit some of the foreign party's money out of the country. Da's response astonished Zhou: "Last Saturday, the director told me that I could not send money out."

"Why?"

"Let us wait until the director comes back from the county people's congress meeting." It was only later Zhou realized that this unusual behavior was the initial shot fired in a whole series of actions taken by workers against the managerial staff. Later, Zhou bumped into Trade-Union Chair Chen Zhaoyuan and Wu Haiying of the Labor and Wage Department, and saw them deeply absorbed in conversation. But the moment they spotted Zhou they stopped talking.

At about 9:00 A.M., Trade-Union Chair Chen brought Zhou and Deputy

General Manager Zhu Zhenlong to General Manager Fang Zhongjun's office. Chen told the three: "The trade union and the cadres are of the opinion that the wage-scale table is not correct."

Fang therefore checked the wage-scale table, which had been drawn up by the Financial Department and which had been approved by the board of directors, against that of the Labor and Wage Department. He found no discrepancy. A bit later, Deputy General Manager Tang Mingqi and Finance Manager Da Zuxing of the Chinese side joined in. Da Zuxing held up an old wage-scale table and pointed out that the company has "left out one level of floating wages." An argument ensued. The Taiwanese side insisted that it was all done in accordance with the decision made at the last board of directors meeting; the other side disagreed. The argument went on for some time without resolution.

At about noon, a rumor was spreading in the factory: "The company is not paying out wages today."

When Fang heard this, he was furious. He went to question Da: "Why are you not paying the workers today? Whose decision was it?" Da could not give any reason. Under Fang's insistence, Da went to the bank to withdraw money for the payroll.

Fang and Zhou Guiliang discussed among themselves what had gone wrong: "In the beginning, Da said he was under orders not to withdraw money, but later, he did go to get the money. Something fishy is going on."

At about 1:15 P.M., Director Wu came back from the county people's congress meeting and immediately called a board meeting to discuss the decision on the "wage reform" that was made on February 28. In addition to the four representatives from the foreign party, the Chinese party included Director Wu, Trade-Union Chair Chen, and Tang Mingqi. When General Manager Zhou left the room to go to the restroom, he saw a lot of workers walking toward the administration building.

"Deputy Director Zhou, this strike is organized. It was planned by Trade-Union Chair Chen two days ago," a worker divulged to Zhou when he was in the restroom.

Zhou was furious. He rushed back to the conference room and berated Trade-Union Chair Chen right there, "You have to take responsibility for this strike."

Chen's face changed color. He shoved Zhou out of the room to the corridor and yelled, "Tell me who told you this!"

By then, about three hundred workers were already gathered downstairs. When they saw the scuffle, some rushed upstairs. About fifty of them were blocking the staircase. When Zhou realized that the situation had become serious, he went back into the conference room. Workers were now crowding outside the room yelling, "Why are you not giving out wages!"

Director Wu took this opportunity to press Zhou and his cohorts to give in. But they refused to capitulate. Meanwhile, the workers outside the room were becoming more and more agitated. Suddenly, "Bang!" A worker had punched his fist through the window. Glass was scattered all over. An explosive atmosphere was hanging in the air. Director Wu asked Chen to call all the mid-level managerial staff to a meeting. Within ten minutes, everyone had arrived. The efficiency was impressive. Normally, it takes half an hour to gather everybody.

Zhou and his associates were told to go to the other end of the room while Wu and the Chinese cadres convened for about twenty minutes. He then came over to Zhou and said "The cadres all want you to agree to the pay raise. What I said as the director is not good enough."

Braving the storm, General Manager Fang insisted, "I am just following the decision made at the board of directors' meeting. The decision is that wages will go up 62 percent. I do not have the authority to decide on anything that was not a board decision."

The production manager, Zhang Kouhua, who was also present, immediately said, "In that case, there is not much I can do [to calm the workers down]. If something untoward happens, I will not intervene."

Meanwhile, the workers outside were roaring: "We have been here for more than an hour! Let's force our way in!" Zhang then led the mid-level cadres out of the conference room. In doing so they raised the curtain for the violent scene to take place.

* * *

The four Taiwanese businesspeople were beaten by the workers, placed under arrest, and victimized for more than ten hours. It was only at 9:00 p.m. that people from the labor bureau and the police arrived. But the first thing they asked the Taiwanese was not whether their personal safety had been in jeopardy or their rights had been violated. They merely asked, "Now that you have agreed to the demands of the workers, how are you going to implement them?"

When Zhou and his company heard this, their hearts sank. They knew that under such circumstances, it was impossible to ask for more. "Please escort us back to our dormitories," they requested. All they could hope for at that moment was to leave the scene.

Comments

The incident was taken very seriously by the Taiwanese newspaper, which gave it the "date name" of the "March 6 Incident." By Chinese convention, only events of historical significance normally merit a "date name." This is certainly too weighty a title for this particular incident, but behind the news-media hype lay the Taiwanese business community's deep anxieties about their personal safety when operating factories in China.³ The report suggested that the Taiwanese managers were victims of a devious plot, and that the violence was instigated by Chinese officials. The report did not delve into the root causes of the Chinese workers' anger against the Taiwanese managers. The immediate cause was said to be a disagreement between the two sides of management over a wage increase. But such a dispute could have been settled peacefully in the boardroom. For it to explode as it did, the workers' resentment and antagonism must have run deep. Taiwanese managers on the mainland have a poor reputation, and it was likely that the Taiwanese leadership in this concrete factory had been abusive. When the trade-union chair stoked the fire, so to speak, the workers felt no inhibition in venting their anger against the Taiwanese. To Taiwanese investors, who were accustomed to enjoying the support of Chinese managers and local authorities, this incident touched off alarm bells. It was obvious that when Chinese authorities sided with workers, the consequences for investors could be disastrous.

Notably, the Jiangsu provincial government did not lend the city authorities and the factory director any public support. There was a news blackout to protect Jiangsu's good investment climate. There was not even a single reference to the incident in the Jiangsu Daily *and the* Jiangsu Workers' News.⁴ *The Taiwanese vehemently lodged complaints to a number of Chinese bureaucracies, including the provincial governor, and were informed that the officials and workers involved in the incident had been reprimanded.⁵*

CASE 22a

The workers at this factory vented their anger against management in a manner very different from the previous case. Workers at a Beijing factory owned by the People's Liberation Army had been pressured to sign one-year employment contracts that would have effectively stripped them of their jobs when the contracts expired. They planned to air their grievances in public and to stage a legal demonstration. Their insistence that they be granted a permit by the police, as stipulated by the Demonstration Law, shifted the focus of their struggle from employment contracts to the right to demonstrate. When the workers insisted on playing by the rules, the authorities did likewise, by finding technical loopholes in the law that prevented the workers from protesting on the streets.⁶

Here, we see workplace collective action emerging that begins to resemble actions taken by an autonomous trade union, with an organizing committee formed to renegotiate employment contracts. The natural leader, Zhu Rui, had an unusual personal history. She was active in the Democracy Wall Movement twenty years ago in 1979–80, when a schoolteacher at this factory. Because of her activities, she was demoted to the shop floor.[7]. Under her leadership the organizing committee took a bold and unusual step, informing the Hong Kong news media of their application to demonstrate.[8]

Three items are included for this case. The first two are undated open letters issued by the organizing committee, calling for solidarity and updating readers on the latest status of the application to stage a street demonstration. The third was written by "a sacked worker from Factory 3501" to the general public, detailing the step-by-step battle the committee fought with the local authorities. Ultimately the demonstration did take place.

OPEN LETTER TO ALL THE STAFF AND WORKERS AT FACTORY 3501*

Fellow 3501 Workers,

Our application to hold a demonstration is a fundamental right of all citizens of China. How could anyone approve of the policies and decisions of the management at Factory 3501? They are using their powers of office to force us to sign one-year contracts. If we refuse to sign, they hide behind the law and say that "the contract has expired and the law is now effective." This is just a weapon to force us to be unemployed. In this manner, they are even denying us the right to claim allowances as laid-off workers.[9] Is this the spirit of the law that the Party Central Committee talks about in the newspapers and on television every day? They are not talking realistically or reasonably. They don't care if the workers have enough to eat, so why shouldn't we use the law to protect our constitutional rights? Everyone here has put the best years of their lives into the factory. Some of us started working here on the military-uniform assembly line on piece rates, earning just 18 yuan a month. We have worked hard for many years to the point that many of us now suffer from serious work-related illnesses. Yet now that we are nearing retirement age, they want to kick us out. Is it not understandable that these experiences have left all of us at 3501 feeling bitter? How many older workers here have put up with this endless hard work? If we were to start all over again, had known how matters would have ended up, none of us would have been prepared to do it again, even if they paid us 100 times over and there weren't half the hardships which we have endured in the past.

Now that China is moving into a new age, those of us over forty have already given our best and are too exhausted to keep up. The 10,000 yuan

---

*Reprinted with permission, from the *China Labor Bulletin*, Issue 40 (January–February 1998), pp. 3–6.

that management has offered in redundancy is nothing more than charity, and anyway, with prices rising the way they are, what's the use of that kind of money? It's simply not enough to exist on. Fellow workers, our past experiences here at 3501 should be a lesson to all of us—young and old.

All the steps we have taken regarding the planned demonstration are in accordance with the legal procedures: if the authorities ratify our application, then the demonstration will be totally legal. We understand that some people are very nervous about taking part, and that not everyone feels the same as we do. However, anyone who contacts the organizing committee can do so anonymously, and will count as one more person opposed to management.

If we are going to change the unreasonable management policies of 3501, and struggle for our own individual interests, we must pull together and make a concerted effort by relying on our collective strength. It is not guaranteed that we will obtain a total victory, but it is guaranteed that the interests of everyone is the first concern, and no one is putting their own interests above the collective interests of all 3501's workers. If people try to drive a wedge between us, anyone at the factory should feel free to check out the whole situation.

If anyone is thinking that we are just doing this as a way of getting more money, then the answer is simple: our financial situation is not good. The factory officials have made it perfectly clear that if we don't take the redundancy money on offer, we will be sacked anyway because our contracts have expired. The paper, ink, and banners for the demonstration are all paid for out of our own pockets, and some people have therefore had to take the money on offer in order to protect their own interests. No one can dare say we haven't put our own sweat and blood into Factory 3501. No one can deny our years of hard work with the factory. No one should deprive us of our rights in such a manner.

Fellow workers, our interests are the same—no one is going to just put on a platter what we are due. We have to stand up and fight for our rights. We have worked for years to win our retirement and pension rights, and management is doing all they can to take them away from us. If just one or a few of us stand up against them, we don't have a chance. But if we all stand together, then they will have to listen to us. We must unite and get the issue solved.

Sacked Workers of Factory 3501
Tel: 62930909
Beeper: 191—2981921

CASE 22b

SECOND LETTER TO THE STAFF AND WORKERS AT FACTORY 3501

To All Workers of Factory 3501:

Twenty days have passed since we applied for permission to hold a demonstration. So far we still have not been given permission. Despite this delay, we have already gained a major victory. Why?

First, more and more people, at all levels of society, are increasingly aware of the situation at Factory 3501 and know that the management's policies are unreasonable. Moreover, as attention focuses on the factory, management and officials at 3501 are beginning to examine their own behavior.

This is at least a step in the right direction! Our sincerity in trying to solve the problems confronting us is also well known. How can the authorities refuse to grant us permission to demonstrate when we apply again?

We hope to achieve a satisfactory settlement to the problems. However, management has acted in a totally insincere manner thus far. They are worried that they will not be able to implement their plans for the factory—plans that threaten the interests of every single one of us. No wonder we all feel that this is an urgent problem requiring immediate action. We need to learn from the mistakes of the past and unite in order to protect our interests; we must get everything ready so that we can hold a street demonstration as soon as we get permission from the police.

If we want to solve the problems, we have to have our say! If they do not give us a say, then we have to adopt another way of firmly expressing our opposition to their unreasonable policies. The organizing committee has already won the support of many people.

Demonstration time: 18 January, 1998. 10:00 A.M.

Slogans:.
- 3501 Workers and our Families Demand the Right to Welfare
- No to Unemployment! Yes to Retirement Rights!
- Kick Out the Unreasonable Policies at 3501
- Protect the Right to Demonstrate

Route:. 3501 Hujialou gate—Dabeiyao—Shuangjing—Dajiaoting—Back to the Factory
Contact Person: Zhu Rui, Tel: 62930909
Beeper: 191–2981921

CASE 22c

News From Beijing Factory 3501

At 3:00 P.M. on December 8, 1997, we distributed several dozen copies of our "Application to Hold a Demonstration" and "Complaint of the Staff and Workers at Factory 3501" to employees at the factory. We also sent materials and information to various newspaper offices, government organizations, and the general office of the Central Committee of the Communist Party of China. At the same time, Zhu Rui went to the Beijing Public Security Bureau (PSB) to complete the application procedures to hold a demonstration. However, because the site for the demonstration was incorrect, she was unable to register.

The following morning, Zhu Rui again went to the PSB office No. 13 in Gongdelin district to complete the procedures. While she was waiting in the office, a police officer from Chaoyang district rushed in and took Zhu Rui to Factory 3501's security office for talks. Their purpose was to bring the application procedures to a halt.

According to the provisions in China's constitution, citizens have the right to freedom of speech, publication, assembly, association, procession, and demonstration (Chapter 2, Article 35). The same section of the constitution also guarantees citizens' labor rights, rest days, the right to existence, as well as material assistance to the aged, those who are ill, or suffer from loss of the capacity to work. Moreover, "the constitutional provisions for the basic rights of citizens are the legal foundation for the rights of all citizens." In light of these rights, Zhu Rui persisted with our application to hold a demonstration.

On the afternoon of December 9, the leader of the Chaoyang district office, along with leaders from the Beijing PSB, held a meeting at Factory 3501. Zhu Rui waited for the results of the talks, but by 8:00 P.M. they still had not persuaded her to withdraw the application. Finally, they decided that those who wanted to demonstrate could continue with their application in accordance with the law, but that they should cease handing out any information to the public about the protest.

While preparing our application to hold a demonstration, we reported the situation at the factory to Party committees at all levels, National People's Congress committees, and government organizations. We also made use of news agencies and other channels of communication to expose the irrational policies of the management at Factory 3501. We made personal visits and sent letters to national bodies and government offices to express our views in the hope of obtaining the support of as many people as possible.

At 11:20 A.M. on December 10, the general office of the Party Central

Committee telephoned us and inquired about the problems. They said they would make preparations to visit the factory to find out more about the situation.

On the morning of December 11, Zhu Rui handed over the notice for holding a demonstration to the No. 13 office. The officer-in-charge said that the problems could be solved through the relevant government departments. If they still weren't happy with the results, then they could resume their application to hold a demonstration.

On the morning of December 17, we went to the Beijing Public Security Bureau No. 13 office to inquire about the situation. An office worker, who did not want to reveal her name, said that the officer-in-charge was not present and asked us to return after two days.

On December 19, we again went to the No. 13 office. The same office worker said that the officer-in-charge was not there and asked us to return the following Monday.

On December 22, we went to No. 13 office for the third time and were received by the officer-in-charge. He told us that the matter concerning Factory 3501 had already been passed on to a higher government level. We replied that at no time had anyone from the government come to talk to us, and the problems at the factory itself were far from being solved. We demanded that we be allowed to formally complete the procedures for holding a demonstration. Because eleven days had already passed and the problems at the factory were nowhere near being resolved, our patience was proof of our sincerity. We said: "Since you have not solved the problems, we want to make use of our rights as citizens and express our opinions to society in general. All we are demanding is our right to survive, not golden handshakes or positions on high-ranking Party committees. We feel that it is our own sweat and blood that has gone into the factory, and now even our rice bowls have been taken away."

As our labor insurance has been expropriated by Factory 3501 [in itself an illegal act—Ed.], we believe the opinions which we expressed are entirely within legal means and are rational. The officer-in-charge was sympathetic to our plight and explanations, asked us to wait another day, and he would personally go to the central authorities to encourage them to deal with the issues. As a further expression of goodwill, we again promised to wait.

On December 24, we were again received by the officer-in-charge. He told us that over the previous two days, they had been in constant talks with the relevant departments: the government, Factory 3501, and the higher government office responsible for Factory 3501. The problems could definitely be solved. Over the past few days, the person responsible from the factory's Party committee, the factory head, and the factory security department had also been holding meetings to study the situation, and had made a report to the government office expressing their sincerity in finding solutions to the problems.

The officer-in-charge also said that further visits to the factory over the next two days were planned and urged us to wait patiently. Our position was clear: the aim of the planned demonstration depended on finding solutions to the problems. With the above assurance of the factory management's goodwill, we would again wait.

On December 25, the officer-in-charge telephoned us, and told Zhu Rui to go to No. 13 office the following day.

On December 26, Zhu Rui went to the office feeling reasonably optimistic. The officer-in-charge picked up the December 24 edition of "News" and started to speak: "They are not happy with this type of news bulletin. However, the PSB has no business interfering in the internal business of an enterprise. We are already fully aware of the situation at the factory, and if you want to express your opinions about it through a demonstration, then fill in the forms."

Zhu Rui replied, "Why didn't you tell us earlier? There are now only two days before the day fixed for the demonstration. Also, when you rang yesterday, you asked me to come to the office and talk about the situation 'in general,' so I haven't brought the information for the application forms."

The officer said, "Check your demonstration route. If the march is in Chaoyang, then you must apply for permission at the Chaoyang police station. Here we can only deal with [routes] that cross districts."

It had taken nearly three weeks, from December 8 until December 26, to get permission to hold a demonstration!

The following day, a reporter from Hong Kong Cable TV interviewed Zhu Rui at the factory gate. That same afternoon, she was taken away to Hujialou police station by four policemen who said that the interview tape had already been confiscated.

On December 28, Zhu Rui was allowed to go home. The attitude of the police toward her had been polite at all times. On January 1, 1998, the sacked staff and workers from Factory 3501 formally applied for permission to hold a demonstration.

A sacked worker from Factory 3501,
January 4, 1998.

CASE 23

This is the case of a migrant from Sichuan province who became a legal advocate for workers claiming industrial injury compensation in Guangdong province. His career pattern did not suggest he would be a likely person to fight for migrant worker rights. He had first been in the army, then in the police force, and later he had worked as a private security guard in a factory in Guangdong. His empathy with the workers launched him into a new career as a mentor for injured migrant workers in the area.

Had the local authorities not tolerated his activities, he could not have openly practiced his profession. That he was able to do so was a reflection of the changed political and social environment in Guangdong province in the late 1990s. It is now possible to litigate, especially for compensation for industrial accidents. The rate of accidents has become so abominably high (see chapter 4) that the authorities have realized there is a need to curb the problem.

THE MIGRANT "LAWYER" WHO SPECIALIZES IN "SPEAKING OUT" FOR OTHER MIGRANTS*

After migrant worker Deng Yuguo's two fingers were chopped off by a cutting machine in Jianghui Footwear Company in Panyu city in Guangdong province, the company would not compensate him a cent. Just as he was feeling helpless, he got in touch with Liao Xiaofeng. Liao made use of the law to fight hard on his behalf. In seven days, the boss handed over to Deng 65,000 yuan in cash.

Liao Xiaofeng, while being considered by some as a troublemaker, has become the savior of the migrants around Panyu area.

Fired after Four Years of Working for a Boss

It is not hard to get hold of Liao Xiaofeng. Many migrants know his pager number.

This stout and sharp-looking youngster from Sichuan is only twenty-eight years old. After graduating from middle technical school, he joined the army, where he became a news reporter in one of the corps of the Beijing Army District. There, he gained a third-level merit. After being discharged in 1991, he worked as a team leader in the police station of Langzhong city in Sichuan province, and then as a public security subdivisional head at North Chengdu Railway Station.

In 1993, he quit those fairly decent jobs in the interior provinces and came south to Panyu city, where he took up several jobs in a row: as a deputy private security guard and then as a public security team leader in a few companies in Lianhua Shan Tax-Free Processing Zone. The pay was only a pitiful few hundred yuan and he could not stand having to be accommodat-

---

*From the Chinese text: Zeng Huafeng and Tan Yangchun, "Zhuan wei dagongzai tao 'shuofa' de dagongzai 'lushi,'" *Laodong daobao* (Labor News), May 5, 1998. Translated by Anita Chan.

ing all the time. It was under such circumstances that he developed a profound empathy for the plight of migrants.

In 1996, when he was working as a security guard in Jidelong Company, a fellow villager, Zeng Guojian, came to him for help. Zeng had been working in a Hong Kong–invested coconut-candy factory and had two fingers cut off while sawing coconuts. The Labor Bureau had classed it as a ninth-level injury, and the factory gave him 6,000 yuan in compensation. Zeng felt cheated, and so went to his friend Liao for help. When Liao could not get anywhere after going to talk to the factory boss, he looked up the labor laws and regulations in some Panyu city bookstores and discovered that for a ninth-level injury, the compensation should be 10,000 yuan. So he stayed up the whole night and composed a letter of complaint addressed to the labor-arbitration committee of the labor bureau, demanding a higher compensation. Twenty-five days later, Zeng was awarded 12,000 yuan.

This was the first time that Liao Xiaofeng had gotten involved in a case, and surprisingly, he was successful. But it had not occurred to him then to take this up as a "profession."

Life passed by quickly and uneventfully until April 13, 1997, a day that was unforgettable for Liao. When the management committee of Lianhua Shan Tax-Free Processing Zone inspected the workers' dormitory of Jidelong Company and uncovered some seventy gas burners, security guard Liao Xiaofeng got the sack, all because he was too softhearted to confiscate the gas burners from the workers.

This incident changed Liao's life.

Twenty Cases: All Successful

Unemployed for a while, Liao felt lost and anxious. A friend came up with an idea for a way out—learn more about the labor laws and help people to file charges.

So Liao rented a room in Shiliu township and went to a Guangzhou bookshop to buy a whole lot of books on labor law, civil law, criminal law, civil litigation, marriage law, and so on. He studied them on his own, seeking some help from people in the legal profession, and began putting what he had learned into practice. Within a month, acting in the capacity as an authorized representative, he successfully helped several migrant workers involved in labor disputes. He started accumulating experience.

On May 22 last year, an arbitration case over an industrial injury was brewing in Shangfei Garment Factory in Lingxing Industrial District. A migrant worker in the factory, Zhang Donghua, slipped and broke her right leg as she came down the unlit staircase of the factory at 11:00 P.M. after working overtime. The next morning, she authorized her husband to go and claim work insurance. But not only did the company refuse to pay, it made her terminate her employment on June 9, giving her 200 yuan as compensation.

After Liao took up Zhang's case as her representative, he consulted a large number of laws and regulations. But when negotiations with the company broke down, he brought the case to the Panyu City Labor Arbitration Committee. On October 5, the arbitration committee ruled in Zhang's favor and demanded the company compensate Zhang with more than 13,000 yuan.

Last February migrant worker Chen Jizhao's foot was crushed by a pile of shoe lasts on the shop floor, but the company refused to pay her any compensation after taking care of her medical expenses. Liao fought on her behalf and got 12,000 yuan for her.

That year, Liao took up twenty cases. Most of them were related to disputes over compensation for workplace injuries, traffic accidents, marriage problems, and unpaid wages. In all cases, the complainants were awarded with some sort of compensation. Now, it is not only in Panyu city that people know of Liao, he is much sought after by migrant workers from Zhuhai, Dongguan, and even Hainan. People call him asking for legal advice or for him to take up their cases. Each day he receives up to twenty phone calls. He has become so busy that, except for when he is asleep, he is out all day.

Only He Himself Knows the Difficulties

For a young person coming from a faraway province, and without any connections, the difficulties Liao has encounterd in fighting for justice for migrant workers are simply too numerous to count.

The greatest obstacle Liao faces comes from none other than the labor bureau's departments. Because of a lack of staff, their attitude is: the less trouble, the better. To them, Liao is nothing but a troublemaker.

Of course, obstacles also come from the companies. Bosses and managers refuse to see him, give him the cold shoulder, or treat him rudely. Once, a boss even called in the local police to arrest him. For his personal safety, Liao is careful not to tell others where he lives.

When it comes to the sensitive question of fees, Liao said he asks for very little, usually 200 yuan for a case. After the case is won, then it is up to the clients to give him as much as they want, and usually is it around 500 to 1,000 yuan. The largest amount he has ever received for one case was Deng's case mentioned in the very beginning of this report. Out of the 65,000 yuan Deng got, Liao got 2,000 yuan. "Making money is not my goal; it is redressing social justice. The compensation the migrant workers get after industrial accidents is for their blood and sweat. I feel bad taking it, but then I also have to make a living."

Liao Xiaofeng's present ambition is to become a certified lawyer, a real people's lawyer. He hopes his work can give migrant workers hope that their problems will have a silver lining.

Comments

Liao never became a certified lawyer, and in 1999, a non-governmental labor organization in Hong Kong received news that "he was driven out of Guangdong province."[10] But advocacy work for victims of industrial accidents did not disappear with Liao's departure. Soon, a certified lawyer, Zhou Litai, also from Sichuan province, became even better known. Zhou went further—he set up a shelter for his clients, who were all injured workers. Since 90 percent of injured workers get dismissed and are penniless and homeless, Zhou provides them with shelter while they file compensation claims in court. These claims can take months, even up to a couple of years. Zhou's home (comprised of two apartments) is an extended family of young men and women who are all disabled in one way or another, mainly by losing arms or fingers.[11] Thus far, he has handled about two hundred cases, including those in process. Of these, about forty are on behalf of women workers.[12] Males are more likely to be employed in physically hazardous jobs, and are therefore more likely to be maimed through workplace injuries.

Like Liao, Zhou finds that his main antagonists are local bureaucracies. The bureaucracies connive to undercompensate workers who are covered by local government industrial-insurance schemes by paying compensation at rates that have not kept up with inflation.

Zhou's actions have started to attract nationwide publicity. In 1999, he appeared on numerous Chinese television programs and in the Chinese and Hong Kong press,[13] and was even interviewed by the Washington Post.[14] *Publicity is probably his best protection against revenge and suppression. But he still has to walk a fine line to avoid the same fate as Liao.*

Notes

1. Li Yuwei, "Lawyers in China—A 'Flourishing' Profession in a Rapidly Changing Society," *China Perspectives*, No. 27 (January–February 2000), pp. 20–34.

2. In this incident, a boatload of Taiwanese tourists visiting China were slaughtered on a lake in the middle of the night.

3. When I conducted field research with Taiwanese owners/managers in Dongguan city in Guangdong province in 1996, they expressed fears for their personal safety. Many of the Taiwanese managers had hired bodyguards.

4. In the editions of March 30 and 31, and all the April issues of these two newspapers, there was not a single word about the incident.

5. *Central Daily*, March 31, 1995.

6. "Organizing Against All Odds," *China Labor Bulletin*, Issue 40 (January–February, 1998), p. 2.

7. Ibid.

8. Jin Yi, "Gongchao—dalu de dingshi zhadan" (Strike Waves—The Time Bomb of Chinese Mainland), *Dongxiang* (The Trend), No. 2, 1998, pp. 28–31.

9. To be unemployed (*shiye*) means a worker's relationship is completely severed from the work unit and the worker is no longer entitled to any subsidies or benefits from the work unit. To be "laid off" or to be "taken off the post" (*xiagang*) is technically a suspension from work. A worker continues to be an employee of the work unit, and so is entitled to *xiagang* subsidies and other benefits, including a pension. By making the workers sign year-long contracts, the management would have been able to make the workers unemployed a year later.

10. I was not able to acquire more information about Liao.

11. In August 1999, I was able to interview Zhou Litai at the shelter and met about a dozen workers there.

12. However, women workers are more likely to contract chronic occupational safety and health diseases caused by toxic chemicals, such as in case 11 of the shoe factory workers in Putian.

13. Yu Bin, "Cangtian zai shang, ti tequ dagongzu daguansi de 'zhuanye'—Chongqing lushi Zhou Litai zai Shenzhen de zhuanqi gushi" (Heaven From On High Provides the Migrant Workers in Shenzhen Special Economic Zone with Someone Who Litigates on Behalf of the Workers—the Story of Chongqing Lawyer Zhou Litai), *Jiayuan* (Home), Vol. 13, No. 1 (1999), pp. 13–16. Zhang Shen, "Dagongzai yingong zhican chuangao wumen, Zhou lushi pai an erqi baoda guansi" (Migrant Workers Handicapped by Industrial Accidents Have Nowhere to Appeal. Lawyer Zhou Rose to the Occasion to Take Their Cases to Court), *Xin bao* (New News), August 19, 1999. Wang Xiaoding, "Youxia Zhou lushi, Shenzhen chuangguan ji" (Lawyer Zhou, the Robin Hood of Shenzhen), *Fazhi zongheng* (Crisscrossing the Legal System), March 30, 1999, pp. 4–11. Lun Gu, "One Man's Bid for Workers' Justice," *South China Morning Post*, March 26, 2000, p. 9.

14. John Pomfret, "In China, No Workers' Paradise: Lawyer Fights for Clients Injured in Factories Placing Money Before Safety," *Washington Post*, January 11, 2000, pp. A11 and A13.

Chapter 9
In Pursuit of Labor Rights

Today, there is growing recognition that the objectives of development go beyond simply an increase in GDP: we are concerned with promoting democratic, equitable, sustainable development. If that is our objective, then it is natural that we should pay particular attention to the issue of how the plight of workers changes in the course of development; and we should look not only at their incomes, but broader measures—at their health and safety, and even at their democratic participation, both at the workplace, and within the broader political arena. Workers' rights should be a central focus of a development institution such as the World Bank.

Joseph E. Stiglitz
January 8, 2000[1]

From the point four years ago when I first thought about writing this book to the time of penning this conclusion, the Western mass media's attitude toward sweatshop labor in developing countries has changed enormously. The expression "labor standards" was once used almost exclusively within labor and government circles. I, for one, had never heard the expression, nor had it appeared in print in academic writings about China. But the term has now found its rightful place in ordinary conversations, in political speeches, and in the mainstream press. The impact of globalization on nations and on the world economy is now recognized to be integrally related to labor, and to labor rights. The above quote from Joseph Stiglitz, the World Bank's former vice-president and chief economist, symbolizes this shift in the views of a number of senior policymakers in the international arena.

Four years ago, it was also unthinkable that the rights of Chinese workers could become a controversial issue in the United States, yet this became a factor in the 2000 Congressional debate over whether to grant China permanent normal trade relations (PNTR). The U.S. government and international public opinion have long been critical of China's human-rights record, but the concerns had always focused on the rights of a few political dissidents, the existence of prison labor, and the suppression of Tibetans. Times have changed. When the Democratic whip in the House of Representatives, David Bonior, a leading opponent of granting China PNTR, ordered his list of rights in his Congressional debate speech, labor rights came first: "That is what this debate is about today: labor rights, human rights, environmental concerns, religious rights."[2]

This increased recognition among American politicians of the important relationship between labor rights and trade owes much to the publicity generated by vocal critics of the exploitation of third-world labor from nongovernmental organizations (NGOs), labor unions, students, and consumer groups. The anti-Nike campaign in particular has attracted considerable media attention. But it was the massive protests in Seattle in November 1999 at the World Trade Organization (WTO) Ministerial Conference that forcefully brought the world's attention to the link between globalization and the exploitation of labor and destruction of the environment.[3]

The close timing of three controversial issues—China's accession to the WTO, the Seattle protests, and the PNTR vote in Congress—suddenly made the exploitative working conditions faced by many Chinese workers, especially workers in foreign and joint-venture enterprises, highly relevant. A book project that began without an international context in mind ended up with a global dimension. This is highly appropriate, given that Chinese workers produce vast quantities of products for export to the developed world, particularly the United States. As shown in this book, most workers producing products for export are migrants from the poorer provinces, at times working under degrading and even slave-like conditions. Their plight has set in motion a "race to the bottom," in which low wages and high unemployment among the unskilled have spread to Chinese workers in other sectors, as well as depressing wage levels in other countries. It is therefore fitting that this concluding chapter should explore possible ways to help alleviate the conditions faced by Chinese workers in a global economy.

The Five Core Labor Rights

Five core labor rights were enshrined in the International Labor Organization (ILO) Conventions, and reaffirmed in the ILO Declaration of Fundamental Principles at Work in 1998,[4] and have been championed by the international trade union movement:

1. freedom of association;
2. the rights to organize and bargain collectively;
3. a minimum age of employment;
4. no forced or slave labor; and
5. a prohibition against discrimination.[5]

Inasmuch as the ILO is a tripartite organization made up of government, employer, and labor representatives, this means that even governments and employers endorse these rights as core rights. The first two—freedom of association and freedom to organize and collectively bargain—are the most fundamental of these rights[6] (henceforth, they will be referred to as the two main core rights). What is truly ironic is that the United States has only ratified one of the core rights, the one on forced labor.[7]

In contrast, the chapter titles of this book highlight other labor standards, sometimes known as non-core labor standards, such as wages and work hours.[8] I would debate the pertinence of merely pushing for compliance with the five core rights in a country like China. I hope that readers will become convinced by the end of this chapter that violations of the non-core labor rights of Chinese workers should be considered no less serious than violations of the five core rights.

The chapters are organized to highlight the violations that daily affect workers most immediately and directly. Although not all are violations of core rights, all have been guaranteed in ILO conventions, and some are rights contained in articles of the United Nations' Universal Declaration of Human Rights. Only two chapters pertain to the core rights: chapter 6, on violations of the right to take collective action and organize unions; and chapter 7, on indentured labor abroad (which can be considered as within the parameters of forced labor). Thus far, international concern regarding forced Chinese labor has been limited to prison labor.[9]

The book does not have a chapter on industrial child labor because this is a less serious problem than in many other developing countries. In a country the size of China, it does of course exist in pockets, but hiring children as wage labor is not pervasive in China, unlike in India and Pakistan.

International organizations have almost completely focused on the two main core rights, of freedom of association and of collective bargaining. They are rights that all workers should enjoy, but they are not the overriding focus of this book because these issues are not at the forefront of Chinese workers' concerns and grievances, especially among migrant workers.[10] Miserable wages, very long work hours, and dangerous working conditions are the problems that most directly affect workers' physical well-being and are in need of immediate solution. To this end, this chapter will make three main arguments:

1. To improve the conditions of Chinese workers, we need to expand our focus from the five core rights to include a range of other labor rights.
2. Labor rights, including the non-core rights, should be seen as human rights and should be fully integrated into the international human-rights discourses and practices.
3. NGOs should apply pressure on the Chinese government, which professes to champion the cause of labor, to persuade it to play a more positive role in regulating labor conditions.

The Historical Relationships Between Core Rights and Non-Core Rights

It may surprise those who are unfamiliar with international labor history that this history at one time was centrally concerned with the adoption of what we today classify as non-core rights. Industrialization in the West in the nineteenth century created a new class of industrial laborers who worked in horrific conditions. There were efforts made across the political spectrum to alleviate the onerous conditions of workers. Thus, "at the Paris Congress of 1890 that led to the formation of the Second International, considerable attention was given to the problem of achieving an eight-hour day."[11] Even the conservative political establishment was aware of an international need to improve working conditions, and, in 1905, the Swiss government convened an intergovernmental conference in Berne—the first international labor conference. At this and a later conference, the first two international labor conventions were adopted, dealing with "the limitation of night work for women in industry and the prohibition of the manufacture of and trade in matches containing white phosphorus."[12]

At Versailles in 1919, a Labor Charter of nineteen principles was drawn up, nine of which obtained a two-thirds majority vote, were adopted, and were embodied in the Peace Treaty:

i.   that labor should not be regarded merely as a commodity or article of commerce;
ii. the right of association;
iii. the payment of an adequate wage to maintain a reasonable standard of living;

   iv. an eight-hour day or forty-eight-hour week;

   v. a weekly rest of at least twenty-four hours;

   vi. the abolition of child labor;

  vii. equal pay for equal work;

 viii. equitable economic treatment of all workers in a country (i.e., immigrants as well as nationals); and

   ix. an inspection system to ensure the enforcement of the laws for worker protection.[13]

It can be said that these nine principles were the core labor rights of that era in history. Of these nine, principles ii, vi, and viii were precursors of today's five core rights. Of the six remaining principles, three—a living wage, limited work hours, and a right to rest—had a direct impact on workers' physical well-being and were agreed to be of prime importance.

After World War I, the ILO was established as the first international tripartite institution in which governments, employers, and workers had equal voting power. In October 1919, the first ILO Conference was held in Washington, D.C., and its first conventions were adopted.[14] The work of the conference was dominated by two themes: hours of work and unemployment. Employment was a major issue because of the massive unemployment after the war, while reining in long work hours was a traditional aim of labor. It was held at the time that this:

> would prolong the useful life of the worker. If he worked for ten to twelve hours a day his useful life would only last some ten years. Second, reduction of working hours increased the time available for leisure, family life and education. Third, during the war the workers had been sustained by the belief that they would be rewarded by a reduction of hours in the peace.[15]

It was only after World War II that the international trade-union movement was able to better establish itself, and in 1948, Convention 87 on the right to freedom of association was passed, followed a year later by Convention 98 on the right to organize and collectively bargain.

In short, international labor history from the second half of the nineteenth century to the end of World War II focused largely on so-called industrial labor problems rather than on the freedom to form trade unions. One could argue that this was because the international trade-union movement was still weak, and in a tripartite arrangement, was not able to force attention to matters of greatest organizational interest to itself.[16] But it can also be argued that prior to World War II, precisely because organized labor was still weak, the "sweating" of labor was the biggest problem—wages were too low to provide a minimally decent livelihood, and work hours were sometimes so long that they endangered health and safety. The international trade-union movement agitated for these "industrial" rights, and they were not alone. The conditions endured by so many workers aroused humanitarian concerns, and even governments recognized their role in regulating working conditions.

After World War II, when human rights began to become a focus of international covenants, labor rights were included among them. In 1947, the ILO and the United Nations concluded an agreement on "the inclusion in their respective agendas of items proposed by the other."[17] Many of the issues debated, principles adopted, and conventions passed in the ILO were precursors of articles in the 1948 Universal Declaration of Human Rights (UDHR).[18] A number of these articles directly concern workers as human beings. It is also important to note that many of these overlapping articles embody both civil-political rights and social, economic, and cultural rights. The five core labor rights fall within the rubric of civil and political rights, whereas the non-core rights are considered economic and social rights. Those that specifically relate to the so-called non-core rights of workers are contained in article 22 (a right to social security); article 23 (a right to work, no discrimination, equal pay for equal work, and reasonable remuneration); article 24 (a right to rest and leisure, including a reasonable limitation of work hours and periodic holidays with pay); article 25 (a right to a standard of living adequate for the health and well-being of the worker and his or her family); and article 26 (a right to education). In other words, what today are not regarded as important enough to be classified as core labor rights occupied a prominent place in the UDHR in 1948. In particular, the right to rest and leisure (which we have seen is of paramount importance to Chinese workers today) occupied a full article.[19]

However, as time passed, these rights concerning the physical well-being of workers became less important to the ILO and human-rights organizations. As welfare states were established, and as legislation was passed to limit maximum working hours and to provide overtime rates—successes due in part to the effectiveness of the international trade-union movement—the movement shifted its priorities toward matters that remained of immediate concern to Western trade unions in their own organizing efforts; that is, Conventions 87 and 98, sanctifying freedom of worker association, a right to organize workers, and a right to collective bargaining.

During these same years, the onset of the Cold War also undermined the status of the economic and social rights that had been included in the Universal Declaration of Human Rights. These rights became casualties of the antagonism between the capitalist camp led by the United States and the communist camp led by the Soviet Union, partly because the latter emphasized these rights in its attacks on capitalism and proclamations of the superiority of socialism.[20] The United States developed an "aversion" to mentioning social and economic rights[21] and, as the most powerful country, it set the agenda of the international rights discourse.

The lack of commitment to this set of rights in the UN is clearly demonstrated in institutional negligence. In the UN Center for Human Rights, according to Philip Alston, an authority on international human-rights law, "Special rapporteurs, country rapporteurs, advisory services experts, members of treaty bodies, officials of other UN agencies, and nongovernmental experts have not even one person within the Centre to whom they can turn for expert advice or assistance in relation to these [social and economic] rights. The Centre has no meaningful collection of materials, books or documents relating to these issues."[22] The United Nations Committee on Economic, Social, and Cultural Rights receives very few resources. Its members meet annually for a single session and do not even have borrowing privileges at the United Nations library in Geneva.[23] Such is the sorry state of economic and social rights within the international human-rights arena.

The Relationship Between Labor Rights and Human Rights

Readers introduced by this book to the harsh lives endured by many Chinese workers probably have unwittingly—and correctly—associated the violations of their labor rights with violations of human rights. But there are many reasons—theoretical, practical, historical, political, institutional—why the non-core labor rights have not always been regarded as human rights[24] or, if recognized, why they have been situated far down in the hierarchy of human rights. The examples in this book show how imperative it is that labor rights are put on an equal footing with other kinds of human rights. It is ironic that we need to belabor this point, as it was recognized more than fifty years ago.

Yet between 1948 and 1999, the internationally agreed-upon recognition of what I call the "non-core labor rights" lost their importance in international discourse and have been short-changed in international human-rights diplomacy.[25] In the accusations and counter-accusations about human rights violations, there has been silence on issues of excessively low wages, extremely long working hours, and dangerous and degrading labor conditions. References to Chinese labor rights over the past two decades have generally been restricted to complaints about barriers to forming trade unions, the imprisonment of specific labor activists, or prison labor. For instance, the U.S. government, one of the most vehement critics of China's human-rights record, issues annual Country Reports on Human-Rights Practices, which include a section called "Reporting on Worker Rights."[26] Although, in principle, the

American government recognizes labor rights as human rights, when China's human-rights violations were raised, labor-rights violations were barely mentioned.[27]

The Chinese government has countered criticism of its human rights record by refusing to recognize that it violates political and civil rights. It argues that the U.S. government is picking on China, which, as an erstwhile victim of imperialism and as a developing country, needs to place its emphasis on social, economic, and cultural rights. China claims to honor what it calls "socialist human rights with Chinese characteristics."[28] Amidst this verbal jousting, Beijing strategically released dissidents from jail like trump cards—one at a time, each time international pressure mounted too high or when it wanted something in return, such as to host the 2000 Olympic Games.[29]

China is not the only Asian country to claim "special characteristics" in interpreting human rights. In 1993, several Asian countries issued the Bangkok Declaration as a counteroffensive to Western criticisms, arguing that there exists an "Asian conception of human rights."[30] The argument was posed in terms of cultural and historical specificities rather than universality in the application of human rights.[31]

In addition to pointing to its "excellent" record of honoring social and economic rights, in 1996, the Chinese government issued a report that included a section entitled "Protection of Workers' Rights." It stated that China had instituted a minimum-wage system and provided employment and social security to its people. The report made no mention of the widespread violations of non-core rights such as illegally low wages and long work hours that have been widely reported in China's own news media and documented in this book.[32] China subsequently signed the International Convention on Economic, Social, and Cultural Rights in 1997.[33] But the timing of China's signing was particularly ironic. Prior to the 1990s, Beijing could have prided itself for providing secure employment and a range of benefits to state-sector workers. But in 1997, the labor rights of many of its workers, and in particular their social and economic rights, were increasingly being systematically abused.

Western human-rights NGOs have traditionally addressed a very narrow range of rights that are mainly civil and political in nature,[34] and within this range, the concern is directed toward political dissidents jailed for their beliefs. Workers locked up in factories toiling day and night for low wages and given inadequate food and little rest do not come within the purview of human rights. This downgrading of the rights of ordinary workers is a universal problem, and not limited to China.

One of the many causes of this problem involves semantics. Let us look again at Representative Bonior's statement quoted above. When Bonior listed "labor rights, human rights, environmental concerns, religious rights," what was on his mind? Are labor rights a kind of human rights? Do labor rights differ in kind from human rights? Or are they a form of human rights, but superior (only recently) to what he called "human rights?" From this quote it can be seen that the status of labor rights as human rights is confusing and elusive. In this instance, Bonior did not seem to be thinking of labor rights as human rights or as a kind of human right. He most likely was equating human rights with civil and political rights only, which is generally how the term is understood in the United States.

During the past several years, human-rights NGOs have become more inclusive in their human-rights concerns. Amnesty International, for example, has begun urging companies to uphold human-rights standards in their operations.[35] While freeing prisoners of conscience continues to be its priority, in early 1998 Amnesty drew up a document called "Human Rights Principles for Companies."[36] The issue has also been pressed by smaller human-rights groups such as Human Rights Watch/Asia[37] and Human Rights in China. But these are only initial efforts, and it will be some time before the labor rights of the ordinary worker will become an integral part of the discourse of international human-rights organizations.

The loudest, most energetic, and most visible critiques of labor rights have emanated from labor NGOs, trade unions, consumer groups, church groups, community groups, and, within the past three years, American university students.[38] These loosely coordinated groups have formed an anti-sweatshop movement. This movement started as a one-person campaign in the early 1990s by Jeffrey Ballinger against Nike's exploitative labor practices in Indonesia, and now, linked by e-mail, it has developed into an international protest movement.[39] The protests have attracted considerable media coverage and put enormous pressure on a few multinationals to improve their labor standards in the factories from which they outsource their products, a large volume of which derives from China. The multinationals have been embarrassed by the exposure of low wages, long working hours, poor health and safety conditions, and the existence of corporal punishment in these plants. An increasing number of multinationals seek to preempt criticism by drawing up their own corporate codes of conduct.[40] About 90 percent of American multinationals had developed their own codes by 1999.[41] Some created new labor-relations departments, which also double as public-relations departments to stave off criticism. A small number have hired the equivalent of labor inspectors to internally monitor conditions in their subcontractors' factories.[42] Even the most vocal NGO critics have to admit that the unrelenting pressure from the anti-sweatshop campaign has improved conditions for workers in the factories of a few of the multinationals' suppliers.

The anti-sweatshop campaign also prompted President Clinton to commission the establishment of an Apparel Industry Partnership in which multinationals and their critics negotiated the terms for the formation of a Fair Labor Association (FLA). Signatories to the FLA are required to abide by the association's rules to improve workers' conditions.[43] As of September 2000, twelve companies had joined the FLA, and 141 colleges and universities had become affiliates. The founding NGO members are the International Labor Rights Fund, the Lawyers Committee for Human Rights, the National Consumers League, and the Robert F. Kennedy Memorial Center for Human Rights.[44] Most multinationals find the FLA's terms too restrictive for their management practices, while trade unions and a number of NGOs would not participate, mainly because the multinationals refused to agree to an effective system of independent external monitoring of factories. American campus protests, including student sit-ins, continue to dog corporations such as Nike, whose owner has retaliated by withdrawing multimillion-dollar donations to universities. Students, university administrations, and corporate donors remain locked in an unending series of protests and negotiations.[45]

There is a difference in emphasis between trade-union organizations, especially at the international level, and the anti-sweatshop NGOs and student groups. Trade-union organizations hold the five core labor rights sacrosanct. The International Confederation of Free Trade Unions (ICFTU), the umbrella trade-union organization that claims to represent 125 million members of 215 affiliated unions in 145 countries, and the International Trades Secretariat, which is the umbrella organization for international trade-sector unions, are the driving forces for the inclusion of a "social clause" in WTO trade negotiations.[46] This social clause basically amounts to the five core labor rights.[47]

In comparison, the labor-rights NGOs and grass-roots trade unions that work closely with grass-roots associations in the developing world tend to have a broader and more flexible stand on the social clause than the international trade-union organizations.[48] Although they see the importance of the five core labor rights, they campaign mostly for standards regarding a minimum living wage, occupational safety and health, maximum length of working hours, social security, and environmental protection.

In sum, whether or not labor rights are recognized as human rights varies from arena to arena. The arena of international politics dominates the discourse, and the peak international organizations in this arena, such as the WTO, the International Monetary Fund, and the World Bank, have refused to consider labor rights as a factor in their agendas. On the other end of the spectrum are the labor-rights advocates, who vehemently attack these world organizations for ignoring labor rights.

Balancing Priorities

The question we need to ask: Is the strategy of prioritizing the two main core labor rights necessarily the most appropriate one for working people in the developing world? Over the past twenty years, globalization has accelerated, with investors scouring poor countries to find the best and cheapest labor. We have seen the return with a vengeance of the "sweating" of labor in developing countries, especially in Asia. In China, where the political system renders it nigh impossible to organize independent unions, but where working conditions urgently need alleviation, what role can outsiders play?

For migrant workers in China, for instance, what rights are the most concrete and most urgent to them? They want to be paid regularly, on time, and to be paid at least U.S.$2 a day (not $2 an hour) rather than $1.50 a day. Workers want to retain their human dignity, to have some leisure time (not the luxury of paid vacations as stipulated by the Universal Declaration of Human Rights), to be free of occupational hazards that threaten their lives and limbs, and to be free from fear of being put into detention centers for not having the right residential (*hukou*) papers. Their wants are concrete and tangible. A small handful of Chinese intellectuals such as Li Wenming and Guo Baosheng (case 17) have tried to organize workers at great personal risk, but this has only invited suppression and incarceration—a picture that is not likely to change soon.

Even for urban state workers, independent trade unionism seems far from their most pressing demand. The immediate need is to eke out a livelihood—the right to a job, to wages, and to a pension. Even when not paid for months, they take to the streets only as a last resort.[49] Head-on confrontation spells upheaval, something Chinese workers try to avoid, preferring to work through existing structures and, sometimes, their official workplace union, which may show some sympathy. Thus, even Han Dongfang, who tried to organize fellow workers during the 1989 Tiananmen protests and now works for Chinese worker rights from Hong Kong, today advises Chinese workers to initially go to the official trade unions for help.[50] In a similar vein, our role as outsiders should be to campaign for the protection of the economic and social rights of Chinese workers in light of the present realities, in addition to their civil and political rights.

The Tactics of the Anti-Sweatshop Movement

The anti-sweatshop coalition has targeted specific multinationals, largely for violating three types of rights (in the following order of priority): paying workers less than a living wage, long mandatory overtime work, and occupational health and safety issues. But activists have not been self-consciously aware that they are championing issues that have not historically been deemed "core" rights, in part because the activists are unaware of the artificial divide that has been made between these two sets of rights. Although the anti-sweatshop campaign also calls for honoring the five core rights, some of the people who prioritize trade-union rights feel uncomfortable about or even opposed to the campaign's call for independent workplace monitors, as they feel external monitoring does not lead to a situation where the workers can self-consciously protect their own rights.[51]

Efforts to fight for a living wage for workers in developing countries have absorbed much of the campaigners' energy. How to define a living wage and set one for each country has become both an academic and a practical issue. The movement conducts research to compare wages against the minimum-wage standards. They gather workers' pay slips, calculate the cost of food baskets, measure with great precision the workers' wages against their expenditures and against inflation, and calculate the workers' wages as a percentage of the retail price of the products the workers manufacture. Conferences have been held to determine a conceptual and working definition of a living wage, and findings of the research have been circulated through the news media and organizational channels.[52] Citations of incredibly low wages paid to workers in the producing countries tend to draw more sympathy from consumers and the general public in high-income countries than any other violations of labor standards.

The movement and the multinationals come into conflict over monitoring. The anti-sweatshop activists demand to be free to enter factories to conduct independent monitoring, a request that many multinationals try to preempt by saying they are conducting their own internal monitoring. In a historical perspective, the movement is trying to revive an inspection system that was contained in one of the principles adopted by the first ILO conference in 1919. The difference here is that instead of being monitored by government, the system today would be monitored by the NGOs.

The anti-sweatshop movement needs to explicitly frame the campaign as one to upgrade the status of economic and social rights in the international labor-rights and human-rights communities. This is the thrust of their movement and it should be portrayed as such. With time and effort, they might be able to help redress what is now an unbalanced approach to labor rights, and increase the awareness that labor rights should also include rights concerning the survival and well-being of workers.

The Role of the State

The anti-sweatshop campaign, in my view, would further its cause if it reoriented its strategy toward the role of the state. Currently, the movement does not apply any pressure on the governments of the developing countries where the products are produced. Yet they are important players. These governments today are the main opponents to the inclusion of a social clause in WTO agreements.[53] Many such governments, far from representing the interests of their workers, are instead preoccupied with competing with other poor countries to sell cheap labor. This is of course shortsighted, in that a race to the bottom has emerged in the developing countries to the detriment of all, especially workers. Instead of rejecting the social clause while undercutting each other's price to sell their labor in the international labor market, the developing countries should form a bloc to collectively bargain with the industrialized nations, much as some of the developing countries have organized, at times successfully, to protect commodity prices such as coffee and oil. They should set a floor price for the labor they are selling in the world labor market and join hands with international labor activists to protect against exploitation by foreign investors. Not only will their workers benefit, this will also aid economic development. The anti-sweatshop movement would do well to divert some of its efforts into pressuring and persuading these governments to accept the social clause and other non-core-rights standards as the best way to stem the downward spiral in wages.

The movement has to understand that its current targets are only a handful of the many thousands of firms outsourcing in developing countries. Locking a few multinationals into high-profile confrontations can spotlight the issues, but the impact in terms of improving the conditions of the masses of workers in the developing countries can only be limited. In China, for example, a relatively small number of workers are directly employed by giant multinationals; by contrast, far more are employed by enterprises owned by small and medium-sized firms. By comparison to the impact of the movement, in many of these countries, the state's capacity to change the situation for workers is far reaching. A government that enforces good labor laws can accomplish far more than the movement's campaign against individual manufacturers.

A professedly "socialist" state, China is vulnerable to pressures to live up to its own rhetorical claims that it champions the cause of workers. As we have seen in previous chapters, the Chinese state, including one of its arms, the official trade union, might be drafted into playing a more active role in protecting labor rights. The legacy of an official socialist ideology may yet be used to good ends. According to Jude Howell, a British specialist on Chinese labor issues, the anti-sweatshop activists "need to work with the [Chinese] government at the national, provincial and municipal levels." Athar Hussain, another expert, notes, "I would strongly support the inclusion of government. You would find allies there."[54]

Recent measures adopted by Guangzhou city in southern China illustrate how the state, where it has the will, can intervene positively to enforce labor laws. One of the city's districts is pioneering a wage-inspection system to ensure workers are being paid. More than a thousand local officials have been assigned to oversee the district's 2,000 mostly Asian-funded enterprises. Local government bodies that rent out buildings and land to factories are responsible for paying any unpaid wages for factories that default.[55] Another innovation in Guangzhou city is a scheme to ensure that companies and factories contribute to social-security funds for their employees, with the funds collected by the local tax department.[56] Before the scheme, only 33 percent of the Hong Kong–owned and Taiwanese-owned enterprises and 24 percent of the private enterprises in the district made social-security contributions, as opposed to 97 percent of the state enterprises.

Conclusion

I believe that the non-core rights should have the same status as the core rights. The right to a living wage, the right to rest, and the right to an intact body are all fundamental. International dialogue may be on the verge of recognizing these non-core rights as essential human rights. Among other things, the international labor movement has begun to see that workers in the developing world have different circumstances and needs from those of organized labor in the industrialized countries. In light of these differences, the international labor movement now needs to shift its priorities and campaign for the very basic rights that were the foundation of the labor movement at the start of the twentieth century. There are causes for optimism. As an example, in a 1997 report on "The ILO, Standard Setting and Globalization," the ILO director-general recognized that the ILO needed to shift course. He suggested that "workers' clauses" ought to be internationally implemented to cover such areas as minimum wages, working hours, weekly hours of rest, and occupational safety and health standards.[57] These critical labor standards had long been neglected by the ILO.

The international labor movement, as represented by the International Confederation of Free Trade Unions (ICFTU), is now searching for new strategies and solutions. While continuing to press the international community to honor the five core rights, at the ICFTU World Congress held in Durban, South Africa, in April 2000, the organization's general secretary declared:

> The new thing is that our movement will seek to establish a global social safety net and will expand far beyond traditional collective bargaining to

encompass hundreds of millions of workers and their families to end once and for all the scourge of poverty which deprives billions of people of a decent life in dignity.

The AFL-CIO president, John Sweeney, concurred that the ICFTU, "which has fought for political democracy for the past fifty years," needs to fight for "economic democracy." To promote this aim, a resolution to form coalitions with NGOs on a case-by-case basis was adopted.[58] And, with the anti-sweatshop movement gathering momentum, this book ends on a more optimistic note than I believed possible when I first thought about drafting it four years ago.

Notes

1. Joseph E. Stiglitz, "Democratic Development as the Fruits of Labor," keynote address to the Industrial Relations Research Association, American Economic Association Meeting, January 8, 2000. See http:/www.worldbank.org/knowledge/chiefecon/articles/boston/htm
2. "Transcript: Democrats in House Argue Against China PNTR, May 16," United States Information Service, EPF308 5/17/00, p. 1. In the academic field of China studies, Andrew Nathan, longtime China human-rights advocate, used the expression "labor standard" in his discussion of Chinese human rights for the first time (Andrew J. Nathan, "WTO Is Not a Human Rights Policy—Neither Granting nor Withholding PNTR Is Likely to Have a Clear Net Effect on Human Rights in China," *Asian Wall Street Journal*, April 12, 2000).
3. There was an enormous amount of reporting on the "Battle in Seattle." The following selections present different sides to the issue. Richard Lacayo, "Rage Against the Machine: Despite, and Because of Violence, Anti-WTO Protesters were Heard," *Time*, December 31, 1999, pp. 24–29; "After Seattle: A Global Disaster," *The Economist*, December 11, 1999, pp. 17–19; David Moberg, "After Seattle," *In These Times*, No. 15 (January 10, 2000), pp. 15–17.
4. The Declaration was passed by the 86th session, International Labor Conference, Geneva, June 1998. The four principles adopted were basically the five core labor standards with freedom of association and freedom to organize collapsed into one. See http://www.ilo.org/public/English/10ilc)ilc86/com-dtxt.htm.
5. David Chin, *A Social Clause for Labour's Cause—a Challenge for the New Millennium*, London: Institute of Employment Rights, 1998, p. 8; Erika de Wet, "Labor Standards in the Globalized Economy: The Inclusion of a Social Clause in the General Agreement on Tariffs and Trade/World Trade Organization," *Human Rights Quarterly*, No. 17 (1995), pp. 443–452.
6. For articles emphasizing these two rights, see, "Introduction" to special issue: Labor Rights, Human Rights, *International Labour Review*, Vol. 137, No. 2 1998, pp. 127–133; Lance Compa, "Labor Rights and Labor Standards in International Trade," *Law and Policy in International Business*, Vol. 25, No. 1 (Fall 1993), pp. 165–191.
7. In fact, the ICFTU report of July 1999 called on the United States to ratify the other core ILO conventions. Cited in a message "Campaign Against Deregulation and for Labor Rights for All!" issued by the Open World Conference in Defense of Trade Union Independence and Democratic Rights, owc@energy-net.org; September 28, 2000.

8. Ibid., pp. 169–191.

9. The attention the West has paid to Chinese prison labor has resulted from a successful anti-*laogai* (prison camp) campaign launched by Harry Wu, a former prison-camp inmate. See the Laogai Research Foundation website http://www.laogai.org/welcome.htm

10. Not even one out of some sixty private letters of migrant workers that I have analyzed contained any reference to trade unionism. See Anita Chan, "Culture of Survival: Lives of Migrant Workers Through the Prism of Private Letters," in Perry Link, Richard Madsen, and Paul Pickowicz (eds.), *Popular Thought in Post-Socialist China*, Boulder: Rowman and Littlefield, forthcoming.

11. Antony Alcock, *History of the International Labor Organization*, London: Macmillan, 1971, p. 9.

12. Harold Dunning, "The Origins of Convention 87 on Freedom of Association and the Right to Organize," *Industrial Labour Review*, Vol. 137, No. 2, 1998, p. 153.

13. Alcock, *History of the International Labor Organization*, p. 35.

14. Nicolas Valticos and Geraldo W. von Potobsky, *International Labour Law*, Boston: Kluwer Law and Taxation Publishers, 1995, p. 19.

15. Alcock, *History of the International Labor Organization*, p. 42.

16. Ibid., p. 9.

17. Dunning, "The Origins of Convention No. 87," p. 159.

18. Universal Declaration of Human Rights (thereafter, UDHR), adopted December 10, 1948. Reprinted in *The United Nations and Human Rights, 1945–1995*, New York: United Nations, Blue Books Series, Volume VII, 1995, pp. 153–155.

19. Ibid.

20. Philip Alston, "Economic and Social Rights," in Louis Henkin and John Lawrence Hargrove (eds.), *Human Rights: An Agenda for the Next Century*, Washington, D.C.: The American Society of International Law, Studies in Transnational Legal Policy, No. 26, 1994, p. 152.

21. Ibid., p. 137.

22. Ibid., pp. 156–157.

23. Ibid., p. 162.

24. This is pointed out, for example, in Roy Adams and Sheldon Friedman, "The Emerging International Consensus on Human Rights in Employment," *Perspectives on Work*, Vol. 2, No. 2, 1998, pp. 24–27.

25. See Peter Van Ness, "Asia and Human Rights Diplomacy," *Current Affairs Bulletin*, December 1993, pp. 27–29; see also Ann Kent, "Human Rights in Australia-China Relations, 1985–95," in Colin Mackerras (ed.), *Australia and China: Partners in Asia*, Melbourne: Macmillan Education Australia, 1996, pp. 57–68.

26. For example, see the 1,376–page report of 1996. For China, listed under "Section 6, Workers Rights," are subsections on: the right of association, the right to organize and bargain collectively, the prohibition of forced and compulsory labor, a minimum age for the employment of children, and acceptable conditions of work (pp. 591–594).

27. See Hilary K. Josephs, "Labor Law in a 'Socialist Market Economy': The Case of China," *Columbia Journal of Transnational Law*, No. 33, 1995, pp. 577–578. Josephs thinks that China's labor record has not been addressed because the United States has ratified fewer ILO conventions than China, and because the United States' own labor record is tarnished.

28. Information Office of State Council (China's Cabinet), "Progress in China's

Human Rights Cause in 1996" (March 31, 1997), in *Beijing Review*, Vol. 40, No. 16 (April 21, 1997), p. 15. Within China, the term "labor rights" is politically sensitive, however, and as yet, the term and concept have not appeared at all in China's mass media. I was told in China that those who want to use the term, even in specialized publications, are warned by their superiors about the personal risks involved. One of the rare books published with the term "labor rights" in the title is Chang Kai, *Laodong guanxi, laodongzhe, laoquan* (Labor Relations, Laborers, Labor Rights), Beijing: Chinese Labor Press, 1995.

29. For a discussion of this tactic of the Chinese government toward well-known political activists, see Anita Chan, "The Changing Ruling Elite and Political Opposition in China," in Garry Rodan (ed.), *Political Oppositions in Industrializing Asia*, London: Routledge, 1996, pp. 161–187. This government tactic was confirmed by John Kamm, Executive Director of an NGO called the Dui Hua Foundation, who, as a private individual, has been negotiating with various bureaucracies of the Chinese government since 1989 for the release or reduction of the sentences of Chinese political prisoners. This information is based on a talk he presented at The Australian National University in June 2000.

30. See, for example, Christian M. Cera, "Universality of Human Rights and Cultural Diversity: Implementation of Human Rights in Different Social-Cultural Contexts," *Human Rights Quarterly*, Vol. 16 (1994), pp. 740–752.

31. Marina Svensson, *The Chinese Conception of Human Rights: The Debate on Human Rights in China, 1998–1949*, Lund: University of Lund Press, 1996, pp. 10–11.

32. Information Office of State Council, "Progress in China's Human Rights Cause in 1996," *Beijing Review*, Vol. 40, No. 16 (April 21–27, 1997), pp. 11–16.

33. *China Rights Forum*, Winter 1997–98, p. 6.

34. Alston, "Economic and Social Rights," pp. 159–160.

35. See, for instance, the speech by Pierre Sane, Secretary General of Amnesty International, "Does Human Rights Make Business Sense?" presented at the One World Conference: Companies Caught in Conflict, March 18, 1997, London.

36. Amnesty International, "Human Rights Principles for Companies," January 1998 (AI Index: ACT 70/01/98).

37. The introduction to the *World Report 1997: Events of 1996* includes two pages on "Labor Rights and the Global Economy," pp. xxi–xxii.

38. Steven Greenhouse, "Activism Surges at Campuses Nationwide, and Labor is at Issue," *New York Times*, March 29, 1999; Duncan Campbell, "U.S. Students Leave Shopping Malls to Sign up for Protests," *The Guardian Weekly*, November 25–December 1, 1999. No such student activism has flared up on university campuses in other Western countries.

39. Harvard Business School, "Hitting the Wall: Nike and International Labor Practices," unpublished manuscript N1–700–047k, January 19, 2000, pp. 3–4.

40. Celia Mather, "Do It Just—Campaigning on Company Codes of Conduct," *IRENE*, Nos. 24 and 25 (February 1997), pp. 6–13.

41. "Hong Kong NGO Seminar on Codes of Conduct, 15 July 1999," *Labor Rights in China Seminar Report*, Hong Kong, unpublished, 1999, p. 2.

42. Robert Collier, "Some U.S. Firms Work to Cut Abuses in Chinese Factories," *San Francisco Chronicle*, May 17, 2000.

43. *Washington Post*, April 10, 1997.

44. The companies participating in the FLA include Adidas-Saloman, Eddie Bauer,

Gear for Sports, Kathie Lee Gifford, Levi Strauss, Liz Clairborne, L.L. Bean, Nicole Miller, Nike, Patagonia, Phillip-Van Heusen, and Reebok.

45. Martin Van Der Werf, "Miffed by Sweatshop Code, Nike Moves to End Agreement to Supply Sports Equipment to Brown University," *The Chronicle of Higher Education*, March 31, 2000; Associated Press, "Nike Kills University of Michigan Talks," April 27, 2000.

46. But even within this arena, there is no consensus over including a social clause. See *Asian Labor Update* (November 1995–March 1996), an issue specially devoted to the debate over the social clause.

47. "Workers in Global Economy Project," International Labor Rights Fund website, http://www.laborrights.org/projects/globalecon/index.html

48. For example, a Workers' Relations Branch of the ILO observed that non-core standards are of less concern to ILO than the core standards. Statement made at the Sixth World Congress of the International Textile, Garment, and Leather Workers Federation, published in the "Sixth World Congress Summary of Proceedings," distributed at the Seventh World Congress of the ITGLWF held in April 1996 in Melbourne, p. 81.

49. Feng Chen, "Subsistence Crises, Managerial Corruption and Labour Protests in China," *The China Journal*, No. 44 (July 2000), pp. 41–63.

50. Han Dongfang, *Reform, Corruption and Livelihood—Recorded Conversation Between Han Dongfang and Chinese Workers, Vol. 1* (Gaige, wubi, minsheng—Han Dongfang yu Zhongguo gongren duihualu, di yi ji), Hong Kong: Chinese Labor Bulletin, 1998, pp. vii, 4–5.

51. Trini Leung, "Labor Rights Without Labor—Not Only Impossible, But Unacceptable," *China Rights Forum*, Spring 2000, pp. 30–33. For a different position advocating that NGOs work with corporations to monitor their codes of conduct, see Bama Athreya, "Governing the Ungovernable? Corporations and Human Rights," ibid., pp. 36–39, 52. For a debate among labor advocates on this controversial issue, see Labor Rights in China (LARIC), "Hong Kong NGO Seminar on Codes of Conduct, 15 July 1999," Seminar Report, 1999.

52. For an example of such research, see Melissa Connor, Tara Gruzen, Larry Sacks, Jude Sunderland, Darcy Tromanhauser, Faculty Advisor: Shubham Chaudhuri, "The Case for Corporate Responsibility: Paying a Living Wage to Maquila Workers in El Salvador," unpublished report for the National Labor Committee, New York, Columbia University, Program in Economic and Political Development, School of International Public Affairs, May 14, 1999.

53. "After Seattle: A Global Disaster," *The Economist*, December 11, 1999, pp. 17–18; Leif Pagrostsky (Sweden's Trade Minister), "Put All Workers' Rights On the Trade Agenda," *International Herald Tribune*, February 16, 2000.

54. Ethical Trading Initiative Seminar Report 4, "Governance in China: What are the Implications for Ethical Trading?" September 1999, at http://www//eti.org.uk/_html/events/seminar_04/framesets/f_page.shtml

55. *Nanfang ribao* (Southern Daily), March 31, 2000.

56. *Nanfang ribao*, April 19, 2000.

57. International Labour Conference, 85th Session 1997, *Report of the Director-General: Executive Summary, The ILO, Standard Setting and Globalization*, June 3, 1997, available at http://www.ilo.org/public/english/10ilc/ilc85dg.rep.htm (visited September 22, 1998).

58. "All About the ICFTU World Congress, Durban, 3–7 April 2000: The Future Shape of the Trade Union Movement," ICFTU Online, 0810000510/LD.

Selected Bibliography

Adams, Roy J. (2001) "Choice or Voice? Rethinking American Labor Policy in Light of the International Human Rights Consensus," *Employee Rights and Employment Policy Journal*, Vol. 5, No. 2, forthcoming.

Chan, Anita (1993) "Revolution or Corporatism? Workers and Trade Unions in Post-Mao China," *The Australian Journal of Chinese Affairs*, No. 29, pp. 31–61.

Chan, Anita (1997a) "The Regimentation of Workers in China's Free Labour Market," *Chinese Perspectives*, No. 9, January/February, pp. 12–15; this article also appears in the French-language edition of the same journal, *Chinoises Perspectives*.

Chan, Anita (1997b) "Whither the Chinese Work Unit?: Toward Enterprise 'Familism' or the Market?," in Lu Xiaobo and Elizabeth Perry (eds.), *Danwei: The Changing Chinese Workplace in Historical and Comparative Perspective*, Armonk, N.Y.: M.E. Sharpe, pp. 91–113.

Chan, Anita (1998) "Labor Standards and Human Rights: The Case of Chinese Workers under Market Socialism," *Human Rights Quarterly*, Vol. 20, No. 4, pp. 886–904.

Chan, Anita (2000a) "Chinese Trade Unions and Workplace Relations in the State-Owned and Joint-Venture Enterprises," in Malcolm Warner (ed.), *Changing Workplace Relations in the Chinese Economy*, London: Macmillan, pp. 34–56.

Chan, Anita (2000b) "Globalization, China's Free (Read Bonded) Labour Market, and the Chinese Trade Union," *Asia Pacific Business Review*, Vol. 6 (3 and 4), pp. 260–79.

Chan, Anita (2001) "Culture of Survival: Lives of Migrant Workers Through the Prism of Private Letters," in Perry Link, Richard Madsen and Paul Pickowicz (eds.), *Popular Thought in Post-Socialist China*, Boulder: Rowman and Littlefield.

Chen, Meei-shia, and Anita Chan (1999) "China's 'Market Economics in Command': Footwear Workers' Health in Jeopardy," *International Journal of Health Services*, Vol. 29, No. 4, pp. 793–811.

Child, John (1991) "A Foreign Perspective on the Management of People in China," *The International Journal of Human Resource Management*, Vol. 2, No. 1, pp. 93–107.

Child, John (1994) *Management in China during the Age of Reform*, Cambridge: Cambridge University Press.

Collingsworth, Terry F., William Goold, Pharis F. Harvey (1994) "Time for a Global New Deal," *Foreign Affairs*, Vol. 73, No. 1, January/February, pp. 8–20.

Feng Tongqing (1994) "Zhongguo zhigong zhuangkuang diaocha de zonghe fenxi" (An Analysis of a Survey of the Situation of Chinese Staff and Workers) in Jiang

Liu et al., *Zhongguo 1993–1994: Shehui xingshi fenxi yu yuce* (China 1993–1994: Analysis and Prognosis of the Social Situation in China), Beijing: Social Sciences Academy, pp. 237–55.

Gao, Mobo (1998) "The Rural Situation in Post-Mao China and the Conditions of Migrant Workers: The Case of Gao Village," *Bulletin of Concerned Asian Scholars*, Vol. 20, No. 4, pp. 70–77.

Greenfield, Gerard, and Apo Leong (1997) "China's Communist Capitalism: The Real World of Market Socialism," in Leo Panitch, *Ruthless Criticism of all that Exists, Socialist Register*, New York: Monthly Review Press, pp. 96–122.

Hannan, Kate (1998) *Industrial Change in China: Economic Restructuring and Conflicting Interests*, London: Routledge.

Howard, Pat, and Roger Howard (1995) "The Campaign to Eliminate Job Security in China," *Journal of Contemporary Asia*, Vol. 25, No. 3, pp. 338–55.

Howell, Jude (1993) "The Fate of Labour," Chapter 6 in Jude Howell, *China Opens its Doors – The Politics of Economic Transition*, Boulder and London: Lynne Rienner Publishers, pp. 209–43.

Howell, Jude (1997) "Looking Beyond Incorporation: Chinese Trade Unions in the Reform Era," *Mondes en Developpement*, Tome 99, pp. 73–90.

Howell, Jude (2000) "Organising around Women and Labour in China: Uneasy Shadows, Uncomfortable Alliances," *Communist and Post-Communist Studies*, No. 33, pp. 355–77.

Human Rights in China (1999) "Not Welcome at the Party: Behind the 'Clean-up' of China's Cities – A Report on Administrative Detention under 'Custody and Repatriation,'" *Human Rights in China*, September, HRIC Arbitrary Detention Series, No. 2, pp. 1–57.

Hsing, You-tien (1998) *Making Capitalism in China: The Taiwan Connection*, New York: Oxford University Press.

Huang, Cen (1998) "The Organization and Management of Chinese Transnational Enterprises in South China," *Issues and Studies*, Vol. 34, No. 3, pp. 51–70.

Jacka, Tamara (1998) "Working Sisters Answer Back: The Presentation and Self-Presentation of Women in China's Floating Population," *China Information*, Vol. 13, No. 1 (Summer), pp. 43–75.

Jiang Kaiwen (1996) "Gonghui yu dang-guojia de chongtu: bashi niandai yilai de Zhongguo gonghui gaige" (The Conflicts between Trade Unions and the Party-State: The Reform of Chinese Trade Unions in the 1980s), *Xianggang shehui kexue jikan* (Hong Kong Journal of Social Science), No. 8, pp. 121–6.

Kernen, Antoine (1997) "Shenyang Learns to Manage its Poor," *China Perspectives*, No. 11, May/June, pp. 17–21.

Lambert, Robert, and Anita Chan (1999) "Global Dance: Factory Regimes, Asian Labour Standards and Corporate Restructuring," in Jeremy Waddington (ed.), *Globalisation and Labour Resistance*, London: Mansell, pp. 72–104.

Lee, Ching Kwan (1995) "Engendering the Worlds of Labor: Women Workers, Labor Markets, and Production Politics in the South China Economic Miracle," *American Sociological Review*, No. 60 (June), pp. 378–97.

Lee, Ching Kwan, (1998a) *Gender and the South China Miracle: The Worlds of Factory Women*, Berkeley: University of California Press.

Lee, Ching Kwan, (1998b) "The Labor Politics of Market Socialism—Collective Inaction and Class Experiences among State Workers in Guangzhou," *Modern China*, January, pp. 1–33.

Lee, Ching Kwan, (1999) "From Organized Dependence to Disorganized Despotism: Changing Labour Regimes in Chinese Factories," *The China Quarterly*, No. 157, March, pp. 44–71.

Leung, Trini Wing-Yue (1996) "Trade Unions and Labour Relations under Market Socialism in China," in Gerd Schienstock, Paul Thompson, and Franz Traxler (eds.), *Industrial Relations between Command and Market*, Commack, NY: Nova Science Publishers Inc., pp. 239–289.

Mallee, Hein (1995) "China's Household Registration System under Reform," *Development and Change*, Vol. 26, No. 1, January, pp. 1-29.

Ng, Sek Hong and Olivia K.M. Ip (1994) "The Public Domain and Labour Organizations," in Maurice Brosseau and Lo Chi Kin (eds.), *China Review 1994*. Hong Kong: Chinese University Press, pp. 14.1–14.33.

Ng, Sek Hong and Malcolm Warner (1998) *China's Trade Unions and Management*, London: Macmillan.

O'Leary, Greg (ed.) (1998) *Adjusting to Capitalism: Chinese Workers and the State*, Armonk, NY: M.E. Sharpe.

Pun, Ngai (1999) "Becoming *Dagongmei* (Working Girls): The Politics of Identity and Difference in Reform China," *The China Journal*, No. 42, pp. 1–18.

Pun, Ngai (2000) "Opening a Minor Genre of Resistance in Reform China: Scream, Dream and Transgression in a Workplace," *Positions*, Vol. 8, No. 2, Fall.

Rofel, Lisa (1999) *Other Modernities: Gendered Yearnings in China after Socialism*, Berkeley: University of California Press.

Senser, Robert A. (1998) "Exploring a New Frontier—Bringing Human Rights Standards into the World Trade Organization," *China Rights Forum*, Summer, pp. 25–40.

Smart, Josephine, and Alan Smart, (1993) "Obligation and Control: Employment in Capitalist Labour Management in China," *Critique of Anthropology*, Vol. 13, No. 1, pp. 7–31.

Society for the Promotion of Human Rights in Employment Newsletter (*SPHRE*), http://www.mericleinc.com/Sphre

Solinger, Dorothy (1995) "The Chinese Work Unit and Transient Labor in the Transition from Socialism," *Modern China*, Vol. 21, No. 2, pp. 155–83.

Solinger, Dorothy (1999) *Contesting Citizenship in Urban China: Peasant Migrants, the State, and the Logic of the Market*, Berkeley: University of California Press.

Tan, Shen (2000) "The Relationship between Foreign Enterprises, Local Governments, and Women Migrant Workers in the Pearl River Delta," in Loraine A. West and Yaohui Zho (eds.), *Rural Labor Flows in China*, Berkeley: University of California Press, pp. 292–310.

Tang, Wenfang, and Tongqing Feng (1996) "Zhongguo qiye de laodong guanxi" (Labor Relations in Chinese Enterprises), *Hong Kong Journal of Social Sciences*, No. 8, Autumn, pp. 85–120.

Tang, Wenfang, William L. Parish, and Tongqing Feng (1996) "Chinese Labor Relations in a Changing Work Environment," *Journal of Contemporary China*, Vol. 5, No. 13, pp. 367–89.

Unger, Jonathan, and Anita Chan (1996) "Corporatism in China: A Developmental State in an East Asian Context," in Barrett L. McCormick and Jonathan Unger (eds.), *China after Socialism: In the Footsteps of Eastern Europe or East Asia?*, Armonk, NY: M.E. Sharpe, pp. 95–129.

Walder, Andrew G. (1983) "Organized Dependency and Cultures of Authority in Chinese Industry," *Journal of Asian Studies*, Vol. 43, No. 1, November, pp. 51–76.

Walder, Andrew (1986) *Communist Neo-Traditionalism: Work and Authority in Chinese Industry*, Berkeley: University of California Press.

Wang, Fei-ling (1998) "Floaters, Moonlighters, and the Underemployed: A National Labor Market with Chinese Characteristics," *Journal of Contemporary China*, Vol. 7, No. 19, pp. 459–75.

Warner, Malcolm (1996) "Chinese Enterprise Reform, Human Resources and the 1994 Labour Law," *The International Journal of Human Resource Management*, Vol. 4, No. 4, December, pp. 779–96.

Warner, Malcolm (ed.) (2000) *Changing Workplace Relations in the Chinese Economy*, London: Macmillan Press.

Warner, Malcolm, and Ng Sek Hong (1998) "The Ongoing Evolution of Chinese Industrial Relations: The Negotiation of 'Collective Contracts' in the Shenzhen Special Economic Zone," *China Information*, Vol. 12, No. 4, pp. 1–20.

White, Gordon, Jude Howell, and Shang Xiaoyuan (1996) *In Search of Civil Society: Market Reform and Social Change in Contemporary China*, New York: Oxford University Press.

Wilson, Jeanne (1990) " 'The Polish Lesson': China and Poland 1980–1990," *Studies in Comparative Communism*, No. 3/4, pp. 259–80.

Wong, Linda (1999) "Unemployment," in Jutta Hebel and Gunter Schucher (eds.), *Der Chinesische Arbeitsmarkt*, Hamburg: Mitteilungen des Instituts fur Asienkunde, pp. 219–35.

Wu, Jieh-min (1997) "Strange Bedfellows: Dynamics of Government–Business Relations between Chinese Local Authorities and Taiwanese Investors," *Journal of Contemporary China*, Vol. 6, No. 15, pp. 319–46.

Zhao, Minghua, and Theo Nichols (1996) "Management Control of Labour in State-Owned Enterprises: Cases from the Textile Industry," *The China Journal*, No. 36, pp. 1–21.

Zhu, Ying, and Iain Campbell (1996) "Economic Reform and the Challenge of Transforming Labour Regulation in China," *Labour and Industry*, Vol. 7, No. 1, June, pp. 29–49.

Index

Adidas, 12, 54
Administration fee, 186–189
All-China Federation of Trade Unions
(ACFTU), 4, 6, 15, 91, 96, 106, 141,
161, 184–185
All-China Women's Federation (ACWF),
5, 83, 91
Alston, Philip, 229
Amnesty International, 231
Anti-sweatshop movement, 232–234
state's role and, 234–236
tactics of, 233–234
Apparel Industry Partnership, 232
Arbitration, 149, 153, 158, 160, 201–202
Asian Law Caucus, 195

Ballinger, Jeffrey, 231
Beijing Public Security Bureau (PBS),
215–216
"Big rice bowl" work ethic, 53
Body searches, 68, 70
Bonded workers, 20
Bonior, David, 224, 230–231
Bribery, 15
"Bride price," 196
Bureaucratic capitalism, 15, 21, 143

Capitalism, 111–112, 118, 123
Caritas, 133
Censorship, 5
Child labor, 22–23, 44, 225

China Seafarers' Union, 185
China's Xiamen International Economic
and Technology Cooperation
Company (CXIETCC), 196–203
Chinese Academy of Preventive
Medicine, 87
Chinese Communist Party, 33, 127, 129,
152, 165–167
Chinese Companies Coordinating Group,
194
Chinese Industrial Relations Regulation,
149
Clinton, William J., 232
Collective action; see Right to organize/
collective action
Collective bargaining, 14, 225
Collective-sector workers, 13–14
Commonwealth of the Northern Marianas
Islands (CNMI), 5, 185–195
Communist Youth League, 5
Compensation payouts, 23, 56, 104, 126,
133, 217–221
Construction industry, 76–80
Corporal punishment, 10, 21–23
case studies of, 46–80
Corporate tax, 15, 71, 75, 87
Corruption
bribery, 15
environmental pollution and, 90
foreign-invested enterprises and, 92
occupational safety and, 123–125

Anita Chan has a Ph.D. in Sociology from the University of Sussex. She is currently an Australian Research Council Senior Research Fellow hosted by the Australian National University, and co-editor of *The China Journal*. Her six books include *Children of Mao* and, as co-author, *Chen Village under Mao and Deng*. In recent years, her research has focused on management styles, worker-management relations in Chinese enterprises, and Chinese trade unions. She has published more than a dozen articles on these topics in a variety of journals and edited volumes.